Global Governance in Crisis

New practices and institutions of global governance are often one of the most enduring consequences of global crises. The contemporary architecture of global governance has been widely criticised for failing to prevent the global financial crisis and Eurozone debt crises, for failing to provide robust international crisis management and leadership, and for failing to generate a consensus around new ideas for regulating markets in the broader public interest. *Global Governance in Crisis* explores the impact of the global financial crisis of 2008–2009 on the architecture and practice of contemporary global governance, and traces the long-term implications of the crisis for the future of the global order. Combining innovative theoretical approaches with rich empirical cases, the book examines how the impact of the global financial crisis has played out across a range of global governance domains, including development, finance and debt, trade, and security.

This book was originally published as a special issue of *Global Society*.

André Broome is Associate Professor at the University of Warwick. His book publications include *Issues and Actors in the Global Political Economy* (Palgrave, 2014), *Seeing Like an International Organization* (Routledge, 2014, with Leonard Seabrooke), and *The Currency of Power: The IMF and Monetary Reform in Central Asia* (Palgrave, 2010).

Liam Clegg is Lecturer at the University of York. His research explores the evolving roles of international organisations in global economic governance, especially the IMF and World Bank. He is the author of *Controlling the World Bank and IMF: Shareholders, Stakeholders, and the Politics of Concessional Lending* (Palgrave, 2013).

Lena Rethel is Assistant Professor at the University of Warwick. She works on global financial governance, the relationship between finance and development, and Islamic finance. Her book, *The Problem with Banks* (co-authored with Timothy J. Sinclair) was published by Zed Books in 2012.

Global Governance in Crisis

Edited by
André Broome, Liam Clegg and
Lena Rethel

Routledge
Taylor & Francis Group

LONDON AND NEW YORK

First published 2015 by Routledge

2 Park Square, Milton Park, Abingdon, Oxon OX14 4RN
711 Third Avenue, New York, NY 10017, USA

Routledge is an imprint of the Taylor & Francis Group, an informa business

First issued in paperback 2017

British Library Cataloguing in Publication Data
A catalogue record for this book is available from the British Library

ISBN 13: 978-1-138-84514-5 (hbk)
ISBN 13: 978-1-138-05685-5 (pbk)

Typeset in Palatino
by RefineCatch Limited, Bungay, Suffolk

Publisher's Note
The publisher accepts responsibility for any inconsistencies that may have
arisen during the conversion of this book from journal articles to book chapters,
namely the possible inclusion of journal terminology.

Disclaimer
Every effort has been made to contact copyright holders for their permission to
reprint material in this book. The publishers would be grateful to hear from any
copyright holder who is not here acknowledged and will undertake to rectify
any errors or omissions in future editions of this book.

Contents

Citation Information

The chapters in this book were originally published in *Global Society*, volume 26, issue 1 (January 2012). When citing this material, please use the original page numbering for each article, as follows:

Chapter 1
Global Governance and the Politics of Crisis
André Broome, Liam Clegg and Lena Rethel
Global Society, volume 26, issue 1 (January 2012) pp. 3–18

Chapter 2
Crisis is Governance: Sub-prime, the Traumatic Event, and Bare Life
James Brassett and Nick Vaughan-Williams
Global Society, volume 26, issue 1 (January 2012) pp. 19–42

Chapter 3
IMF Surveillance in Crisis: The Past, Present and Future of the Reform Process
Manuela Moschella
Global Society, volume 26, issue 1 (January 2012) pp. 43–60

Chapter 4
Post-crisis Reform at the IMF: Learning to be (Seen to be) a Long-term Development Partner
Liam Clegg
Global Society, volume 26, issue 1 (January 2012) pp. 61–82

Chapter 5
Global Trade Governance and the Challenges of African Activism in the Doha Development Agenda Negotiations
Donna Lee
Global Society, volume 26, issue 1 (January 2012) pp. 83–102

Chapter 6
Multilateralism in Crisis? The Character of US International Engagement under Obama
Alexandra Homolar
Global Society, volume 26, issue 1 (January 2012) pp. 103–122

Chapter 7
Each Time is Different! The Shifting Boundaries of Emerging Market Debt
Lena Rethel
Global Society, volume 26, issue 1 (January 2012) pp. 123–144

Please direct any queries you may have about the citations to
clsuk.permissions@cengage.com

Global Governance and the Politics of Crisis

ANDRÉ BROOME, LIAM CLEGG and LENA RETHEL

The notion of global governance has always been intimately linked to that of crisis. In recent crisis episodes the architecture of global governance has been held responsible for weak or ineffective regulatory mechanisms that failed to either prevent systemic crises or to at least give an "early warning" of impending disasters, while in other episodes global governance institutions have been blamed for poor crisis responses and management. Global governance institutions have also been blamed for failing to expand the scope of their jurisdictions to incorporate new systemic risks and new market players, as well as for their inability to adapt to new political, economic, social and environmental challenges. The framing article for this special issue on "Global Governance in Crisis" examines four key features of global governance in the context of the global financial crisis: (1) the dynamic role played by ideas in making global governance "hang together" during periods of crisis; (2) how crisis serves as a driver of change in global governance (and why it sometimes does not); (3) how ubiquitous the global financial crisis was as an event in world politics; and (4) the conditions that constitute an event as a crisis. Due to the complexity and institutional "stickiness" of the contemporary architecture of global governance, the article concludes that a far-reaching overhaul and structural reforms in global governance processes is both costly and improbable in the short-term.

The notion of global governance has always been intimately linked to that of crisis. In the post-World War Two period, the decision to seek solutions to a range of domestic and international problems at the global level and subsequent efforts to create organisational blueprints to underpin these arrangements—most famously at international conferences such as those of Bretton Woods and Dumbarton Oaks—was a direct response to the economic turmoil of the 1930s and the cataclysmic wars of the first half of the twentieth century. Indeed, the period since then has been characterised by the proliferation of global governance institutions. At the same time, however, claims of a crisis in global governance have been repeated at an accelerating pace, especially following the breakdown of the Bretton Woods exchange rates system, the oil shocks and the rise of global finance in the early 1970s. If we look at global financial governance in particular, it seems as if crisis has been the norm rather than the exception, which is illustrated by the string of financial crises in both the developed and developing world in the 1980s and

---

*The authors wish to express their gratitude to the reviewers of this special issue.

1990s.[1] Unsurprisingly, these crises have also led to heated debates questioning the efficacy and legitimacy of contemporary forms of global governance.

In each of these crisis episodes, part of the blame has been sheeted home to global governance institutions. In some cases, the existing architecture of global governance has been held responsible for weak or ineffective regulatory mechanisms that failed to either prevent systemic crises or to at least give an "early warning" of impending disasters, while in other episodes global governance institutions have been blamed for poor crisis responses and management. More recently, we can also add to this litany of allegations that global governance institutions failed to expand the scope of their jurisdictions to incorporate new systemic risks and new market players, and more generally their seeming incapacity to adapt to new political, economic, social and environmental challenges. Indeed, with the benefit of hindsight the latter half of the twentieth century seems simultaneously to have been both the era of "global governance" and the era of global governance *crises*.

This trend has continued apace into the new millennium. The first decade of the twenty-first century was characterised by landmark governance failures at multiple regulatory levels, such as the bursting of the internet bubble in 2000, the Argentine debt crisis in 2001–2002 and global asset price bubbles, including booms not only in residential property but also in key commodities such as oil and foodstuffs. These events culminated in the US sub-prime crash in 2007 that gave way to the global "credit crunch" of 2007–2008, turning into a wholesale "global financial crisis" in 2008–2009, with the latest twist in the tale being the rapid transformation of the private sector financial crisis into a public sector fiscal crisis with unprecedented levels of sovereign debt in many economies (especially in Europe).

Despite (or perhaps as a consequence of) lacking many of the levers of hard power—and the broader social legitimacy—available to most national governments, global governance institutions often carry the blame for (responses to) global catastrophes. In this respect, the global credit crunch was a singularly dramatic event in world politics. The revelation that, far from being the product of a perfect science, measures of value in complex financial systems were subject to sudden fluctuations—and sudden fluctuations of an almost incomprehensible magnitude—came as a shock to market actors, regulators and governments alike across the industrialised world. Likewise, the speed and vigour with which problems in financial markets fed through into the real economy and spread around the globe caught almost all observers off guard. Although it is already common to speak about the global financial crisis (GFC) in the past tense, we are very clearly still living through the consequences of the bursting of what had become a particularly large bubble. Attempts by state actors to step in to plug banks' liquidity gaps and to provide stimulus spending have been followed by a widespread reframing of domestic policymaking as being, to borrow a favoured phrase of the UK Chancellor, squeezed by the "nation's credit card bill". In the light of this disciplinary pressure, politicians of all

---

1. These include the international debt crisis of the 1980s; the 1987 Wall Street crash and more generally the late 1980s and early 1990s savings and loans crisis in the US; a series of debt crises linked to the post-communist "transition" in the early 1990s; the Exchange Rate Mechanism (ERM) crises of 1992; the 1995 "Tequila" crisis in Mexico; and the Asian financial crisis of 1997–1998 and its spread to Russia and Latin America at the end of that decade.

stripes have picked up the mantra that "there is no alternative" to public sector retrenchment, and a new "age of austerity" has dawned (in recent memory a comparatively new experience for much of the developed world, but a familiar experience for most developing countries).

Although there is a broad spectrum of opinion on the issue,[2] the high water mark of the GFC can be drawn somewhere between September 2007, when the crisis visibly broke onto UK shores with the run on Northern Rock, and September 2008, with the collapse of US investment bank Lehman Brothers and the bailout of American International Group (AIG) (the following month, Iceland became the first Western economy to seek to borrow from the International Monetary Fund (IMF) in three decades).[3] This means that, at the time of writing, we have had a period of around three years from its *dénouement* to reflect on the lessons to be learnt from the global financial crisis. Historically, Political Science and International Relations (IR) scholarship has been propelled forward by crises in the "real world": the trauma of World War One;[4] the failure to "predict" the onset of World War Two and the demise of the Soviet Union;[5] the "hot" Cold War in the early 1960s;[6] and the breakdown of the Bretton Woods System.[7] The GFC is no exception to this rule. It has already sparked a huge proliferation of crisis and post-crisis analyses. Notwithstanding this wealth of GFC-related output, an important question remains: is three years a sufficient time to be publishing scholarly analyses on the impact of the financial crisis?

The answer to this question, we believe, is an emphatic "yes". While the depth of analysis of much popular commentary on the GFC remains shallow, with complex structural dynamics often reduced to simplistic narratives focusing on the personalities of key players,[8] or concentrating on which section of public spending is merely down and which is devastated in the austerity stakes, recent academic insights have begun to fruitfully explore what the GFC reveals about deep changes and imminent contradictions within the ongoing financialisation of global capitalism. As well as shedding substantial light on the structural features of the global economy that helped fuel asset prices in the industrialised countries by funnelling capital "uphill" from developing countries,[9] contributions to this endeavour have begun to use the GFC as an opportunity to problematise the "common sense" of highly leveraged trading, and to explore the political and ethical implications of the securitisation techniques that became a bedrock of banking profitability through the "good

---

2. For an overview of these "eye of the storm" events, see Andrew Gamble, *The Spectre at the Feast: Capitalist Crisis and the Politics of Recession* (Basingstoke: Palgrave, 2009), p. 23.

3. André Broome, "Negotiating Crisis: The IMF and Disaster Capitalism in Small States", *The Round Table*, Vol. 100, No. 413 (2011), pp. 155–167.

4. Edward Hallett Carr, *The Twenty Years' Crisis* (Basingstoke: Palgrave, 2001), p. 3.

5. Mark Blyth, "Great Punctuations: Prediction, Randomness, and the Evolution of Comparative Political Science", *American Political Science Review*, Vol. 100, No. 4 (2006), pp. 493–498.

6. David Baldwin, "Security Studies and the End of the Cold War", *World Politics*, Vol. 48, No. 1 (1996), pp. 117–141.

7. Benjamin Cohen, *International Political Economy: An Intellectual History* (Princeton, NJ: Princeton University, 2008), p. 23.

8. For example, Michael Lewis, *The Big Short: Inside the Doomsday Machine* (London: Allen Lane, 2010); Paul Mason, *Meltdown: The End of the Age of Greed* (London: Verso, 2009).

9. Mervyn King, "Global Imbalances: The Perspective of the Bank of England", *Banque de France Financial Stability Review*, Vol. 15, No. 1 (2011), pp. 73–80.

times".[10] And although many valuable insights into the deeper causes and consequences of the GFC have been delivered, one question has remained conspicuously absent: what impact have the events of the last three years had on the contemporary architecture, practices, and normative goals of global governance?[11]

The political salience of the GFC is acute and emphatically global in dimension. As a consequence, there is a pressing requirement to provide intellectually rigorous and critical interrogations of its implications for processes and mechanisms of transnationalisation, globalisation and governance. By focusing on the question of global governance, the contributions to this special issue allow for a second-order analysis which looks both at the subject (the way that existing international regulatory arrangements have coped with the crisis) but also the social dimension (the social networks and power structures that make up global governance). Concentrating on the question of governance also enables the contributors to this special issue to bring an explicitly normative dimension to the subject.

In exploring this broad question, the articles in this special issue contribute to the task of overcoming a significant gap in the extant crisis literature. The works included are six original research articles, with each one providing fresh insight into the dynamics surrounding global governance during an episode of systemic crisis. Individually, these articles contribute to a range of debates in a manner that adds significantly to our conceptual and empirical grasp of the relationship between global governance and crisis-type events. These particularities are reviewed in the closing section of this framing article. Collectively, however, these works deliver a provocative series of insights to scholars across the disciplines of International Relations and International Political Economy (IPE), and it is to the exploration of these crosscutting themes that we dedicate the majority of our efforts here. By taking a historically informed view of modes of crisis production, the politics of change in formal arenas of global governance, trends in intergovernmentalism and shifting patterns of debt throughout this and previous crisis events, the authors outline four closely linked themes that require further investigation. Contributors identify the need for future scholarship to be directed towards the following questions:

- What makes global governance "hang together" during periods of crisis?
- How potent is "crisis" as a driver of change in global governance?
- How ubiquitous is/was the global financial crisis as an event in world politics?
- Finally, what makes an event become a crisis?

---

10. See, for example, James Brassett, Lena Rethel and Matthew Watson, "The Political Economy of the Subprime Crisis: The Politics, Economics, and Ethics of Response", *New Political Economy*, Vol. 15, No. 1 (2010), pp. 1–7 and other contributors to the special issue; Johnna Montgomerie, "Bridging the Critical Divide: Global Finance, Financialisation, and Contemporary Capitalism", *Contemporary Politics*, Vol. 14, No. 3 (2008), pp. 233–252 and other contributors to the special issue.

11. This was the issue that the participants were asked to address at a two-day workshop on "Global Governance in Crisis?", from which the papers in this special issue are drawn. The workshop was held at the University of Birmingham on 27–28 May 2010, and we gratefully acknowledge the financial support from the host institution, the Economic and Social Research Council (RES 062 23 0369 and PTA 026 27 2807), and the British International Studies Association's International Political Economy Group.

In the following sections, the contribution of this special issue to each of these questions shall be addressed in turn.

What Makes Global Governance "Hang Together" during Periods of Crisis?

Big ideas matter in world politics. When at their most potent, big ideas can serve to unite otherwise disparate international actors around a coherent narrative for understanding the causes of systemic challenges and prescribing the range of possible solutions, and may help to foster a sense of shared purpose around which arenas of global governance can be made to hang together. For example, in the long transition from the Gold Standard to the Bretton Woods international monetary regime, a growing acceptance of the ideal of "embedded liberalism" provided the intellectual map in accordance with which the blueprints for specific governance spaces were laid out. Through this period, a cluster of related themes—including the key tropes of "national autonomy" and "industrial planning"—provided a shared language through which harnessing the potential benefits of global economic integration to the service of domestic policy became the "common sense" aim of global governance.[12] In the aftermath of the collapse of the Bretton Woods System in the early 1970s, it is widely agreed that we have witnessed something of a dis-embedding of liberalism from its previously held goals. Not only have structural changes been enacted that have served to compel national economies to adapt to the vagaries of international market pressures, but—perhaps more significantly—this inversion of the relationship between global interconnectedness and domestic policy has been constituted as *an end in itself*. Under this "neoliberal" reframing, the disciplinary power of globally active networks of capital became understood as a positive force for trimming state structures to allow allocatively efficient free markets to take hold, at least in theory. It was assumed that collective welfare and individual liberty would thus be ultimately expanded.[13] Nevertheless, this transition was accompanied by a series of financial crises of which the 1987 Wall Street Crash, the post-communist "transition" in the early 1990s, the 1995 "Tequila" crisis in Mexico and the Asian financial crises of 1997–1998 are only a few examples.

How does the most recent financial crisis slot into this constellation of evolving ordering principles in global governance? Efforts are underway (or, perhaps, are already exhausted) to paint the present juncture as an epoch-shaping moment: the dawn of "post-neoliberalism", or even of the arrival of "post-capitalism". According to these narratives, the GFC should be read as a signal event, a watershed moment from which a process of re-embedding global liberalism will begin.[14] The analyses contained in this special issue stand firmly in opposition to these interpretations of the financial crisis as a fundamental challenge to the prevailing norms of global economic governance. Rather than seeing contests over big ideas, there is a broad

12. John Gerard Ruggie, "What Makes the World Hang Together? Neo-Utilitarianism and the Social Constructivist Challenge", *International Organization*, Vol. 52, No. 4 (1998), pp. 855–885; John Gerard Ruggie, "International Regimes, Transactions, and Change: Embedded Liberalism in the Postwar Economic Order", *International Organisation*, Vol. 36, No. 2 (1982), pp. 379–415.

13. A high profile proponent of this line of narrative is Thomas Friedman, *The Lexus and the Olive Tree* (New York: Anchor, 2000).

14. Elmar Altvater, "The Failure of Neoliberalism in the Financial Market Crisis", *Development Dialogue*, Vol. 51, No. 1 (2009), pp. 73–85.

consensus that global governance remains bonded together by the glue of more routine little ideas. At the IMF, we see a tinkering around the edges of the mechanics of surveillance and conditionality,[15] and yet another attempt to pull the organisation in the direction of being a "long-term development partner". At the World Trade Organisation (WTO), the search for "trade fairness" goes on through the Doha Development Agenda round of negotiations. Although the realisation of this aspiration remains as elusive as ever, it is this "everyday" idea rather than more foundational contests that animates activity in this area of global governance.

The long-term shape and size of structural reform always comes with a significant time lag. Institutional change at the global level is most often a painstakingly slow process, as the sustained period of time from the initial policy experiments with expanded economic management during World War One, the 1920s and the 1930s Great Depression to the post-World War Two international economic order aptly illustrate.[16] It is of course possible that the incremental shifts in the ideational frameworks at the heart of global economic governance will cascade, and begin to evolve into something that looks more like a reconstitution of first-order norms. There is room for the developments examined at the IMF and WTO, for example, to be seen as components of a wider drift into a "post-Washington Consensus", and the legitimisation of a more active approach to public management of the persistent dysfunction of deregulated markets. While we readily acknowledge the plausibility of such an interpretation of events, we are hesitant to place (responses to) the GFC at the heart of this process of changing the big picture norms that make global governance hang together. Indeed, this special issue demonstrates that rather than exerting a transformational dynamic, the crisis has in fact acted as a centripetal force holding the current order together. Instead of pushing global policymakers to question the hitherto accepted foundations of global economic governance, the dominant conceptualisation of the 2007–2008 liquidity dearth as a pseudo-physical trauma presented governments with a patient in need of emergency treatment.

Rather than fundamental reorientations, governments have fought hard to resuscitate the *status quo ante*. Indeed, it has been governments, rather than the IMF, that urgently called first for "shock therapy" cuts in public spending and retrenching the role of the state, at least in the case of developed economies. The overall message from this special issue is that, contrary to some reports, suggestions of radical changes to political-economic "business as usual"—whether this is called "neoliberalism", "market fundamentalism", or the "Washington consensus"—are premature.

How Potent is "Crisis" as a Driver of Change in Global Governance?

The conventional wisdom in International Relations and IPE scholarship suggests that crisis serves to open a window for substantive structural change, whereby

---

15. See the following articles in this special issue: Liam Clegg, "Post-crisis Reform at the IMF: Learning to be (Seen to be) a Long-term Development Partner", *Global Society*, Vol. 26, No. 1 (2012), pp. 61–81, and Manuela Moschella, "IMF Surveillance in Crisis: The Past, Present and Future of the Reform Process", *ibid.*, pp. 43–60; also André Broome, "The International Monetary Fund, Crisis Management and the Credit Crunch", *Australian Journal of International Affairs*, Vol. 64, No. 1 (2010), pp. 37–54.

16. Leonard Seabrooke, "The Everyday Social Sources of Economic Crises: From 'Great Frustrations' to 'Great Revelations' in Interwar Britain", *International Studies Quarterly*, Vol. 51, No. 4 (2007), pp. 795–810.

"ordinary" policy routines, regulatory habits and institutional frameworks are unsettled, reconfigured, demolished or recreated.[17] There are four main dimensions of the idea of crisis as a driver of change which are useful to consider here. First, crisis may be used by both elite and non-elite actors to challenge existing cognitive assumptions about how the world works, what counts as a policy "problem" and how particular problems should be regulated (such as the 1930s Great Depression, or the early 1990s collapse of centrally planned economies in East and Central Europe and the former Soviet Union).[18] In this sense, crisis can lead to structural changes in dominant ideas by introducing new "knowledge regimes" at both the national and global level. Second, crisis may prompt policy responses that reconfigure the style and scope of government or intergovernmental intervention in the economy (which may be legitimised by changes in dominant ideas).[19] Short-term policy responses, such as the decision to pour billions into ailing banking sectors, can create new path dependencies that delineate the possibilities of future reforms. Third, crisis can function as a catalyst for shifts in the "centre of gravity" in the world economy or world politics more broadly (such as World War Two or the 1970s oil shocks), with many observers suggesting that the current crisis is an important stepping stone to a more Asia-centred or sino-centric world economy with respect to the balance of material power among states. Finally, systemic economic crisis may stimulate a reordering of private power in the world economy, whereby some observers expect to find a diminished role for the financial sector as a driver of growth (and tax receipts) in the aftermath of the global financial crisis.

Of these four potential paths for crisis to act as a driver of change, the first and second—changes in knowledge regimes and in the style and scope of policy action—appear most likely to result in (substantial) global governance reforms in the short term. If crisis drives changes or accelerates existing shifts in the centre of gravity in the world economy and the reordering of private power, this is more likely to prove significant for the architecture of global governance over a long-term time horizon. Indeed, the most prominent global governance institutions often view their core roles as shaping ideas about global "best practice" with respect to different areas of social and economic governance,[20] and fostering the development of new regulatory regimes.[21]

Thus far, the global financial crisis has proved to be at best a potential catalyst for change in global governance, rather than ushering in a new era of revamped institutional frameworks and processes. Headline reforms like the substitution of the Group of Twenty for the Group of Seven/Eight, upgrading the Financial

---

17. Stephen D. Krasner, "Approaches to the State: Alternative Conceptions and Historical Dynamics", *Comparative Politics*, Vol. 16, No. 2 (1984), pp. 223–246; John T.S. Keeler, "Opening the Window for Reform: Mandates, Crises, and Extraordinary Policy-Making", *Comparative Political Studies*, Vol. 25, No. 4 (1993), pp. 433–486.

18. André Broome, "Money for Nothing: Everyday Actors and Monetary Crises", *Journal of International Relations and Development*, Vol. 12, No. 1 (2009), pp. 3–30.

19. See, for example, Lena Rethel, "The New Financial Development Paradigm and Asian Bond Markets", *New Political Economy*, Vol. 15, No. 4 (2010), pp. 493–517.

20. See Liam Clegg, "Our Dream is a World Full of Poverty Indicators: The US, the World Bank, and the Power of Numbers", *New Political Economy*, Vol. 15, No. 4 (2010), pp. 473–492; André Broome, "Global Monitor: The Joint Vienna Institute", *New Political Economy*, Vol. 15, No. 4 (2010), pp. 609–624.

21. Cf. the chapters in Susan Park and Antje Vetterlein (eds), *Owning Development: Creating Policy Norms in the IMF and the World Bank* (Cambridge: Cambridge University Press, 2010).

Stability Forum to the Financial Stability Board, and the substantial increase in the IMF's lending resources, as well as regional "solutions" such as the creation of a European bailout mechanism for distressed Euro zone economies, appear in the fine print to represent changes in style rather than substance. Less visible changes that occurred "under the radar", such as the greater role played by emerging market economies like Brazil, India, China and others in lending funds *to* the IMF, have the potential to snowball into more substantive reforms in global governance down the track, but are unlikely to bear fruit in the short term. Above all else, the global financial crisis has served as a reminder that substantive structural change at the global level is a long game, the outcome of which is especially hard to accurately predict this close to the peak of a systemic crisis.

How Ubiquitous is/Was the Global Financial Crisis as an Event in World Politics?

During the eye of the global financial storm, media reporting of falling asset prices, political leaders' efforts to "save the world", and tales of everyday financial woe went into overdrive. With 24-hour rolling news coverage of what was satirically relabelled the "cash-pocalypse",[22] the hitherto hidden world of global finance became a central feature of everyday life across the advanced industrialised world. We know that the mass media plays a highly significant role in shaping how publics and political actors interpret and react to major events, and that this is true in relation to both routine, predictable events (elections) and more "out of the blue", unpredictable (crises) events.[23] Indeed, recent analysis of the impact on regulators' judgements from the mass media's "storytelling" over the deleterious effects of mark-to-market accounting demonstrates the continuing relevance of this source of information as a filter of events.[24] What has been less deeply reflected on, however, is the effect of this form of immersion on analysts of the political world.

To an unprecedented extent, the global financial crisis placed European and North American analysts of international political economy at the centre of unfolding events. Whereas many contemporary subject-defining moments— including the Latin American debt crisis, the Asian financial crisis and the slow unwinding of the low-income country debt malaise—were located in an "other" geographical realm, the GFC was very much a home event. This local point of view has led to the creation of the financial crisis as something of a ubiquitous event in IPE.[25] In contrast, this special issue delivers a more measured evaluation.

22. The phrase was coined by Charlie Brooker, "Newswipe", Episode 1, Series 1. Broadcast on BBC4, 24 June 2009. Cited in this issue by James Brassett and Nick Vaughan-Williams in the article "Crisis *is* Governance: Sub-prime, the Traumatic Event, and Bare Life", *Global Society*, Vol. 26, No. 1 (2012), pp. 19–42.

23. James Dearing and Everett Rogers, *Agenda Setting: Communication Concepts* (London: Sage, 1996).

24. William Smith, David Boje and Kevin Melendrez, "The Financial Crisis and Mark-to-market Accounting: An Analysis of Cascading Media Rhetoric and Storytelling", *Qualitative Research in Accounting and Management*, Vol. 7, No. 3 (2010), pp. 281–303.

25. From 2007 to 2010, for example, 148 articles appeared in Thomson-Reuters ranked journals that made a direct reference to the "global financial crisis". This is over three times the number of articles that appeared relating to the "Asian financial crisis" in the four years from 1997. Authors' analysis of ISI Web of Knowledge database.

Just as the GFC has unfolded in a manner that has left the big ideas overlaying global governance largely intact, it is important to realise, too, that functional spheres of global governance have remained aloof from the disruptions of the financial crisis as we see, for example, in the ongoing deadlock in the Doha Round of trade negotiations.

Contributions to the special issue remind us that the intensity of the impact of the "global" financial crisis is geographically patterned. The contemporary dynamics of debt restructuring in emerging markets, and in particular across key East Asian states, have been in evidence for the last two decades. Governance structures surrounding the global trading regime have remained largely untouched.[26] And following the classic distinction established by Keohane,[27] we see that the tendency of state actors to behave in an atomised manner in the "high politics" of security governance remains the case through the current period.

What Makes an Event Become a Crisis?

Critical events that have a global impact often become recognised in retrospect as crises that served as "turning points" to usher in new political and economic orders.[28] In this process of translating an event or a series of events into a "crisis", brute facts matter—such as the loss of value from stock markets, or the volume of liquidity injections in a particular economy. But facts require an *interpretive framework* for actors to make sense of them, as well as for specific events to be recognised as representing a "crisis". For example, because it does not smell like burning toast, emerging market debt recomposition has not set off smoke alarms. Likewise, political and economic elites, as well as the media, have held up the "mirror of history" to link current understandings of the global financial crisis to earlier crisis frames such as the 1930s Great Depression.[29] These framings are inherently political phenomena. With this in mind, an essential ingredient in any crisis is the development of an effective *crisis narrative*. Systemic shocks ramp up the level of uncertainty that actors face in making decisions, both in terms of household budgeting and public policy, thereby generating confusion over how an event or series of events should be interpreted and acted upon. Through the dynamic process of crisis narration, a series of discrete events become discursively linked—whether or not they may be deemed to be *causally* connected—and a "crisis" is constructed through iterated acts of framing and interpretation.[30]

26. A recent WTO review concluded that during the height of the financial crisis, "governments largely resisted resort to trade barriers". WTO Trade Policy Review Body, "Report to the TPRB from the Director-General on Trade-related Developments", 14 June 2010. See WTO official website, available: <http://www.wto.org/english/news_e/news10_e/report_tprb_june10_e.pdf> (accessed 20 April 2011).

27. Robert Keohane, "Realism, Neorealism and the Study of World Politics", in Robert Keohane (ed.), *Neorealism and Its Critics* (New York: Columbia University Press, 1986), pp. 1–26.

28. See Wesley W. Widmaier, Mark Blyth and Leonard Seabrooke, "Exogenous Shocks or Endogenous Constructions? The Meanings of Wars and Crises", *International Studies Quarterly*, Vol. 51, No. 4 (2007), pp. 747–759.

29. Amin Samman, "The 1930s as Black Mirror: Visions of Historical Repetition in the Global Financial Press, 2007–2009", *Journal of Cultural Economy*, Vol. 5 (2012, forthcoming).

30. Alexandra Homolar, "Rebels without a Conscience: The Evolution of the Rogue States Narrative in US Security Policy", *European Journal of International Relations*, Vol. 17 (2011), pp. 705–727.

Learning new ways of interpreting unforeseen events is not a "clean" process that actors can always control, but is more likely to be messy and characterised by mixed messages, especially in the early stages of narrative development. The leading actors here include political elites but also the media, opinion shapers, institutional actors (at the national level, such as central bank governors, and at the global level, such as the IMF) and market actors (such as major commercial banks and firms, credit rating agencies and industry representatives, among others). The incremental creation of crisis narratives enables actors to construct a template of cognitive order that can be imposed upon political, social and economic instability, which may serve as a means to rationalise uncertainty and to facilitate negotiation of the terms of an appropriate response to both immediate and longer-term challenges.[31] The contributions to this special issue test and contest these narratives, as is outlined in further detail below.

Global Governance in Crisis?

In the opening article of the special issue, James Brassett and Nick Vaughan-Williams present an innovative and compelling argument that "Crisis *Is* Governance". With its intellectual roots in the conceptual framework advanced by Giorgio Agamben, the article outlines the need to problematise discourses of trauma surrounding the sub-prime crisis. Whereas much existing analysis of the GFC either ignores the extreme imagery within mainstream media narratives, or else selectively draws on this hyperbole as a kind of advertising tool, for the authors of this article the deeper implications of the repeated invocations of crisis as trauma—heart attack, fear, tsunami, volcano—are yet to be explored. For Brassett and Vaughan-Williams, in order to do this it is necessary to invert the dominant line of thinking on the GFC in IR and IPE scholarship. Rather than following the well-trodden reformist path of asking how governance should be altered in the light of the crisis, Brassett and Vaughan-Williams argue that we need to ask how the traumatic representations of the crisis sowed the seeds of its own resolution, and explore how (representations of) crisis functioned as imminent forms of governance.

By packaging together a series of discrete happenings into one mega-event, the narrative of financial crisis has, for Brassett and Vaughan-Williams, displayed analogous properties to the story of the "war on terror".[32] And just as the politics of exception in the war on terror has served to make room for extraordinary forms of government action, the traumatic narrative of the recent financial crisis too has cleared the way for extreme interventions. Indeed, policymakers have explicitly—and repeatedly—invoked the discourse of trauma as a justification for their use of "emergency" powers, with parallels drawn to humanitarian relief after natural disasters. By constituting everyday savers and lenders as "traumatised financial subjects", this narrative interpellated "ordinary people" as the victims of the banking collapse, and therefore helped frame government injections of liquidity as ultimately being directed towards helping everyday financial actors. Through this analysis, Brassett and Vaughan-Williams present a cogent message that

---

31. *Ibid.*

32. See also Wesley W. Widmaier, "Emotions before Paradigms: Elite Anxiety and Populist Resentment from the Asian to Subprime Crises", *Millennium*, Vol. 39, No. 1 (2010), pp. 127–144.

there is an urgent need for discourse in general—and discourses of crisis in particular—to be understood as sites of primary political importance.

Following on from Brassett and Vaughan-Williams, the second and third articles of this special issue are provided by Manuela Moschella and Liam Clegg respectively. Both of these works focus on the IMF, which, given the organisation's historic role as fire fighter of the global financial system, is highly appropriate to the central theme of the special issue. By exploring contrasting areas of the IMF's operations that exhibit similar dynamics, the papers complement each other while revealing significant lessons about the politics of change at this key institution of global economic governance. Moschella's contribution focuses on the evolution of surveillance at the IMF,[33] and specifically the incorporation of financial sector issues into surveillance practices. By taking a detailed, medium-term perspective on the issue, Moschella traces the IMF's engagement in financial sector surveillance back to the 1990s, and the organisation's response to the Mexican and Asian crises of 1994–1995 and 1997–1998 respectively. By laying bare shortcomings in the organisation's capacity to identify destabilising tendencies in members' financial sectors, these crises were followed by a series of relatively low-key reforms including, *inter alia*, the expansion of staff expertise, the creation of a new functional group in the form of the International Capital Market Department, and the launch of the Financial Sector Assessment Programme (FSAP). Operational change at the IMF, for Moschella, is most effective when it takes place through incremental processes of "layering" new practices onto old, and the "conversion" of existing activities to serve amended goals.

Having established these important insights, Moschella proceeds to examine the most recent post-crisis reforms to the IMF's surveillance activities. Two lines of reform are identified. On the one hand, efforts are underway to redouble the IMF's efforts to explore the links between the "real" and financial sectors by more fully integrating FSAPs into its existing surveillance channels. On the other hand, internal and external pressures are propelling the organisation into the realm of "systemic surveillance", supplementing the existing focus on the *domestic* implications of financial sector development with an additional line of analysis on their *spillover* effects. Although the IMF, with its growing knowledge base and increasingly established practices in the area, is well placed to take the former operational change in its stride, question marks over the organisation's data collection and interpretation capabilities mean that the latter is likely to prove a step too far.[34] Restrictions in the IMF's Articles of Agreement mean that the organisation cannot compel members to release data on the private corporations that are likely to be at the centre of the transmission of systemic risk, and—even if these informational gaps could be filled—the assumption that the IMF's existing analytic tool kit would be able to cope with this transformed goal is unrealistic. To head off these problems, Moschella suggests that (in line with past dynamics) more focus is needed on the "nuts and bolts" of the reform process to ensure that there is an appropriate fit between new aims and existing

---

33. For a comprehensive overview of this aspect of the Fund's work, see Manuela Moschella, *Governing Risk: The IMF and Global Financial Crises* (Basingstoke: Palgrave, 2010).

34. On the construction of cognitive authority in global governance, see André Broome and Leonard Seabrooke, "Seeing Like an International Organisation", *New Political Economy*, Vol. 17, No. 1 (2012, forthcoming).

practices. At the IMF, the process of operational reform matters. Slow and steady, it seems, wins the race.

In its analysis of the roots of the IMF's recent reforms to its concessional lending activities, Clegg's paper adopts a similar historically informed approach to that of Moschella. By going back to the beginnings of the IMF's lending engagements with low-income members, which began with the launch of the Oil Facility and Trust Fund in response to earlier crisis episodes during the 1970s, Clegg outlines the distance that began to open up between the IMF's "traditional" area of macro-economic expertise and its steady drift into the world of structural adjustment. Moreover, by drawing on a combination of archival and interview data, Clegg reveals that there is a deeply embedded split between the US and European views of the appropriateness of the IMF's move. This division has remained apparent over a period of several decades, during which time the Europeans have consistently used the provision of supplementary finance as a means of pulling the organisation in a direction against the expressed wishes of its most powerful member state. The recent commitment to double the organisation's concessional lending resources, which accompanied the post-GFC reforms to the IMF's lending and surveillance operations, represents another stage in this overall journey.

In addition to showing that the IMF's largest quota holder is not as omnipotent as many analyses suggest, Clegg also advances our conceptual understanding of another dimension of the politics of change in international organisations. In order to cement a move into a new field, it is necessary for an organisation like the IMF to develop an effective mechanism for collating and communicating evidence of policy success.[35] Historically the IMF has been a poor salesman for its concessional lending activities, and has indeed been consistently subject to heavy criticism on this front. However, with recently announced plans to use monitored conditionality to push borrowers to meet poverty reduction expenditure targets, there is evidence of a significant change here. Indeed, Clegg shows that the data collected by the Fund has already begun to be used by the organisation as a kind of "legitimation device", concisely proving that it is "doing good" in its low-income country lending operations.[36] Overall, and in common with Moschella, Clegg demonstrates that crises play an important catalytic role in processes of long-term change at the Fund, and that, at the end of the day, unglamorous capacity-building measures (in this case, expenditure tracking systems) are the basis on which successful operational transformations are built.

Through the fourth article the special issue shifts focus from finance to trade, as Donna Lee sheds new light on the state of play in the ongoing round of negotiations at the WTO. With a reminder that the regime surrounding the governance of international trade has continued to function according to established patterns during the past couple of years, Lee's article provides a call for calm amongst analysts of global governance. The central focus of Lee's analysis is on the multiple dynamics that are currently aligning to enhance developing countries' agency at the WTO, which collectively are working to facilitate the emergence of a "new

---

35. For an overview of parallel pressures at the World Bank, see Liam Clegg, "Our Dream is a World Full of Poverty Indicators", *op. cit.*

36. The phrase comes from Tamar Gutner, "When 'Doing Good' Does Not: The IMF and the Millennium Development Goals", in Deborah Avant, Martha Finnemore and Susan Sell (eds), *Who Governs the Globe?* (Cambridge: Cambridge University Press, 2010), pp. 266–291.

activism" in the Doha Development Agenda (DDA). With rising export values providing a propitious material background, developing countries have been discursively placed at centre stage in the ongoing negotiations over *development-friendly* trade. In addition, incremental efforts to bolster developing country members' administrative capacity have helped to enhance the knowledge base and skills set needed to effectively participate in negotiations. This has been accomplished, Lee reveals, through high take-up rates of WTO-sponsored training sessions, collaboration with highly specialised NGO activists and participation in the innovative "Focal Point" system to ensure that an African voice is present at all significant negotiating forums.

Under the influence of these complimentary dynamics, African countries have, for Lee, recently found their voice in the WTO. In a reactive fashion, a willingness to say "No" means that it is unlikely that the Doha Round will be completed without an agreement on the vitally important issue of cotton. In a more proactive fashion, the increasingly coherent African bloc has become an attractive partner in strategic negotiations, and members of the Africa Group are increasingly acting as Chairs of negotiating committees and submitting proposals to be discussed. This newfound agency, however, is a double-edged sword. The more effectively African activism is able to assert the collective interests of this group of traditionally marginalised countries by bargaining hard through the Doha Round, the greater the danger that key developed nations will "venue shift" into regional trade agreements where their control is more complete. Whether the moral force of the normative discourse surrounding the Doha Development Agenda will forestall this possibility, for Lee, remains an open question.

In many ways, the "business as usual" message of Lee's paper is mirrored by the penultimate article of the special issue, provided by Alexandra Homolar's exploration of "Multilateralism in the Age of Obama". In presenting a conceptually rich analysis of the changed practices of international engagement between the current and previous US administrations, Homolar's article begins by outlining the surprising lack of clarity surrounding the concept of "multilateralism" in the existing IR literature. In the place of current definitions that either rely on negative descriptions that frame multilateralism in terms of what it *is not* (such as unilateralism, bilateralism), or lack the specificity needed to be analytically tractable, Homolar proposes a novel interpretation of multilateralism "as process". By differentiating between "inclusive" and "exclusive" multilateralism and presenting a typology of observable indicators of political leadership within multilateral processes, Homolar's conceptual framework serves to bring order into a subject that, historically, has all too often been characterised by analyses talking *across* rather than *to* each other.

With this framework in place, Homolar proceeds to explore two policy areas where the need to find global solutions to global problems is at its greatest: nuclear non-proliferation, and the politico-normative bases for humanitarian intervention by force. In relation to the former, although there is some evidence of inclusive multilateralism emerging to match Obama's discursive shift (in particular through efforts to strengthen the UN-monitored Non-Proliferation Treaty), the main thrust of policy initiatives has come through unilateral and bilateral channels. In relation to the latter, although Obama's lofty rhetoric on the "responsibility to protect" (R2P) has drawn a line in the sand under the Bush administration's *post hoc* employment of R2P as a means of legitimising the

2003 Iraq invasion, as yet there is little evidence of the present US presidential administration clarifying its position on the circumstances under which this UN-sponsored norm should be acted on. Unfolding events across the Middle East and North Africa demonstrate the pressing importance of this issue, and reiterate the utility of Homolar's framework as a powerful analytic tool.

Through the final article the special issue returns to the "big picture" analysis of the GFC, with Lena Rethel's article serving to both complement and contrast the contribution from Brassett and Vaughan-Williams. In common with Brassett and Vaughan-Williams, Rethel pushes us to de-naturalise financial crises, and to explore their inner dynamics in greater depth. However, where Brassett and Vaughan-Williams focus on the constitutive power of crisis discourse, Rethel focuses more squarely on material dynamics. Driven by a frustration with mainstream economists' unreflexive use of the sovereign defaults and restructurings of the 1980s as an intellectual roadmap for understanding (and studying) financial crises *en tout*, Rethel outlines a call for a more nuanced approach. Indeed, by focusing on trends in emerging market debt, Rethel demonstrates that rather than being merely desirable, it is imperative that such an analytic shift is made.

By demonstrating that, since the 1980s, emerging market debt has become disintermediated, domesticised, privatised and individualised, Rethel illustrates that the existing "cookie cutter" framework is ill equipped to capture major contemporary dynamics. Because these debt dynamics have not been of a "sovereign eurobond" shape, they have evolved below the mainstream radar and not featured in discussions over the (global) governance of debt. However, as Rethel succinctly puts it, with the transformation of the power to borrow "from being a largely sovereign prerogative to being a matter of the everyday, the politics of debt have changed substantially". Rethel argues persuasively that there is a pressing need to explore the implications of this changed landscape. By demonstrating conclusively that the topography of emerging market debt has shifted, this article lays the foundations on which such a line of investigation can and should be built, and from which broader lessons for the design of global governance arrangements can be derived.

Conclusion

Global governance institutions have played a series of critical roles in the current crisis, including the promotion of international policy coordination, international crisis management and emergency financing, monitoring (and, in some cases, *enforcing*) norm compliance, and diagnosing the proximate causes of—and potential long-term solutions for—regulatory and market failure in the international financial system. Yet the existing architecture of global governance failed to either prevent or to clearly forecast the onset of financial disaster in the core economies of global capitalism. Collectively the contributions to this special issue illustrate how, while the events of the past several years point to a crisis *of* global governance, the contemporary architecture of global governance is not *in* crisis *per se*. On the one hand, the main causes of and responses to the global financial crisis highlight striking regulatory and governance failures on the part of global governance institutions, as well as raising substantive normative questions about the socially appropriate goals for governance at the global level. On the other hand, the pre-crisis institutional arrangements for global governance have thus far either survived intact, or have been reinforced and strengthened rather than reformed and recreated. In part, this is hardly surprising for IR and IPE scholars. Global governance processes and institutions reflect a patchwork of regulatory spheres and actors, which seldom coordinate their actions effectively and more often act at cross-purposes due to their competing institutional agendas, membership pressures, mandates and bureaucratic interests.

Precisely because it is often difficult for both elite and non-elite actors to identify *the* problem in contemporary global governance structures, and where blame for global catastrophes should properly lie, negotiating a clear and coherent set of substantive reforms that sweeps away existing institutional habits and policy routines is both costly and improbable, at least in the short term. By highlighting many under-appreciated dimensions of the crisis/non-crisis with respect to global governance, the contributors to this special issue expand the scope of political imagination with respect to: (1) how the current crisis should be understood from a global governance perspective; (2) what crisis "means" and how crisis diagnosis, management and long-term solutions are interpreted, narrated and deployed; and (3) how actors can potentially utilise crisis episodes to stimulate, expand and also to close down avenues for more radical political and economic change.

Crisis *is* Governance: Sub-prime, the Traumatic Event, and Bare Life

JAMES BRASSETT and NICK VAUGHAN-WILLIAMS

This article provides a critical analysis of how discourses of trauma and the traumatic
event *constituted the ethico-political possibilities and limits of the sub-prime crisis.
Metaphors of a "financial tsunami" and pervasive media focus on emotional "responses"
such as fear, anger and blame constituted the sub-prime crisis as a singular, traumatic
"event" demanding particular (humanitarian) responses. Drawing upon the work of
Giorgio Agamben, we render this constituted logic of event and response in terms of
the securing of sovereign power and the concomitant production of* bare life; *the
savers and homeowners who became "helpless victims" in need of rescue. Using Agamben's recent arguments about "the apparatus" and processes of subjectification and
de-subjectification, we illustrate this theoretical approach by addressing the position of
the British economy, bankers and homeowners. On this view, it was the movement
between subject positions—from safe to vulnerable, from entrepreneurial to greedy,
from victim to survivor—that marked out the effective manner of governance during
the sub-prime crisis. In the process sovereign categories of financial citizenship, asset-
based welfare and securitisation (which many would posit as the very problem) were
confirmed as central to our future "survival". In short, (the way that the) crisis (was
constituted) is* governance.

"Financial Tsunami: The End Of The World As We Knew It"
(Market Oracle Headline, 30 September 2008)

"The time for half-measures is over. Britain is no longer in the grips of a
credit crunch or even a financial crisis; *it is suffering a full-on financial
heart attack.*"
(Legrain, 7 October 2008)

---

* An earlier version of this paper was presented at the "Governing Traumatic Events" workshop,
Department of Politics and International Studies, University of Warwick, 20–21 January 2011. The
authors would like to thank participants at the workshop, the guest editors of this special issue, and
three anonymous reviewers for their input into the development of the article. Helpful comments
and suggestions on the development of the argument were also received from Chris Clarke, Chris
Holmes, Chris Rogers, Nigel Thrift and Mat Watson. Finally, James Brassett would like to thank the
Department of Political Science and International Studies, University of Queensland, for generous
support in the form of a visiting fellowship during which aspects of this article were completed. All
remaining errors of fact or interpretation are our own.

Introduction

Media and policy discussions of the sub-prime crisis were marked by a prevalence of catastrophic and traumatic imagery.[1] References to a financial "tsunami" and "heart attack" brought a sense of urgency to the discussion of sub-prime. But such representations also worked to constitute the sub-prime crisis at a more fundamental level: as an "event" that required a response. Thus, although the "crisis" was months in production, and is arguably still exerting an influence on world affairs some years hence, we have become accustomed to thinking about "it" as a specific and time bound "event".[2]

The traumatic qualities and characteristics of this event can be found in media portrayals that represented it in terms of shock, fear, anger and shame. Emotional categories were echoed in policy discourses that sought to address the "financial tsunami" engulfing the world economy; as something we had a duty to respond to, but also to anticipate through the construction of "early warning systems".[3] Furthermore, a sense of "emergency" was palpable in reporting on this issue and, indeed, emergency powers (including anti-terror legislation) were invoked in policy responses, such as the UK government's move to freeze £4 billion of Icelandic finances and various efforts, sometimes overnight, to bail out the banks.

Interestingly, early work on the sub-prime crisis within academia has done little to question the representation of the crisis as traumatic. With some notable exceptions,[4] authors within economics and International Political Economy (IPE) have been content to *either* ignore the traumatic imagery, seeing it as the usual puff of infotainment, *or* capitalise upon it in order to underline the gravity of the sub-prime crisis within the history of global finance.[5] For scholars who employ the tropes of trauma, crisis and catastrophe, the suggestion is clearly, and perhaps quite understandably, that "something must be done" to reign in global finance and subject it to the same disciplines as other sectors of the economy. In this sense, it might be argued, if any "positives" can come from trauma and the traumatic imagery surrounding the sub-prime crisis then it may serve to add weight to reformist objectives. Indeed, media, policy and academic discourses seem to have coalesced around the question of governance as a "response" to this "traumatic

---

1. James Brassett and Chris Clarke, "Performing the Sub-prime Crisis: Trauma and the Financial Event", in *International Political Sociology*, forthcoming (2012).

2. As an indication of the kinds of timespans that were involved in the emergence of what was called the sub-prime crisis, see <http://news.bbc.co.uk/1/hi/business/7096845.stm> (accessed 25 April 2011).

3. Gordon Brown, "Speech to the Lord Mayor's Banquet", 10 November 2008, transcript available: <http://webarchive.nationalarchives.gov.uk/+/number10.gov.uk/news/speechesand-transcripts/2008/11/speech-to-the-lord-mayors-banquet-17419> (accessed 31 May 2010).

4. Grahame Thompson "What's in the Frame? How the Financial Crisis is Being Packaged for Consumption", *Economy and Society*, Vol. 38, No. 3 (2009), pp. 520–524; Matthew Watson, "Headlong into the Polanyian Dilemma: The Impact of Middle-class Moral Panic on the British Government's Response to the Sub-prime Crisis", *British Journal of Politics and International Relations*, Vol. 11, No. 3 (2009), pp. 422–437.

5. Peter Preston, "The Other Side of the Coin: Reading the Politics of the 2008 Financial Tsunami", *British Journal of Politics and International Relations*, Vol. 11, No. 3 (2009), pp. 504–517; Ngaire Woods, "Analysis: Financial Tsunami", BBC Radio Documentary, 19 March 2009, transcript available: <http://news.bbc.co.uk/nol/shared/spl/hi/programmes/analysis/transcripts/19_03_09.txt> (accessed 31 May 2010).

event". Do we need more or less governance? Do we need more just or democratic forms?

While this discussion of global governance in times of crisis is an understandable and important response, this article takes a different approach. It aims to draw out the constitutive effects of the invocation of trauma within the discourse of the sub-prime crisis. Taking a lead from recent discussions about the politics of exception in the war on terror, it is argued that there are commonalities between the discursive production of the traumatic event of the financial crisis and the terrorist attacks of 9-11. In particular, by drawing on the work of Giorgio Agamben,[6] we argue that the discourse of trauma provides ready ingredients for the (re)production of sovereign power, liberal financial subjects and the very market practices that were implicated in the crisis. In this sense, we step back from the current round of reformism in global governance scholarship, to reverse the line of enquiry and ask how crisis itself, and more specifically *the traumatic discourse of the sub-prime crisis*, can serve as a form of governance.

According to mainstream psychology, trauma involves the identification of an "extreme" event beyond the range of normal expectations that requires a set of exceptional responses.[7] In the psychological and humanitarian literature, the traumatised subject is produced in direct relation to this extreme event, and is assumed in certain circumstances to develop pathological reactions which require intervention and therapy. More critical approaches to trauma suggest that these logics are increasingly generalised through techniques of psycho-social intervention and psychological debriefing to form a new regime of "therapeutic governance".[8] Indeed as Fassin and Rechtman argue, "Trauma is not confined to the psychiatric vocabulary; it is embedded in everyday usage. It has, in fact, created a new language of the event."[9]

In the first section of this article, we suggest that this narrative of trauma was at work within the discourse of the sub-prime crisis. Sub-prime was constituted as an extreme event that required certain responses; concomitantly financial subjects, borrowers and homeowners were portrayed as the helpless, needy victims of a traumatic event. Emotional responses including shock and fear soon gave way to a moral discussion that centred upon a sense of guilt and shame for borrowing so excessively, and anger at "greedy bankers" for lending so wildly.[10] A discourse of deviance quickly emerged with common critiques of "seriously delinquent finance" and "predatory lending". The very notion of the "sub-prime borrower",

---

6. Giorgio Agamben, *Homo Sacer: Sovereign Power and Bare Life* (Stanford: Stanford University Press, 1998); Giorgio Agamben, *Means Without Ends: Notes on Politics*, trans. V. Binetti and C. Casarino (Minnesota: University of Minneapolis Press, 2000); Giorgio Agamben, *State of Exception* (Chicago and London: University of Chicago Press, 2005).

7. Jon Bisson, "Post-traumatic Stress Disorder", *British Medical Journal*, Vol. 334 (2007), pp. 789–793; Royal College of Psychiatrists, "Health Leaflet: Post-traumatic Stress Disorder", 2010, available: <http://www.rcpsych.ac.uk/mentalhealthinfo/problems/ptsd/posttraumaticstressdisorder.aspx> (accessed 7 April 2010).

8. Vanessa Pupavac, "Therapeutic Governance: Psycho-social Intervention and Trauma Risk Management", *Disasters*, Vol. 25, No. 4 (2001), pp. 358–372.

9. Didier Fassin and Richard Rechtman, *The Empire of Trauma: An Inquiry into the Condition of Victimhood* (Princeton, NJ and Oxford: Princeton University Press, 2007), p. 6.

10. Wesley Widmaier, "Emotions before Paradigms: Elite Anxiety and Populist Resentment from the Asian Crisis to the Subprime Crisis", *Millennium*, Vol. 39, No. 1 (2010), pp. 127–144.

a broad category in itself, was filled out with racial and geographical "data".[11] The effect of such "othering" practices was to affirm an apparently "normal" realm of stable finance and honourable financial subjects who must be secured.[12]

Section 2 of this article interrogates the trauma narrative by reflecting on Giorgio Agamben's arguments about the relationship between what he calls "sovereign power" and the production of certain subjects as "bare life". Agamben works with Michel Foucault's paradigmatic notion of biopolitics as a liberal rationality of governance that takes life itself as its object of rule. However, in a modification of the Foucauldian position, Agamben fuses this account with Carl Schmitt's influential notion of sovereignty as the decision on the exception and Jean-Luc Nancy's concept of the ban. For Agamben, as is already well rehearsed in the critical international politics literature, bare life is produced as an "exceptional" form of subjectivity via a decision about its unworthiness as a form of life. Such a decision, which may take the form of specific intervention or a more general stance arising from a policy or attitude, bans people, particularly those perceived to be of a particular racial background, who are not deemed to be worthy from "normal" juridical-political—and to this we seek to add socio-economic—structures and the protection they usually afford. Here Nancy's concept of the "ban" is central because, on Agamben's account, bare life is not simply excluded from political community, but held in abeyance in relation to it and thus more "amenable to the sway" of sovereign power.[13] Crucially, bare life is not merely an accidental by-product of liberal biopolitics, but rather a necessary component of the continuation of that rationality of governance in the face of its inherent instabilities and limits. Indeed, according to Agamben, it is precisely through the reproduction of bare life that the "normal" liberal citizen-subject is performed into existence: a performance that is ultimately said to define the inner workings of Western sovereign biopolitics.

Applying Agamben's core thesis, we argue that the traumatic narrative of the sub-prime crisis served to produce bare life as a mechanism for ensuring the continuation of "normal" sovereign power relations. Against the grain of much IPE and International Relations (IR) scholarship, we do not regard "finance" as somehow removed from, separate to, or working against "sovereign power". Such a position implies that sovereign power can only be located and understood in the context of the state, which, in turn, is said to be somehow undermined by "global" finance. Rather, we see the ability to define who and/or what can count as "viable" or "non-viable" liberal financial citizen-subjects as an act of sovereign power *per se*: in other words, as a *logic* of governance that is not the sole preserve of the state, but involves other actors such as multinational corporations, regional security communities and diverse institutions whose interests are bound up with ensuring the maximum efficiency of liberal governmental rationality.[14]

11. Johnna Montgomerie, "Spectre of the Subprime Borrower: Beyond a Credit Score Perspective", CRESC Working Paper Series, No. 58 (2008); Len Seabrooke, "What Do I Get? The Everyday Politics of Expectations and the Subprime Crisis", *New Political Economy*, Vol. 15, No. 1 (2010), pp. 51–70.

12. James Brassett, Lena Rethel and Matthew Watson, "The Political Economy of the Sub-prime Crisis: The Economics, Politics and Ethics of Response", *New Political Economy*, Vol. 15, No. 1 (2010), pp. 1–8.

13. Michael Dillon, "Virtual Security: A Life Science of (Dis)order", *Millennium: Journal of International Studies*, Vol. 32 (2003), pp. 531–558.

14. Jenny Edkins, Michael J. Shapiro and Véronique Pin-Fat (eds), *Sovereign Lives: Power in World Politics* (London and New York: Routledge, 2004); Jacqueline Best, "Why the Economy is Often the

In this way, we seek to complement the rich Foucauldian literature on technologies of finance such as credit scoring and the moral personage of everyday financial subjects by drawing on Agamben to further elucidate how such systems are reliant on sovereign logics that decide on the status of different lives.[15] The value added of an Agambenian account is that it leads to a fuller appreciation of the way in which decisions about creditworthiness play an important but otherwise unexamined role in defining the worthiness of the subject more generally. As Jacqueline Best succinctly puts it, "[i]f Foucault's concept of governmentality provides important insights into the kinds of tactics and rationalities being deployed [. . .], Agamben's ideas reveal the violence implicit in these governmental strategies".[16]

Finally, the third section of this article illustrates this primarily theoretical argument through the identification of three examples, which we hope might serve as pointers for the future empirical development of an Agambenian approach to global finance. Firstly, the invocation of emergency powers by the UK government was executed in precisely the terms established through the traumatic discourse; without such actions, the British economy—and accompanying "way of life"—was said to face an existential threat. Secondly, we look at the production of individual bankers as greedy/deviant. For a short period, individual bankers entertained widespread hatred and condemnation, even receiving death threats. The effect of such a construction was to individualise the crisis, focusing attention on the "greedy banker", for example "Fred the Shred", and away from the normal finance that needed to be secured. Thirdly, returning to the issue of survival, we look at a range of interventions that sought to re-empower liberal financial subjects and move them from the category of "passive victim" to "survivor". In particular, the category of survivor was secured through the state protection of only "cautious investors" and at the expense of "foolhardy borrowers".[17]

Once this dividing practice had been initiated, cautious victims were secured and the banks were recapitalised. Attention then turned instead to the issue of welfare reform. The effect of such shifts was to mobilise the bare life of the financial subject to the perpetuation of sovereign power, such that individual financial fears were harnessed to collective responses that render unquestioned the financial category of homeowner/mortgager, while simultaneously removing the social welfare that might secure anyone not able to fulfil the requirements of that category. Thus, securitisation and credit-fuelled property ownership were ultimately ensured through the manner of the movement between victim and survivor, or, put differently, from trauma to "recovery".[18] In conclusion, we offer a

---

Exception to Politics as Usual", 2007, available: <http://aix1.uottawa.ca/~jbest/Exception-JBest. pdf> (accessed 10 November 2011).

15. Paul Langley, "Sub-prime Mortgage Lending: A Cultural Economy", *Economy and Society*, Vol. 37, No. 4 (2008), pp. 469–494.

16. Best, *op. cit.*, p. 21.

17. Montgomerie, *op. cit.*; Watson, *op. cit.*

18. Extending this line of thought, an implication of our argument is that while the moral and critical attraction of debates about global governance is clearly apparent—indeed we have elsewhere contributed to them (see William Smith and James Brassett, "Deliberation and Global Governance: Liberal Cosmopolitan and Critical Perspectives", *Ethics and International Affairs*, Vol. 22, No. 1 (2008), pp. 69–92)—it is also important to reflect upon how discourses of crisis act as a form of governance themselves, within which resistance can also be effectively thought/practised. By this we mean to suggest that, in line with Foucault, governance/resistance is an enduring dilemma in and across

discussion of potentially new ways of thinking/practising resistance that may emerge from our reconfigured approach to the sub-prime crisis precisely *as* a mode of governance.

1. The Sub-prime Crisis as a Traumatic Event

The subprime crisis that began in the summer of 2007 may rank as one of the most traumatic global developments since World War II. Unlike wars and famine, this crisis and how it was caused seems to have caught the governing elites in rich countries completely unawares.[19]

Finance has long been an area of intense metaphorical work.[20] While contemporary finance has often relied upon metaphors of size and heroism—"global finance" as a "phoenix risen" and populated by "rocket scientists"—the history of finance demonstrates how metaphorical tropes have worked to produce such "positives" against the negative of finance-gone-wrong. For instance, Marieke De Goede has identified how discourses of fortune have drawn upon ideas relating to the goddess Fortuna and the question of whether or not she can be mastered by rational man.[21] A stable rising market is associated with cold reason, mastery of "fundamentals" and so forth. A plummeting market is produced as hysterical, mad, or as David Buick told Radio Four[22] in the midst of one recent crash, the markets were in need of "a good slap" to bring them to their senses. As De Goede argues:

> The argument that situates financial crises in the realm of delusion and madness sustains a discourse of transcendental reality. By locating financial crisis in the aberrant domain of mad behaviour, the normal, regular and sane workings of financial markets are reaffirmed. Irrationality, excess and greed are located externally to the financial system; they may disturb the system from time to time, but have no proper place in it. Thus, the financial system is imagined as a coherent and rational whole.[23]

social contexts, as important in the relations of power embodied in popular culture as it is in the relations between institutions and financial markets. Indeed, the two areas readily overlap, as authors such as Rob Aitken (*Performing Capital: Towards a Cultural Economy of Popular and Global Finance* (New York: Palgrave Macmillan, 2007)) and Marieke De Goede ("Mastering Lady Credit", *International Feminist Journal of Politics*, Vol. 2, No. 1 (2000), pp. 58–81) have demonstrated. While some may be tempted to draw a line between such perspectives, seeing them as fundamentally irreconcilable, an "either-or", we are not persuaded by such dichotomies and see them as a barrier to fruitful and productive dialogue and critical engagement, thus more of a "both-and" (for a sustained discussion of this question see James Brassett and Eleni Tsingou, "The Politics of Legitimate Global Governance", *Review of International Political Economy*, Vol. 18, No. 1 (2011), pp. 1–16).

19. Tim Sinclair, "Round up the Usual Suspects: Blame and the Subprime Crisis", *New Political Economy*, Vol. 15, No. 1 (2010), p. 100.

20. Gordon Clark, "Money Flows Like Mercury: The Geography of Global Finance", *Geografiska Annaler*, Vol. 87, No. 2 (2005), pp. 99–112; P. Kelly, "Metaphors of Meltdown: Political Representations of Economic Space in the Asian Financial Crisis", *Environment and Planning D*, Vol. 19, No. 6 (2001), pp. 719–742.

21. De Goede, *op. cit.*

22. "Live cut away", Radio Four, PM, 17 September 2008.

23. De Goed, *op. cit*, p. 72.

When financial markets go out of control then, there is often a sense that some ungraspable (feminine) power—be it (mad) fortune or nature—is making itself felt. Likewise, in terms of nature, we are also used to thinking about "market turbulence", where traders are forced to "weather the storm". Indeed, the Asian financial crisis was commonly referred to as a hurricane in significant policy papers.[24]

Such metaphors work to construct finance as "natural", rather than the ongoing product of social interactions within structures of power. The political effects of such images are to render financial arrangements as immutable, something we live with, rather than something we make. Interestingly, the discourse of the sub-prime crisis drew upon and developed such metaphors by focusing most directly on their traumatic qualities. Rather than nature, divorced from context, the most commonly used idea was that the sub-prime crisis and resulting credit crunch was like a "financial tsunami" threatening to engulf the world. As Ngaire Woods argued, "Just when many of the world's poor countries have fought their way back – and started building democracies that work, businesses that grow, exports that sell – a tsunami is swelling up out of the banks of the rich world".[25]

This idea of a financial tsunami was common across a range of media commentators and policy actors, including Gordon Brown, who rendered the metaphor according to discussions about transparency. Brown called for an early warning system akin to the one he endorsed after the 2004 tsunami that hit Thailand, Indonesia, Sri Lanka and India. Indeed, the use of imagery like "tsunami" is interesting because it evokes common understandings of mass death. The implicit suggestion is that the sub-prime crisis was not only an example of the awesome power of natural finance, but also an "event" literally capable of threatening the lives of hundreds of thousands of people. This theme of catastrophe was common across a range of commentators who variously referred to heart attacks and "death spirals".[26] In a more light-hearted tone, Charlie Brooker spoke of a "cash-pocalypse". In his BBC weblog Paul Mason wrote:

> There's a lot of catastrophic imagery being thrown around about this crisis, but I think I have finally found one that fits: with the 15 September meltdown, the stock market panic and finally the economic chill that is falling on the world and depressing growth. *It's like the eruption of Krakatoa.*[27]

The intensity of media interest that surrounded the sub-prime crisis meant that there was a near blanket coverage of finance throughout certain weeks. This is interesting and important for a number of reasons, not least because it suggests

---

24. See, for example, M. Goldstein, *Safeguarding Prosperity in a Global Financial System: The Future International Financial Architecture* (A Report of an Independent Task Force Sponsored by the Council on Foreign Relations) (Washington, DC: Institute for International Economics, 1999), p. 6.

25. Woods, *op. cit.*

26. Andrew Rawnsley, "The Weekend Gordon Brown Saved the Banks from the Abyss", *The Observer*, 21 February 2010, available: <http://www.guardian.co.uk/politics/2010/feb/21/gordon-brown-saved-banks> (accessed 31 May 2010).

27. Paul Mason, "This is an Economic Krakatoa", *Idle Scrawl*, 15 October 2008, available: <http://www.bbc.co.uk/blogs/newsnight/paulmason/2008/10/this_is_an_economic_krakatoa.html> (accessed 1 June 2010).

a broader, more everyday interest in the politics of finance than is commonly assumed in much of the literature. Thus, we argue, the role of trauma in the everyday production of knowledge about finance connects abstract financial knowledge with individual financial subjects in interesting and problematic ways.[28]

In ethico-political terms, one of the most interesting questions in finance is the binaries of inclusion and exclusion that operate. As Lena Rethel (this issue) argues,

> ... by looking at the shifting boundaries of debt in the wake of crises, we can gain a better understanding of the economic, political and ultimately normative commitments these entail. Each crisis is a unique social experience, operating as a catalyst for rebalancing various aspects of state–market–society relations. As the politics of adjustment generate new dynamics of inclusion and exclusion, a more nuanced, historically sensitive understanding [...] is necessary.[29]

A key issue we identify is the disjuncture between the way the language of finance is often couched in terms of abstract, arcane and fundamentally elitist mathematical equations and economistic readings of reality on the one hand, and ongoing processes of financialisation that have witnessed the widespread "democratisation" of finance such that everyday citizen-subjects are increasingly rendered as "financial subjects", on the other hand.[30] In this sense, a dilemma emerges in terms of how to (effectively) govern financial subjects increasingly aware of the realities and importance of finance without drawing upon (older) forms of financial elitism that seek to exclude.

The Discourse of the Sub-prime Crisis as a "Traumatic Event"

In order to address these issues we focus on the discursive construction of the sub-prime crisis as a "traumatic event". We adopt a sociologically "thicker" notion of discourse than is commonly portrayed in the literature on constructivism, for instance, one that does not reduce discursive formations to merely "linguistic" phenomena but seeks to recover the political force of materiality.[31] After all, the sub-prime crisis was not just about the words, sentences and speeches of high-profile politicians or media commentators, or the financial models of number crunchers, for that matter. It was also produced in terms of the everyday experiences of Northern Rock customers who could not access their savings, the frustrations of those trying to sell their houses, the bankers who lost their jobs

---

28. More broadly, then, we echo Widmaier, *op. cit.*, p. 129 when he argues: "Even as emotional influences have driven market and policy trends, International Relations (IR) and International Political Economy (IPE) frameworks have neglected their import. To the extent that the recent IPE literature has overlooked emotional influences, it has led scholars to underrate the emotional context of agency, the weight of emotional influences on elites and possibilities for a more pragmatic IR theory that 'speaks the language' of policy and market agents."

29. Lena Rethel, "Each Time is Different! The Shifting Boundaries of Emerging Market Debt", *Global Society*, Vol. 26, No. 1 (2012), p.127.

30. Langley, *op. cit.*; Aitken, *op. cit.*

31. Tom Lundborg and Nick Vaughan-Williams, "Resilience, Critical Infrastructure, and Molecular Security: The Excess of 'Life' in Biopolitics", *International Political Sociology*, Vol. 5, No. 4 (2011), pp. 367–383.

overnight, indeed the widespread demonisation of "greedy bankers", and the crash of the stock markets. In this sense, "discourse" is much more than a set of words and sentences that can be counted or otherwise recorded, but refers to the complex performance of subjects and objects in contested relations of power. The production and governance of financial subjects is therefore a continuous and everyday practice; as tied to the use of graphs and arrows on our 24-hour TV news and the home-owning ideology of the *Daily Mail* as it is financial models or the dominant discourses of economics and politics.[32]

Significantly, the overriding frame in representations of the sub-prime crisis was one that focused on emotional reactions.[33] Savers were depicted in fear for their money, homeowners were quizzed about what they would do if the bank foreclosed or, as became more central, their house prices went down.[34] Understandably, when told about the onset of a "financial tsunami", popular emotions were indeed marked by shock and fear, but interestingly there was also a mobilisation of other traumatic emotions, including shame—both individual and collective—as well as anger towards the alleged perpetrators. The "blame game" that emerged sought to identify numerous candidates and make them feel guilt and shame for their role in the crisis.[35] Clearly the excesses of bankers, predatory lending and high remuneration were major issues, but equally, perhaps, there was a more general reflection upon the way that we were *all personally* responsible; we had borrowed too much, got too used to "Lady Credit" and had not learnt from the mistakes of our predecessors in the Great Depression.[36]

These kinds of emotional responses were not just individual experiences, but were gradually mobilised by the media and interpellated as collective categories for understanding and responding to the crisis. As Matthew Watson argues, the media discourse of the sub-prime crisis, particularly as it was felt within the UK, nurtured and mobilised a sense of "angst" in individual homeowners.[37] The active production of a middle-class panic then served to allow the government to justify incredibly large interventions to recapitalise the banks on behalf of such anxious citizens; the trick of course being that it was actually the citizens who were to subsidise the protection of the very banks that created the excessive lending in the first place. As Watson argues, "[t]he continued newsworthiness of the sub-prime crisis was facilitated by the ease with which the focus on house prices was used to turn a public financial event into a personal struggle to survive global economic pressures unscathed".[38]

Watson cites the constant repetition of individual stories about mis-sold mortgages and first-person perspectives on the effect of declining house prices as a way of tapping into latent insecurities commensurate with modern news reporting. In such a manner, the traumatic discourse of the sub-prime crisis was able to mediate between the elite-driven conception of finance on the one hand—finance

---

32. Gordon Clark, Nigel Thrift and Adam Tickell "Performing Finance: The Industry, the Media and its Image", *Review of International Political Economy,* Vol. 11, No. 2 (2004), pp. 289–310.

33. Watson, *op. cit.*; Widmaier, *op. cit.*

34. BBC News, "Northern Rock Customers Air their Views", BBC News website, 17 September 2007, available: <http://news.bbc.co.uk/1/hi/business/6999272.stm> (accessed 4 June 2010).

35. Sinclair, *op. cit.*

36. Brassett and Clarke, *op. cit.*

37. Watson, *op. cit.*

38. *Ibid.*, p. 427.

as dominated by experts, complex knowledge and powerful players—and the emergence of everyday financial subjects on the other.

Crucially, the traumatic discourse of the sub-prime crisis also served to bind together an otherwise disparate series of happenings, experiences and emotions into a unified whole, an "event". While it may now seem commonsensical to think of the sub-prime crisis in such terms, it is instructive to recall the way in which "it" did not present "itself" as a singular event. At the time of the Northern Rock collapse, for example, it was far from obvious even to some of the most seasoned financial commentators that the UK and the West more generally was heading for a disaster of "tsunami-like" proportions. Rather, the "eventalisation" of the sub-prime crisis took place through the stringing together of multiple occurrences beginning with the Northern Rock episode through to the collapse of Lehman Brothers, as well as the media theatricalisation of that sequence. Retrospectively, the production of the discourse of the sub-prime crisis as an "event" has packaged these various happenings as a coherent and straightforward entity.

As has been pointed out in critical analyses of the by now similarly naturalised sequence of terrorist attacks characterising the "war on terror"—from "9/11" to "Mumbai" via "11/3" and "7/7"—such a rendering obscures the intricacies of different occurrences at various sites, and competing interpretations of them.[39] Furthermore, and importantly for the purposes of our argument here, the framing of the sub-prime crisis specifically as a "traumatic" event also enabled a series of demands to be made in response, which, in turn, conditioned the possibility for certain forms of governance to emerge. In this sense, we seek to draw upon the critical literature of trauma that looks to how psychological knowledge about trauma acts to level down experience, finding commonalities of event and symptoms, which then allow for a more direct and predictable form of response/ governance.

On this view, Western conceptions of trauma embodied within mainstream conceptions of psychology and theories of cognitive behavioural therapy (CBT) are generalised as a universal and "normal" response to catastrophe.[40] While this view is somewhat blind to differences between people and cultures,[41] it carries deeper political implications for how we are able to think about the governance of humanitarian response. Politics is reduced to a narrative of a necessary cause/event, a set of pathological effects and a requirement to "recover". On an individual level, this is problematic since it can be invasive and deterministic. As Jenny Edkins, among others, has argued, diagnoses of post-traumatic stress disorder (PTSD) can depoliticize trauma in that those diagnosed "are to accept the route to cure suggested by therapy. Political action is ruled out. Any attempt at such action ... is interpreted as an expression of their disease. It is an 'acting out' of their symptoms, nothing more".[42] When generalised as an aspect

---

39. Angharad Closs-Stephens and Nick Vaughan-Williams, "Introduction: London, Terror, Time", in Angharad Closs Stephens and Nick Vaughan-Williams (eds.), *Terrorism and the Politics of Response* (London and New York: Routledge, 2008), pp. 1–15.

40. Fassin and Rechtman, *op. cit.*; Allan Young, *The Harmony of Illusions: Inventing Post-Traumatic Stress Disorder* (Princeton, NJ: Princeton University Press, 1997).

41. Christina Zarowsky, "Writing Trauma: Emotion, Ethnography, and the Politics of Suffering among Somali Returnees in Ethiopia", *Culture, Medicine and Society*, Vol. 28, No. 2 (2004), pp. 189–209.

42. Jenny Edkins, Trauma and the Memory of Politics (Cambridge: Cambridge University Press, 2003), p. 50; cf. Alison Howell, "Victims or Madmen? The Diagnostic Competition over 'Terrorist' Detainees at Guantanamo Bay", *International Political Sociology*, Vol. 1, No. 1 (2007), pp. 29–47.

of the managerialist logics of global governance, it emplaces an eventalised conception of the political; governance is reduced to response.

It is precisely these "eventalised" forms of governance that we seek to probe in closer detail. To do so we analyse how the discourse of the sub-prime crisis as a traumatic event led to the (re)production of different forms of subjectivity conducive to the shoring-up of the liberal way of life and rule. More specifically, we want to draw attention to and critically examine the manner in which the everyday liberal financial subject was not merely a "passive recipient of" or "bystander to" the discourse of the sub-prime crisis. Rather, we wish to explore how financial subjects were produced in new and problematic ways, which rendered them up as potentially "traumatised financial victim-subjects", in need of help in ways that contemporary liberal governance could then respond to while reaffirming its own authority.

2. Governance through Traumatic Finance and the Production of Bare Life

The previous section suggested that the discourse of the sub-prime crisis was marked by a prevalence of traumatic imagery and sought to reflect upon the political importance of that fact. On the one hand, it was suggested that the use of such catastrophic imagery connects with broader debates about the role of metaphor in world politics and finance. By rendering financial crisis in terms of natural disaster, finance itself is constructed as natural/feminine—i.e., in need of male mastery/reason—and a sense of widespread fear and vulnerability is nurtured. If the sub-prime crisis were a financial tsunami, we might suggest, the question would be where would it hit land and how many people's lives would be threatened? On the other hand, we also wish to reflect more critically on the specific role played by trauma and traumatic imagery in the discourse of the sub-prime crisis. What is the constitutive politics of invoking trauma? What possibilities and what limits are produced in respect of governance? Who is included/excluded according to these sovereign logics? In this way, we put forward the idea that knowledge about trauma, as it is received and re-produced in the everyday coverage of the sub-prime "disaster", plays a constitutive role in the production of financial subjects and the position of responsibility that policy makers concomitantly find themselves in and/or claim.

In this section we draw upon and develop the work of Giorgio Agamben in order to address these questions. Thus, we develop our claim that more is at stake in the use of traumatic imagery than simply the construction of finance as "natural"—important as that may be. Rather, we seek to uncover the manner in which traumatic finance produces an intimate relationship between finance and the subjects of finance. By constructing the sub-prime crisis as a traumatic event to which we should respond as such, a complex moral and economic apparatus of governance is (re)produced. In this sense, the traumatic discourse of the sub-prime crisis is itself a form of governance—or governmentality—that requires scrutiny on its own terms.

Apparatuses and the (Re)production of Subjectivities

In *What Is an Apparatus?* (2009) Agamben introduces the key term of the essay in relation to his reading of the work of Michel Foucault. According to Agamben, the concept of "apparatus" is a translation of Foucault's use of *dispositif*: a relation of forces that are supported by certain types of knowledge. On this view, an apparatus encompasses both linguistic and non-linguistic phenomena in a complex field of forces throughout social life: "institutions, buildings, laws, police measures, philosophical propositions, and so on".[43] Each of these elements is not an apparatus in and of itself. Rather, the apparatus refers to the network of relations *between* them. Furthermore, Agamben argues that every apparatus implies the production of different forms of subjectivity (or "personhood"). On his view, the subject is (re)produced as a result of the interaction between living beings on the one hand, and apparatuses that attempt to capture and govern life on the other hand. In this way, his usage of the term "apparatus" refers to "literally anything that has in some way the capacity to capture, orient, determine, intercept, model, control, or secure the gestures, behaviours, opinions, or discourses of living beings".[44]

Agamben's hypothesis is that contemporary political life, which he associates with the most "extreme phase of capitalist development", is characterised by an "extreme proliferation in processes of subjectification": "today there is not even a single instant in which the life of individuals is not modelled, contaminated, or controlled by some apparatus".[45] For this reason, it is impossible to think of a stable identity of any given subject since s/he is always already the product of multiple overlapping and often competing apparatuses. Moreover, while there have always been apparatuses of some kind or another, Agamben claims that what is distinctive about the current stage in the development of capitalism is that the nature of subjectivities they produce has changed. Indeed, ironically, the nature of contemporary apparatuses is that they do not produce subjects straightforwardly, but precisely work via the activity of what Agamben calls "de-subjectification". In other words, it is precisely through the performative act of denying or negating subjects' subjectivity that their subject-hood is constituted: "he who lets himself be captured by the 'cellular telephone' cannot acquire a new subjectivity, but only a number through which he can, eventually, be controlled".[46]

Agamben points to the figure of the Catholic who confesses their sins in order that their subject position of "good believer" is constituted directly in terms of their de-subjectification. It is the "movement" between subject positions that becomes understood as the true manner of governance, rather than the straight affirmation of deviance. Indeed, it is the very ability to construct subjects as "salvageable through movement", through a de-subjectification, which renders them docile. We believe this short but pointed intervention on the idea of the apparatus brings an important—but otherwise glossed over—dimension to the sovereign production of bare life with which Agamben is more widely associated and to which we will now turn in greater detail.

Sovereign Power and Bare Life

Much of Agamben's more widely read work centres around one particular apparatus and the form of subjectivity it seeks to produce in order to ensure its own

---

43. Giorgio Agamben, *What Is an Apparatus? And Other Essays*, trans. D. Kishik and S. Pedatella (Stanford: Stanford University Press, 2009), p. 3.

44. *Ibid.*, p. 14.

45. *Ibid.*, p. 15.

46. *Ibid.*

survival: sovereign power and what he calls "bare life"—a form of life without any political voice.[47] Seeking to diagnose the biopolitical conditions under which certain subjects are cultivated as "bare" via their de-subjectification, Agamben again turns to the paradigmatic work of Foucault. As is well known, "biopolitics" is the term Foucault used to refer to the process during the latter half of the eighteenth century by which biological life (*zoē*) became included within the modalities of state power (*bios*). For Foucault, the entry of *zoē* into *bios* constituted a fundamental shift in the relation between politics and life, whereby the simple fact of life was no longer excluded from political calculations and mechanisms, but came to reside at the heart of modern politics. For Foucault then, life itself became an object of governance. However, whereas Foucault reads the movement from politics to biopolitics as a historical transformation, for Agamben the political realm is *originally* biopolitical. On Agamben's view, the West's conception of politics has always been biopolitical, but the nature of the relation between politics and life has become even more visible in the context of the modern state and its sovereign practices.[48] Also, for Agamben, and *contra* Foucault, the activity of the biopolitical machine is inherently linked with Western sovereign politics, rather than a particular phase of liberal governmentality emerging from the latter half of the eighteenth century.

Agamben's approach to sovereignty is influenced by German legal and political theorist Carl Schmitt who defined the sovereign as "he who decides on the exception".[49] According to Schmitt, such a decision declares that a state of emergency exists and suspends the rule of law to allow for whatever measures are deemed to be necessary. However, moving beyond the somewhat elitist potentialities of Schmitt's analysis, Agamben also invokes Walter Benjamin's critique of Schmitt's theory of sovereignty: "the tradition of the oppressed teaches us that the 'state of exception' in which we live is the rule".[50] Agamben draws on Benjamin's insight, written during a period when emergency powers were repeatedly invoked during the Weimar Republic era in Germany, in an attempt to move the notion of the exception away from the issue of emergency provisions towards a more relational and original function within the Western political paradigm.[51] That is to say, the politics of exception may be regarded as very much the norm for much of Western society.

Drawing these different strands together then, for Agamben sovereign power is the central apparatus in Western biopolitical structures, one that relies upon the ability to make a decision about whether certain forms of life are worthy of living. Echoing the discussion in the previous section, such a decision produces a form of subject that is characterised by its very de-subjectification. Agamben calls this subjectivity a bare form of life because it is stripped of the "normal" legal and political rights associated with the modern liberal subject (i.e., "de-subjectified"). Rather, it

47. Agamben, *Homo Sacer*, *op. cit*; Agamben, *Means Without Ends*, *op. cit.*; Agamben, *State of Exception*, *op. cit.*

48. Agamben, *Homo Sacer*, *op. cit.*, p. 6.

49. Carl Schmitt, *Political Theology: Four Chapters on the Concept of Sovereignty*, trans. George Schwab, 3rd ed. (Chicago and London: University of Chicago Press, 2005).

50. Walter Benjamin, "On the Concept of History", in H. Eiland and M. Jennings (eds.), *Walter Benjamin: Selected Writings, Volume 4, 1938–1940* (Cambridge, MA and London: The Bellknap Press of Harvard University Press, 2003), p. 392.

51. Agamben, *State of Exception*, *op. cit.*

appears only as a form of life that can be saved, but which has no political voice. Bare life is thus neither what the Greeks referred to as *zoē* or *bios*. Rather, it is a form of life caught in a permanent state of exception between the two.

According to Agamben, the camp is the most obvious manifestation of a space in which the state of exception has become the rule and bare life is produced. As is by now well documented and illustrated, Agamben says that the most obvious illustration of the contemporary production of bare life is the detention camp at the US naval base in Guantánamo Bay.[52] Other current examples to which we might point include Kandahar and Bagram airbases, detention centres in southern Europe, and Gaza. On the other hand, Agamben refers to "the camp" as something more than these specific sites; it is symptomatic of the deeper workings of the apparatus of sovereign biopolitics. Thus, it is possible to identify logics of exceptionalism and the production of bare life in contexts beyond camps in the conventional sense. In this context, for instance, Agamben has argued that liberal humanitarianism shares a secret alliance with sovereign power in that both can only grasp a form of life reduced to victimhood. Indeed, it is through the designation of a "humanitarian emergency" that global liberal governance attempts to control victims' lives while strengthening its own position. Victims, such as those people caught up in the recent devastating floods in Pakistan and the tsunami in Japan, are produced as passive recipients of aid. By producing such lives as bare, sovereign power in turn shores up its own position as the apparatuses *needed* by the victims it has produced.

This argument holds important implications for understanding the governance of events cast as "traumatic" in general and the sub-prime crisis in particular. In general terms, discourses of and knowledge about trauma can be understood as part of a more general apparatus that renders subjects as bare life. Practices of humanitarian psychology produce "victims of trauma" who require "psychological intervention" in order to become "survivors". Such movements of de-subjectification are intended to avert the so-called pathological effects that can ensue from disaster encapsulated in the diagnosis of PTSD. Indeed, Pupavac sees such practices as a form of "therapeutic governance" that renders subjects as mere recipients of psychological intervention:

> Trauma is displacing hunger in the West's conceptualisation of the impact of wars and disasters in the South. Our attention is drawn to the psychological suffering of victims, their emotional scars, their sense of despair and helplessness. Viewing experiences through a therapeutic lens, trauma counselling, or what is known as psycho-social intervention, has become an integral part of the humanitarian response in wars. Invariably reports flag up the need for counsellors to be brought in to help the community 'come to terms' with its suffering.[53]

This account is particularly reflective of our conception of trauma as an apparatus for the production of bare life, since it points to the way that politics itself is

---

52. Giorgio Agamben, "Interview with Giorgio Agamben—A Life, a Work of Art without an Author: The State of Exception, the Administration of Disorder and Private Life", *German Law Review*, Vol. 5, No. 5 (2004), p. 612.

53. Pupavac, *op. cit.*, p. 358.

subsumed within a medicalised account of the relations between subjects and governance. Pupavac continues:

> Politics becomes both about appealing to and regulating the vulnerable id. Under therapeutic governance, rights are being reconceptualised in terms of psychological recognition and custodianship rather than freedoms, that is, as protection by official bodies, rather than protection from official bodies.[54]

In short, the victims of traumatic events are produced and understood as bare life. Their very subjectivity is understood in relation to the extreme event that has befallen them and their political meaning is simply understood in terms of survival, the movement from "damaged"/"pathological" "individual"/"victim", through therapeutic intervention, to "positive" and "balanced" "survivor".

Traumatic Finance, Economic Security

Collecting these ideas together, we therefore postulate a far more intimate relationship between the traumatic narrative of the sub-prime crisis and the practices of governance that ensued. As Jenny Edkins has argued, "sovereign power produces and is itself produced by trauma: it provokes wars, genocides, and famines".[55] Moreover, in claiming to be the provider of security, sovereign power repeatedly conceals its involvement in the production of the trauma it merely purports to respond to. In this way, we are compelled to reflect upon the violence that produces and is produced by the sovereign power of finance.

It is instructive to note that the discourse of the sub-prime crisis as a "traumatic" event followed a similar logic to that of humanitarianism. Through the invocation of the trauma narrative, a permanent state of emergency in the financial markets—and Western society more generally—was thereby declared and sustained. "Exceptional times call for exceptional measures" was the mantra, which came to legitimise measures beyond the "normal" remit of financial governance. Such a logic of exceptionalism permitted the production of one-time "good" liberal financial subjects as deviant sub-prime borrowers. Like the victims of a humanitarian disaster, these subjects were rendered "needy": not as people who had lost their jobs, homes and livelihoods, and with political views about the socio-economic organisation of society, but mute and undifferentiated financial pariahs who could not do anything about the "crisis" they faced, other than place their faith in the very technologies of liberal governance that created them (and their trauma).

In this way, returning to Agamben, we can see how the discourse of trauma acted as a self-reinforcing apparatus of control. The discourse enabled various forms of sovereign power—not only Western governments, but the liberal capitalist way of life more generally—to reassert authority in the face of "crisis" circumstances it was complicit in creating the conditions of possibility for in the first place. Under the guise of "economic security" the traumatised victims of the

---

54. *Ibid.*, p. 360.
55. Edkins, *op. cit.*, p. xv.

sub-prime crisis were de-subjectified in order to help secure modes of liberal governance.

Against the plight of those sub-prime borrowers, "good" liberal financial subjects were defined who, temporarily at least, could still take out mortgages and life insurance policies and ensure the continued mobility of capital. In this way, as Foucault diagnosed in his series of lectures published as *Society Must Be Defended*,[56] the discourse of traumatic finance resembled a liberal biopolitical apparatus of security. Whereas forms of *disciplinary* power imply apparatuses that structure space by isolating, concentrating and enclosing bodies in order to enable some form of control over them, *biopolitical* apparatuses of security, on the other hand, work precisely by *"allowing* circulations to take place, of controlling them, sifting the good and the bad, ensuring that things are always in movement, constantly moving around, continually going from one point to another, but in such a way that the inherent dangers of this circulation are cancelled out".[57]

Here we might reflect suggestively upon the way that, despite all the traumatic imagery that circulated and the doubtless genuine reflections that ensued regarding the future viability of financial capitalism, the policy compromise that emerged ultimately supported the housing market, protected the banks and then subjected welfare systems across the world to austerity measures. Just as the liberal financial subject is secured, the safety net for anyone unable to meet the criteria of that category is removed.

3. Governing Subjects: The Economy, Bankers and Borrowers

Drawing the discussion of the previous sections together, the use of traumatic imagery in the discourse of the sub-prime crisis constituted the crisis as an event with traumatic characteristics. In emotive terms, responsible savers and borrowers were created as the passive and helpless victims of this "financial tsunami". While the real heat of the sub-prime crisis was perhaps being felt in the market for mortgage-backed securities, the central "effects", as they were relayed in the media, were upon individuals themselves. This was not then just a crisis of balance sheets, but a traumatic event for persons whose entire way of life was in peril. In Agamben's terms, the victims of the sub-prime crisis were produced as bare life, a form of life rendered needy and without significant political voice, incapable of resisting or surviving without the assistance of the sovereign power of governance. In this way, our analysis shares some overlap with the work of theorists on moral panic surrounding financial crises. Indeed, as Mat Watson argues:

> [...] it was the financially literate, financially aware and financially conscientious members of the middle classes who could claim to be the genuinely innocent victims of a sub-prime crisis that was the result of other people's poor decision-making. By downplaying the human interest aspect of stories about being in the sub-prime sector, the idea of being innocently in that sector was progressively lost.[58]

---

56. Michel Foucault, *Society Must Be Defended: Lectures at the Collège de France, 1975–76* (London: Penguin, 2003).

57. *Ibid.,* p. 65.

58. Watson, *op. cit.,* p. 433.

This construction was both enabled by—*and symptomatic of*—a period of inscribing dividing lines between financial subjects. As Watson indicates, "prime" borrowers were divided from "sub-prime" and, further, "predatory" lenders were demonised at the expense of "responsible" lenders. Agamben's account of bare life adds to the literature informed by the sociology of deviance by diagnosing the connection between the production of marginal/deviant financial subjects and the broader operation of biopolitical logics of liberal governmentality. Within the discourse of "delinquent finance", national images came to the fore: the British lambasted the US; the Europeans criticised the Anglo-Saxons; and the "developing world" poured scorn on the North. However, perhaps most interesting about this period, for our purposes, was the way in which the production of the sub-prime crisis as a traumatic event entailed a particular range of "responses".

As we have seen, the nature and politics of response to the crisis echoes the discourse of therapeutic governance. It was not that financial citizens—even the innocent victims—were being *included* in the discussion of how the response should proceed. Quite the reverse in fact; once their status as victims was secured, their political agency was essentially diminished (or "de-subjectified"), and the path was clear for interventions on their behalf. Thus, while some commentators may want to construct—and quite persuasively so—an exclusively class-based analysis of responses to the sub-prime crisis, seeing a classic recalibration of capital and wealth away from labour, we seek to go further and uncover how sovereign power is entrenched through processes of de-subjectification at play. In particular, we are sensitive to the (re)production of financial citizenship that pertains to the traumatic discourse of the sub-prime crisis. In this final section, we examine three sites of response in order to further outline and illustrate our position: the economy, bankers and borrowers.

What is provided here is no more than a snapshot of some of the ways in which our approach might be developed, which finds particular resonance in the British experience of the sub-prime crisis. Other avenues that may be productively explored include bankruptcy, discourses of foreign capital, migrant labour and discussions of the effective "banning" of particular groups (e.g., smokers, the obese, etc.) from public healthcare.[59]

The (British) Economy

On the eve of the recapitalisation of the banks, Gordon Brown released a podcast from Downing Street in which he argued that government intervention was part of a more general "humanitarian" response to the sub-prime crisis. He stressed, "I want you to know, we are doing this for *you*".[60] State intervention to support the banks was thus couched in terms of *saving* individuals. This move, of course, followed previous interventions on behalf of borrowers and savers, and most notably the decision to nationalise parts of Northern Rock. How did the weight of traumatic imagery, the "heart attacks" and "death spirals", resolve themselves into massive interventions to save the banks (institutions that were arguably the cause of the "trauma")?

---

59. Best, *op. cit.*
60. Emphasis added; cf. Rawnsley, *op. cit.*

It follows from our argument that sovereign power requires both the production of bare life to identify its "other" *and* for that other to be enfolded and secured. The way that trauma and the traumatic event were mobilised suggests that this discourse was a particularly effective apparatus for such an exercise. While sub-prime-related issues were identified well before any of the bank runs, credit freezes and stock crashes that we now more commonly associate with "the event", such issues did not constitute a popular news story. Falls in house prices in the US and problems with various mortgage-backed securities simply did not resonate, initially, with the British public. Even the long list of failing sub-prime banks that sprang up through 2006/7 did not occupy much headline space. However, the fall of Northern Rock was a different issue. Simultaneously, anxiety about financial vulnerability, expressed through images of savers queuing round the block to access their savings, was presented alongside the nurturing of a discourse of national shame. This was widely represented as the first run on a British bank for over 100 years and sounded a death knell to the long-felt sense of financial strength based on the City of London. Anxiety and shame were thus mobilised as potent emotional categories. They heightened the urgency of the crisis, nurtured the generalised sense in which these were economically exceptional times, and thereby proffered the question of response in particular (and political) ways.

On the one hand, anxiety became a mainstay of the news reporting on this issue.[61] Members of the public were seen telling their stories of lifetime savings, worries over their future, and even insecurities about their ability to "see" their money. In this context, a helpless victim of the generalised trauma was constructed, bearing witness to a collective tragedy with individual impact.[62] On the other hand, the issue of shame was quickly marshalled to defensive discourses of national pride. This saw a popular discussion over the question of which nations had the "worst" or most exposed financial sectors. Who had taken the greatest risks, endangered the most people?

For a long period Gordon Brown pointed the finger at the US,[63] but soon the story turned to Iceland, a country whose financial system was in a potentially far more precarious state than the UK's. While this turn might reflect a realist logic of securing good relations with the most powerful players, our interest is in the invocation of emergency powers to freeze Icelandic assets. Such an invocation, after all, reflects a Schmittian logic of exceptionalism referred to in the previous section. Normal financial relations were suspended and the declaration of exceptional circumstances came to permit exceptional measures. While the use of these emergency powers related most explicitly to relations with Iceland, it can be argued that a generalised state of exception indeed came to characterise global markets and pervade Western societies in particular.

In the UK context, amidst the turmoil and globally diffuse complexities of the sub-prime crisis, a national image of the economy was produced as a realm to be secured. Indeed, borrowing from the language of the Copenhagen school of security studies, this sector was in effect "securitised": taken outside of the normal workings of

---

61. Watson, *op. cit.*, p. 433.

62. BBC News, *op. cit.*

63. Stephen Webb, "Playing the Financial Crisis Blame Game: Foreign Leaders Were Quick at First to Attack the U.S. for Subprime Woes", ABC News International, 9 October 2008, available: <http://abcnews.go.com/International/story?id=5987055&page=1 (accessed 31 May 2010).

political order and framed via the lens of security.[64] In these terms, an existential threat was posed to the referent objects of "Britain", "the British people", and their "way of life". The securitisation of the British economy and the instantiation of a generalised state of financial emergency entailed the rendering of British subjects as the "real" victims of the banking collapse in desperate need of protection. As Brown put it, "We are taking legal action against the Icelandic authorities . . . We are showing by our action that we stand by people who save".[65] Following an Agambenian logic, the activity of responding to those produced in need of salvation served to reinforce the position of the British government at a time when the security of its own authority was at stake. In this way, and against the grain of extant analyses, the production of the crisis actually created opportunities to govern in ways that reinforced particular visions of sovereign political community.

Bankers

Responses to the constructed trauma of the sub-prime crisis—by the media, politicians and authorities—entailed movements *between* different positions. Thus, for the UK government, the issue of sub-prime went from being a global phenomenon, to an issue for the US, to a national shame, and then on to being a question of national pride (the notion that the UK is still a "stable home" for global finance). Indeed, while in Davos, Brown went to great lengths in order to deny the suggestion found in headlines of the *New York Times* and the Bagehot column of the *Economist* that London was no more than "Reyjkavik-on-Thames".[66] Nowhere is this idea of movement between subject positions, reminiscent of Agamben's notion of the play of subjectification and de-subjectification in contemporary apparatuses of control, more acute than in relation to the discourse on bankers.

According to conventional accounts, a common reaction to traumatic events is to feel anger and blame.[67] Clearly, with the benefit of hindsight, these emotions can be read into the experience of bankers. However, it is possible to identify an initial confusion in popular reactions to the role and position of bankers in the sub-prime crisis. In the early days of reporting, the position of bankers was widely portrayed as an aspect of the traumatic event itself. Bankers were seen in their traditional poses reserved for such occasions—jackets off, rolled up sleeves, shouting, and touching their faces looking aghast.[68] Even when it became clear that there had been a litany of serious errors and excesses within several of the now collapsed big investment banks, the media focused on the job losses. Individual bankers were pictured leaving their office, looking resigned

64. Barry Buzan, Jaap de Wilde and Ole Wæver, *Security: A New Framework for Analysis* (London and Boulder, CO: Lynne Rienner, 1998).

65. Bloomberg, "UK Freezes Icelandic Bank Assets", available: <http://www.bloomberg.com/apps/news?pid=newsarchive&sid=aarH9BaUZJZY> (accessed 10 November 2011).

66. See, *inter alia*, Bagehot, "Reykjavik-on-Thames", *The Economist*, 29 January 2009, available: <http://www.economist.com/node/13021969> (accessed 10 November 2011); D. Smith, "Gordon Brown Says: London is Not 'Reykjavik on the Thames'", *The Times*, 1 February 2009, available: <http://business.timesonline.co.uk/tol/business/economics/article5627301.ece> (accessed 9 May 2011).

67. See Mark Goulston, *Post Traumatic Stress Disorder for Dummies* (London: John Wiley and Sons, 2007).

68. Indeed a semi-satirical blog called "brokers with hands on their faces" was set up to chart this particular aesthetic of the crisis: <http://brokershandsontheirfacesblog.tumblr.com/>.

and carrying their boxes.[69] Of course, as we now know, this confusion did not last long and the mood quickly turned as people realised that the massive sums being used to bail out the banks were going to come from taxpayers' money (current and future).

While we are often taught to think about crisis as an opportunity to re-explore the compromise between capital and labour, it is interesting just how squarely the traumatic discourse of the sub-prime crisis avoided such abstractions. Instead the focus turned quickly to characters like "Fred the Shred" and the details of his salary and pensions; there was even a long period of focus upon his home, with cameras stationed outside his house for some days while he was in another country.[70] In psychological terms, reactions like anger and blame are understood as normal, but potentially counter-productive if excessive or persistent. From an applied Agambenian perspective, it can be noted that through the construction of individual bankers as social pariahs in need of governance, in the form of a ban or heightened regulation, there is a curious pacification of criticism of the structure of banking and finance itself; in other words, a depoliticisation of the context in which their deviance became possible.

In this example, the deviant "greedy banker" is produced concurrently with a discourse of national pride that seeks to save the wider system of banking. While we run the risk of going too far beyond the historical and philosophical specificities of Agamben's argument, it may be suggested that the de-subjectification of the bankers in this way shares a curious similarity with his diagnosis of bare life. The paradigmatic figure of bare life—the *Müsselmänner* of the Nazi *lager*—is of course a far cry from the subject positions of bankers caught up in the sub-prime crisis (and to avoid any confusion it is certainly *not* our intention to draw or imply ethical and political equivalences between the two). Yet, although it would be churlish to overstate these equivalences in empirical terms, the *logic* of the production of the banker-as-outcast from the social-economic order is reminiscent of that which bans *homo sacer* from the city in Agamben's account of sovereign power. Both are subjects who can be saved by humanitarian logics of intervention, but given no place or voice in the "normal" juridical-political from which they are banned.[71]

Borrowers

What of the central victim of the financial tsunami—the borrower? In early reporting of the sub-prime crisis it was widely perceived that the problem was a straightforward "finance gone wrong" scenario. As Montgomerie argued, "the narrative of the subprime crisis has been constructed around two distinct personalities: the credulous and financially illiterate subprime borrower and the greedy and predatory subprime lender".[72] However, the "victims" of the sub-prime crisis

---

69. The collapse of Lehman Brothers was typified by such images. At this stage the dominant narrative was sympathy and Lehman Brothers and its employees were portrayed as victims. As the BBC coverage suggested, "Having survived two World Wars, one Wall Street crash, and 9-11 it now looks like the sub-prime crisis will prove the undoing of Lehman Brothers", available: <http://www.youtube.com/watch?v=4wxeBBYE8pk> (accessed 9 May 2011).

70. BBC website, "Why Does Everyone Hate Fred the Shred?", available: <http://news.bbc.co.uk/1/hi/magazine/7924481.stm> (accessed 10 November 2011).

71. Agamben, *Homo Sacer, op. cit.*

72. Montgomerie, *op. cit.*, p. 2.

who received the most attention, especially in the UK, were the *responsible* borrowers: prudent mortgage holders, ensuring their welfare.[73] For them the "trauma" was most vividly felt in the long and seemingly inexorable decline of house prices and the need to ensure low interest rates. In this way, a crisis of financial citizenship was read into declining asset prices, directly linked to the subject position of liberal financial subjects. Thus, the traumatic discourse of the sub-prime crisis centred narrowly on the recovery of house prices, rather than any more general issues of inequality, or various stratifications due to race or gender (or indeed any broader politics of housing and welfare).

Sovereign dividing lines were inscribed from the start between "prime" and "sub-prime" borrowers. While there was an opportunity perhaps to reflect upon some of the more pernicious practices that entailed the delineation of sub-prime—such as racial profiling and gender and mental issues—what we in fact saw was the generation of patterns of deviance.[74] Such people were commonly portrayed as NINJAs ("No Income, No Job, or Assets") and an example of finance gone mad. The IMF even referred to the whole practice of sub-prime lending as "seriously delinquent finance".[75] In terms of the discourse of trauma, the sub-prime crisis was illustrative of the vexed politics of victimology whereby the very social discussion (often contest) over who can claim victimhood for their cause is of acute political importance.

By claiming victimhood, "responsible" financial subjects in the UK were able to enjoy the promise of rescue and recovery. The panoply of governance responses suggested or implemented during the period of response is breathtaking. Mortgage repayments were guaranteed; the Bank of England rate of interest was brought down to 0.5%; billions upon billions in capital and low interest loans were pumped into the financial sector with the expressed purpose of keeping banks lending; and there was a reduction of stamp duty.[76] In other words, the manner of the movement between victimhood and survival involved an even stronger pact with the sovereign power of finance and the affirmation of the particular category of liberal financial citizenship.

The endemic violence sustained through the production of the imperilled sub-prime borrower as bare life is most obvious when we pause to reflect on the disproportionate effects of the crisis on certain populations. Indeed, while the generalised state of exception implies a pervasive economic insecurity that potentially renders us all bare life or *homines sacri*, as Agamben has controversially argued, evidence shows that the production of the deviant sub-prime other nevertheless was and continues to be a highly racialised apparatus. As Wyly *et al.* have shown in the context of the US, sub-prime lending has always been disproportionately concentrated among ethnic minority individuals and neighbourhoods.[77] At the height of the crisis, however, racial segregation intensified to new levels.

73. Watson, *op. cit.*

74. Langley, *op. cit.*; Seabrooke, *op. cit.*

75. Randall Dodd, "Subprime: Tentacles of a Crisis", *Finance and Development: A Quarterly Magazine of the IMF*, Vol. 44, No. 4 (2007), pp. 15–19.

76. C. Hay, "The 2010 Leonard Schapiro Lecture: Pathology without Crisis? The Strange Demise of the Anglo-Liberal Growth Model", 60th Anniversary Political Studies Association (PSA) Conference, Edinburgh, 29 March–1 April 2010; Langley, *op. cit.*

77. Elvin Wyly, Markus Moos, Daniel Hammel and Emanuel Kabahiz, "Cartographies of Race and Class: Mapping the Class-monopoly Rents of American Sub-prime Mortgage Capital", *International Journal of Urban and Regional Research*, Vol. 33, No. 2 (2009), pp. 332–354.

In 2004 African-Americans were 1.6 times more likely to become "sub-prime borrowers" than non-Hispanic white people; and by 2006 they were 2.3 times more likely.[78] During the same period the share of African-Americans pushed into high cost loans soared from 37% to 54% and inequalities were even more severe in cities such as Cleveland, Chicago, Newark and New York.[79] In this way, the dynamics of the production of sub-prime bare life can be read as part of broader racialised sovereign logics of who is/is not deemed "worthy"—not only of credit, but as part of legitimate political community as defined by liberal biopolitical modes of governance.

Conclusion: Resistance beyond Vulgar Resistance

[...] The prevailing tendency to clearly identify unscrupulous and predatory lenders as the cause of the crisis may actually be politically disabling.
Apportioning blame in this way contributes to securing a foe as a scape-
goat, and leads into the belief that the problems created by predatory
lenders in the sub-prime sector and by excessively greedy Wall Street
Financiers can be regulated away. But apportioning blame also serves to
secure the identity of those who are assumed to oppose that foe. Pointing
the finger at predatory lenders, or their cosy relationships with credit
ratings agencies, for instance, rather conveniently secures the identity of
"prime" lenders and borrowers.[80]

Paul Langley identifies the crux of the problem of thinking resistance to the excesses of global finance beyond a vulgar form of reactionary critique. In the context of a media spotlight on bankers' bonuses, tax avoidance, securitisation and pro-cyclical lending practices, it is somewhat tempting to see the sub-prime crisis as a moment of great opportunity. However, as Langley suggests, such opportunities must be placed in question. On the one hand, following a line of vulgar resistance, and echoing the experiences of numerous previous rounds of financial reformism, it can be observed that very little has changed. Minor "one off" levies on the banking sector combined with minimal scrutiny of *individual* bankers' bonuses are somewhat piecemeal reforms in the context of such levels of anger. While there is clearly some public mood for scrutiny as evidenced in the formation of movements like UK-UNCUT, which deploys important strategies of resistance to question and indeed rephrase conceptions of the public sphere embodied in the current round of cuts in the UK, it is arguably too little, too late. Moreover, the prevailing view that the "answer" lies in state regulation of the apparently errant financial sector is underpinned by a problematic separation between states and markets that further endorses the capacity for sovereign power to "succeed". On the other hand, resisting the line of vulgar resistance involves a deeper questioning of how finance is a social practice produced and re-produced though everyday life. Langley points to the important issue of how blaming particular "excessive" practices like sub-prime lending can have the ironic effect of

---

78. *Ibid.*, p. 346.
79. *Ibid.*, p. 349.
80. Langley, *op. cit.*, p. 490.

securing the identity of "prime" lending. In this sense, critique tranquilises critique; a questioning of the broader practices of governmentality is forgone:

> Given that the calculative devices of risk that have proved so contradictory in sub-prime lending have also made possible prime networks of mortgage and consumer borrowing over the last few decades, the relational representation of a realm occupied by apparently responsible lenders and borrowers is especially problematic.[81]

Indeed, this questioning of the "othering" practices of the sub-prime crisis has been pronounced in early critical work on the topic.[82] Contributing to this line of thought, this article has sought to draw out the "thick" discursive relations between individuals and finance that accompanied the traumatic rendering of the sub-prime crisis. At stake is a notion of how it was not simply practices of "othering" at work, but more complex and ongoing processes of subjectification and de-subjectification. Indeed, as expressed in our title, the production of the sub-prime crisis as a traumatic event and the cultivation of crisis conditions legitimised by that discourse in turn created opportunities for governance precisely through the movement of these subject positions. The relationship between individuals, their houses/homes and their investment and saving habits was suddenly produced as a category of moral analysis in the public sphere. Fear, guilt, shame and anger were mobilised and sovereign responses, typically couched in the humanitarian vocabularies of salvation and helping victims, as we have seen, were not only justified but seen to be necessitated.

While our approach clearly echoes and supports a Foucauldian analysis—indeed, as we have stated, Agamben works within a broadly biopolitical logic—we would also suggest that there are important resources in Agamben that can take us beyond the sometimes "technical" overtones of governmental approaches in IPE. That is to say, it may very well be that technologies of risk, calculative devices and so on, are weaving with particular subject categories—mortgagers/responsible investors, prime borrowers, etc.—but this account does not fully grasp the *violence* of decisions that produce bare life. It is by bringing the violent logics of sovereign power back into the foreground of analyses of the production of subjectivity that we are able to connect and better grasp the effects of the discourse of the sub-prime crisis as a traumatic event. In this sense, and going beyond a logic of vulgar resistance, some curious and perhaps counterintuitive points can be raised.

Firstly, the moral demonisation of sub-prime borrowing, and the salvation of the "real victims" of this crisis, i.e. the responsible prime borrowers, has somewhat overshadowed the potentially transformative effects of sub-prime lending itself. Extending credit to support sustainable asset ownership may very well change the game for many marginalised in society. Thus it is not sub-prime, *per se*, but the specific practices of securitisation, the bundling and re-bundling of risk that led to the expansion of sub-prime lending, which should be questioned.[83] Unfortunately, as Chris Clarke points out, the practice of securitisation has been left

---

81. *Ibid.*

82. See, *inter alia*, James Brassett, *Cosmopolitanism and Global Financial Reform: A Pragmatic Approach to the Tobin Tax* (London: Routledge, 2010); Montgomerie, *op. cit.*; Sinclair, *op. cit.*; Watson, *op. cit.*

83. The authors thank Nigel Thrift for helpful advice on this point.

largely unscathed by even the most "reformist" of the numerous "commissions" on financial reform.[84] Secondly, and perhaps more critically, one of the politically disabling elements of the logic of vulgar resistance is precisely a crowding out of the possibility of asking deeper questions about the centrality of finance to everyday life. The moral certitude of blame simply distracts from other possibilities like de-securitisation, or, on an individual level, de-financialisation, that are not skewed by the moralised divisions between prime and sub-prime, normal and delinquent finance. Indeed, such questions might disrupt the ever more commonsensical conflation of individuals with their home (read: investment) and open up new debates about the politics of housing.

One of the implications of the financialisation of everyday life is that everyday subject positions become a salient component of the operation of global finance. Rather than interrupting the process of governing liberal financial subjects, the sub-prime crisis demonstrates the evolving contours of an ever more entrenched and secure set of arrangements. The discourse of the sub-prime crisis as a traumatic event simultaneously (re)produced the centrality of finance to our future "survival", just as it seemed to question the desirability of such centrality. Drawing from Agamben, we have argued that this was achieved through overlapping processes of subjectification and de-subjectification to construct a financialised form of bare life against which liberal subjects could then be identified, enfolded and secured. The apparatus of invoking the discourse of trauma—and specifically knowledge about the traumatic event—provided ready resources, emotional and psychological categories, for the inscription of dividing lines to shore up the sovereign power of "normal finance". Crucially, we think, it was not simply that certain subjects benefited at the expense of others, but rather that the movement *between* the subject positions of liberal financial subject and bare life—made possible by the discourse of trauma and the crisis conditions it instantiated—was itself the site of governance. Hence, the key question is not how governance should "better" respond to the financial crisis, but how we are to understand that crisis *as* governance.

---

84. Chris Clarke, "The Ethico-political Space of Financial Crisis: Individual Subject Positions in Light of Subprime Regulatory Responses", Paper presented at the International Studies Association Conference, Montreal, 16–19 March 2011.

IMF Surveillance in Crisis: The Past, Present and Future of the Reform Process

MANUELA MOSCHELLA

The global financial crisis of 2007–09, in common with many of the 1990s financial crises that preceded it, has raised important issues regarding the efficacy and legitimacy of the international financial surveillance that lies at the heart of the International Monetary Fund (IMF)'s operations. This article examines post-crisis reform of IMF surveillance activities, placing contemporary reforms in their historical context. A particular focus is placed on the IMF's involvement with financial sector surveillance. By tracing the process of surveillance reform from the 1990s, I show that the absorption of the financial sector into the Fund's surveillance activities continues to be shaped by deeply embedded dynamics. Recent reforms have been designed to enhance the Fund's capacity to assess the systemic spillover effects of developments in key members' financial sectors; however, aspects of the organisation's structure, culture and mandate will limit the extent to which these aims are effectively met. Drawing extensively on Executive Board and archival documents, I show that current proposals fail to fully appreciate the complexity of global financial networks, and that current reforms have their roots in past (failed) experience.

Introduction

The global financial crisis of 2007–09 has brought to the surface serious shortcomings in the regulatory and supervisory mechanisms designed to govern the financial system and prevent financial instability. Against a favourable macroeconomic outlook characterised by ample liquidity and low real interest rates, lax supervision and regulatory forbearance contributed to the build-up of risk that led to the crisis and its contagion.[1] This article addresses the issue of failure of international supervision by focusing on the performance of the International Monetary Fund (IMF).

---

* I would like to thank the participants in the Birmingham workshop on Global Governance in Crisis, including and especially Andrew Baker, Andrè Broome, Liam Clegg, Lena Rethel, Jan Aart Scholte and Colin Thain, who provided important insight and commentary on an earlier draft of this article.

1. The literature on the causes of the subprime crisis is huge and any indication is necessarily selective. Among the analyses conducted by international supervisory bodies and panels of international experts see, for instance, Bank for International Settlements, *Annual Report* (Basel: Bank for International Settlements, 2008), Jacques de Laroisiére, *The High Level Group on Financial Supervision in the EU* (Brussels, 2009); available at <http://ec.europa.eu/internal_market/finances/docs/de_larosiere_report_en.pdf>; and IMF, *Global Financial Stability Report* (Washington, DC: IMF, April 2009).

The IMF has long occupied a primary position within the constellation of international supervisory bodies, which include the Financial Stability Board (FSB), the Bank for International Settlements (BIS) and the G20, among others. Indeed, since the time of its creation in 1944, the IMF has been formally mandated to exercise surveillance over the economic policies of its members and to preside over the stability of the international monetary system. According to the 2007 Surveillance Decision, then, the main objectives of IMF surveillance are "to help head off risks to international monetary and financial stability, alert the institution's 187 member countries to potential risks and vulnerabilities, and advise them of needed policy adjustments".[2] In spite of its mandate and longstanding experience, the IMF conspicuously failed to spot the severe interconnected problems in the world's advanced economies or to provide clear warnings about the risks and vulnerabilities of the global financial system from 2004 to 2007.[3] As the former Managing Director of the IMF recently conceded, in the run-up to the global financial crisis "surveillance lagged behind global economic and financial developments".[4]

The purpose of this article is to examine the reforms to IMF surveillance that have been enacted in response to the weaknesses revealed by the latest crisis. In doing so, the article engages with the literature on the politics of change within International Organizations (IOs) by arguing that today's round of reforms is influenced by the past mechanics of change. That is to say, the way in which IMF surveillance has evolved in the past helps us understand how it will evolve in the future.[5] The argument builds on the historical analysis of the development of IMF surveillance. Indeed, reviewing and explaining the major changes to IMF surveillance that were adopted in the 1990s in response to the Mexican and Asian crises, the article will unveil the characteristics of the institutional development of IMF surveillance that are likely to influence the round of reforms triggered by the global financial crisis.

Specifically, as illustrated at greater length below, two major lessons can be drawn from the analysis of the historical process of change. First, the evolution of IMF surveillance has taken place within the parameters set by the Fund's macroeconomic culture and organisational structure.[6] The lack of financial expertise and of departments dedicated to the analysis of financial sector issues has significantly constrained the expansion of IMF surveillance over time. As a result, IMF surveillance has primarily evolved by small and incremental changes, including layering and conversion, rather than by "big bang" changes.[7] The second

2. IMF, *Bilateral Surveillance over Members' Policies Executive Board Decision*, 15 June 2007.

3. Independent Evaluation Office (IEO), *IMF Performance in the Run-Up to the Financial and Economic Crisis: IMF Surveillance in 2004–07* (Washington, DC: IMF, 2011).

4. Dominique Strauss-Kahn, *Crisis and Beyond—The Next Phase of IMF Reform*, Speech delivered at the Peterson Institute for International Economics, Washington, DC, 29 June 2010.

5. On the legacy of past policies for today's reforms to IMF surveillance, see also Manuela Moschella, "Lagged Learning and the Response to Equilibrium Shock. The Global Financial Crisis and IMF Surveillance", *Journal of Public Policy*, Vol. 31, No. 2 (2011), pp. 1–21.

6. On the importance of organisational culture for the analysis of the politics of change see Catherine Weaver, *Hypocrisy Trap: The World Bank and the Poverty of Reform* (Princeton, NJ: Princeton University Press, 2008).

7. The conceptualisation of layering and conversion draws from the analyses developed in Eric Schickler, *Disjointed Pluralism: Institutional Innovation and the Development of the US Congress* (Princeton, NJ: Princeton University Press, 2001); Wolfgang Streeck and Kathleen Thelen (eds), *Beyond Continuity: Institutional Change in Advanced Political Economies* (Oxford: Oxford University Press, 2005); Kathleen Thelen, "Timing and Temporality in the Analysis of Institutional Evolution and Change", *Studies in American Political Development*, Vol. 14, No. 1 (2000), pp. 101–108; and Kathleen Thelen, *How Institutions*

lesson that can be drawn from the empirical findings is that, next to the constraints set by its culture and internal organisation, the process of change has been shaped by the discretion accorded to the Fund in its mandate. The fact that the Articles of Agreement grant the IMF significant discretion in the conduct of bilateral surveillance has facilitated the process of adaptation over time,[8] but has favoured the adoption of informal changes. Transformation of IMF surveillance was brought about more by changes in organisational practices than by changes in formal rules that need to be adopted by member states.

What do these findings suggest for the reform of IMF surveillance in the aftermath of the 2007–09 financial crisis? In order to answer this question, it is first necessary to look into the reforms that have been recently floated. In particular, one of the reform proposals under discussion is that of giving IMF surveillance a systemic focus. According to this proposal, the IMF will bear the responsibility of assessing members' domestic policies not only against the standard of domestic stability but also in light of international considerations. In line with the recent interest in macroprudential regulation and supervision,[9] the proposed reform suggests that IMF surveillance has to embrace a systemic approach by assessing the international spillovers of domestic policies and suggesting policy adjustments in the presence of negative externalities.[10]

Assessing such a reform proposal against the findings derived from the historical development of IMF surveillance, this article suggests that it is unlikely that the shift towards a systemic approach will materialise in a short time span. As the historical record reveals, the implementation of new reforms has been slowed down by the prevalent macroeconomic culture of the Fund, which is far from having being displaced in spite of the important learning process that has taken place within the organisation since the early 1990s. Furthermore, building on the findings of the historical analysis, what we can expect for the reform of IMF surveillance in the coming months is a progressive adjustment at the level of organisational practices. Exploiting the discretion provided by its mandate, the Fund seems more eager to transform its surveillance by modifying existing operational practices rather than seeking the consensus of Executive Directors on a decision that would give the Fund the explicit mandate over systemic surveillance—i.e., a Multilateral Surveillance Decision.[11]

Evolve. The Political Economy of Skills in Germany, Britain, the United States, and Japan (Cambridge: Cambridge University Press, 2004).

8. On the discretion that characterised the Fund's surveillance work after the end of the Bretton Woods system see, for instance, Manuel Guitiàn, *The Unique Nature of the Responsibilities of the International Monetary Fund* (Washington, DC: IMF, 1992), pp. 8–9.

9. A. Baker, "Financial Booms, Crisis Politics and Macroprudential Regulation: The Political Economy of an Ideational Shift", Paper presented at the AGORA Workshop on Global Knowledge Networks, Brown University, 21–22 June 2010. For an overview of the recent literature on macroprudential regulation and supervision see Gabriele Galati and Richhild Moessner, "Macroprudential Policy—A Literature Review", *BIS Working Papers*, Vol. 337, February 2011.

10. The 2007 Surveillance Decision had already introduced the concept of external stability as an organising principle for bilateral surveillance. Nevertheless, this principle has been extended in the reform proposals contained in IMF, *IMF Executive Board Adopts Surveillance Priorities for 2008–2011*, Press Release No. 08/238, 8 October 2008; IMF, *Bilateral Surveillance Guidance Note* (Washington, DC: IMF, 2009); and IMF, *Communiqué of the International Monetary and Financial Committee of the Board of Governors of the International Monetary Fund*, 25 April 2009.

11. IMF, *Review of the Fund's Mandate—Follow-up on Modernizing Surveillance* (Washington, DC: IMF, 30 July 2010).

The problem with this pattern of change is that it threatens both the efficiency and the legitimacy of the IMF. Switching to systemic surveillance without first securing a formal revision to its mandate cannot but aggravate the crisis of legitimacy of the organisation, especially in light of the scope of the proposed reform.[12] Indeed, the proposal to redress IMF bilateral surveillance in a systemic mode does not solely request a demanding effort from the Fund (i.e., the effort of collecting and pooling information on a wide range of potential sources of financial risks); the reform proposal also requires widespread political support among its membership in order to ensure that IMF warnings do not simply go unheeded. Without significant focus on building both organisational capacity and political support, the reform of IMF surveillance will be less successful than its designers believe.

The article is organised as follows. In the first section, I introduce the characteristics of IMF surveillance as well as the discretion granted to the organisation in its mandate. I then engage with the literature on the politics of change within IOs, delineating the theoretical argument advanced in this article. Section 2 traces the evolution of IMF surveillance that led the Fund to progressively incorporate financial sector issues in its analyses and policy advice. In particular, based on archival documents, the article reviews the evolution that has taken place over the 1990s in response to the Mexican and Asian crises. Section 3 turns to the current reform proposals. Specifically, the article concentrates on the proposal to give the Fund surveillance a systemic thrust. In this section, I also assess the proposal for systemic supervision against the historical record of the evolution of IMF surveillance. In so doing, I use the past in order to obtain some insights regarding the prospects of current reform proposals. In the concluding section I reflect on the conceptual lessons that can be drawn from the analysis of the dynamics of reform surrounding the Fund's surveillance activities, and on likely success of the ongoing attempts to upgrade the IMF's role to that of a systemic supervisor.

From Organisational Change to Dynamics of Change

Along with the provision of financial assistance to member countries facing balance of payments difficulties,[13] the activity that is the most associated with the workings of the IMF is bilateral surveillance.[14] Bilateral surveillance is a regular and obligatory activity. Every year, a team of IMF staff members issues a report that assesses the economic situation for each member country, suggesting

---

12. For an overview of the arguments on legalisation as a form of legitimacy see, for instance, Christian Brütsch and Dirk Lehmkuhl, "Complex Legalization and the Many Moves to Law", in C. Brütsch and D. Lehmkuhl (eds), *Law and Legalisation in Transnational Relations* (London: Routledge, 2007), pp. 9–32. I am indebted to Jan Aart Scholte for drawing my attention to the positive relationship between legalisation and legitimacy.

13. On the Fund's lending to low-income members, see Liam Clegg, "Post-crisis Reform at the IMF: Learning to be (Seen to be) a Long-term Development Partner", *Global Society*, Vol. 26, No. 1 (2012), pp. 61–81.

14. Whereas bilateral surveillance refers to the IMF's oversight activity over the policies of individual countries, multilateral surveillance refers to the analysis of global economic and market developments conducted in the Fund's flagship publications—i.e., the World Economic Outlook and the Global Financial Stability Report. For the purposes of this article, surveillance refers to the bilateral type although, as explained at greater length below, one of the crucial implications of the reforms proposed in the aftermath of the global financial crisis is that of blurring the line between bilateral and multilateral surveillance.

corrective actions where they are deemed needed. These reports are known as Article IV surveillance reports and are based on extensive analytical work by IMF staff and on consultation with national authorities on a large spectrum of economic policies.

Although the scope of IMF surveillance has been significantly extended over time,[15] the core of surveillance is the assessment of domestic macroeconomic policies and, in particular, exchange rate policies, against the rules governing the international monetary system. Under the original par value system created in 1944 at Bretton Woods, the main purpose of IMF bilateral surveillance was that of assessing members' macroeconomic policies against the goal of maintaining the fixed value of national currency. Indeed, the general obligation of Article IV was for member countries to collaborate with the Fund to assure orderly exchange arrangements and to promote a stable system of exchange rates. The Fund would have approved change in the value only if it was satisfied that the change was necessary to correct a "fundamental disequilibrium". The IMF was thereby the guardian of the fixed exchange rate system, and a member that changed the par value of its currency without the concurrence of the Fund became ineligible to use the Fund's resources.

Under the floating exchange rate system that followed the collapse of Bretton Woods at the end of the 1970s, the discretion accorded to the Fund in the conduct of bilateral surveillance increased.[16] Whereas under the Bretton Woods system the par value was the standard against which to assess domestic policies, in the post-Bretton Woods system, where exchange arrangements are left to the choice of countries, "policy assessments need to rely on judgement to a larger extent".[17] The responsibilities of the IMF changed from those of a guardian of members' compliance with the fixed exchange rule to those of an interpreter of members' economic choices. The expansion of the discretion accorded to the Fund, as compared to the one enjoyed under the Bretton Woods system, is also evident from the letter of the amended Article IV where the Fund is mandated to adopt specific principles for the guidance of members with respect to their exchange rate policies (Article IV, Section 3b). These principles have been laid out in the 1977 Decision adopted by the Fund's Executive Board, and have henceforth informed the Fund's procedures for the exercise of surveillance.

As this brief overview reveals, IMF surveillance has undergone significant changes over time, thereby representing an interesting case study for the research agenda on the change in IOs.[18] For instance, borrowing from the rationalist scholarship, it could be argued that the changes in IMF surveillance are explicable either as a deliberate choice made by member states[19] or as the result of information asymmetries and disagreements among members over the precise goals

---

15. Harold James, "The Historical Development of the Principle of Surveillance", *IMF Staff Papers*, Vol. 42, No. 4 (1995), pp. 762–791; Louis W. Pauly, *Who Elected the Bankers? Surveillance and Control in the World Economy* (Ithaca, NY: Cornell University Press, 1997).

16. Discretion here refers "to the characteristics of the act of delegation—that is, a constitution, treaty, legislation, or other type of contract—that establishes the parameters of acceptable agent behaviour". Mark A. Pollack, *The Engines of European Integration. Delegation, Agency, and Agenda Setting on the EU* (Oxford: Oxford University Press, 2003), p. 28.

17. Guitiàn, *op. cit.*, p. 10.

18. For a discussion of this literature see Clegg, "Post-crisis Reform", *op. cit.*

19. Barbara Koremenos, Charles Lipson, and Duncan Snida, "The Rational Design of International Institutions", *International Organization*, Vol. 55, No. 4 (2001), pp. 761–800.

with which to task the IMF. Indeed, using a principal-agent framework, these latter factors may enhance IOs' room for "agency slack"—to engage in activities that are not expressly mandated by member states or that directly contravene members' aims.[20] In contrast, borrowing from the constructivist scholarship, it could be argued that the changes in the Fund's surveillance are a function of endogenous, organisation-specific factors. Indeed, several studies of changes in IOs have convincingly shown how organisational cultures and competition among internal units and departments drive and shape the process of change.[21]

Although the confrontation between PA and constructivist scholars has yielded important forays into the study of organisational change, it is not a purpose of this article to adjudicate between the two explanations; the present analysis builds on the assumption that both are important to explain organisational change.[22] Building on existing studies, the purpose of this article is that of unveiling how the causal factors identified in PA and constructivist scholarship shape the process of change—i.e., the speed and the level of change.[23] Furthermore, the article is interested in assessing whether the way in which change unfolds has an impact on the ultimate outcome of change. That is to say, a question is raised of whether the process of change influences the politics of change.[24]

Anticipating briefly the arguments made in the following sections, the article shows how both the Fund's organisational culture (as constructivists would emphasise) and the discretion enshrined in its terms of delegation (as PA scholars would argue) influenced the *process* through which the Fund reformed its surveillance during the 1990s. Specifically, the Fund's macroeconomic culture slowed down the process of change in response to the Mexican and Asian financial crises. Since financial expertise was limited and no organisational resources existed for comprehensive assessments of financial sector policies, the Fund changed its surveillance by slowly accumulating the required knowledge and by adapting existing instruments to the changed economic circumstances. In short, the Fund's culture and organisational structure contributed to a process of change that was mainly slow and incremental. At the same time, the terms of delegation were also a crucial factor to explain the dynamics of change and, in particular, the level of change that materialised. Indeed, by exploiting the room for manoeuvre provided by its Articles, the Fund reformed its surveillance by

---

20. Darren G. Hawkins, David A. Lake, Daniel L. Nielson, and Michael J. Tierney (eds), *Delegation and Agency in International Organizations* (Cambridge: Cambridge University Press, 2006).

21. Catherine Weaver, *Hypocrisy Trap, op. cit.*; Jeffrey M. Chwieroth, "Normative Change from Within: The International Monetary Fund's Approach to Capital Account Liberalization", *International Studies Quarterly*, Vol. 52, No. 1 (2008), pp. 129–158; Manuela Moschella, *Governing Risk: The IMF and Global Financial Crises* (Basingstoke: Palgrave Macmillan, 2010).

22. For studies that have attempted to bridge the divide between the PA and constructivist scholarship, Daniel L. Nielson, Michael J. Tierney, and Catherine A. Weaver "Bridging the Rationalist-Constructivist Divide: Re-Engineering the Culture of the World Bank", *Journal of International Relations and Development*, Vol. 9, No. 2 (2006), pp. 107–139; Catherine Weaver, "The World's Bank and the Bank's World", *Global Governance*, Vol. 13, No. 4 (2007), pp. 493–512; and Liam Clegg, "In the Loop: Multilevel Feedback and the Politics of Change at the IMF and World Bank", *Journal of International Relations and Development*, Vol. 13, No. 1 (2010), pp. 59–84.

23. This pragmatism is shared by other contributors to this special issue. See Clegg, "Post-crisis Reform", *op. cit.*, and Donna Lee, "Global Trade Governance and the Challenger of African Activism in the Doha Development Agenda Negotiations".

24. Paul Pierson, "When Effect Becomes Cause: Policy Feedback and Political Change", *World Politics*, Vol. 45, No. 4 (1993), pp. 595–628.

relying primarily on informal changes. Rather than transforming surveillance through the adoption of formal decisions or amendments to the Articles, change materialised by changes in the operational practices of IMF staff members. In short, the speed (slow and incremental) of the changes in IMF surveillance has been shaped by the Fund's organisational culture, and the type of change (mainly informal) has been shaped by the terms of delegation.

In advancing this argument, the article mixes the insights developed within International Relations (IR) and International Political Economy (IPE) with those developed within comparative politics, especially within the historical institutionalist tradition that has long studied the process of institutional change. In particular, historical institutionalist scholars have emphasised how institutions (or policies) are the product of concrete temporal processes and political struggles and how these processes constrain change.[25] In the attempt to explain how change takes place in spite of such constraining effects, historical institutionalists have identified a variety of change dynamics among which two figure prominently in the sections that follow: conversion and layering. Conversion takes place when existing institutions are slowly redirected to new goals. In other words, what changes is the objective the institution or policy is meant to pursue. As far as layering is concerned, this type of change "occurs when new rules are attached to existing ones, thereby changing the ways in which the original rules structure behaviour".[26] That is to say, change takes place by adding new elements to stable policies rather than dismantling the old.[27] Similarly to conversion, layering is not a quick process of change but entails incremental and slow-moving transformations.

Building on the insights developed from the institutionalist literature, the article shows how conversion and layering have marked the evolution of IMF surveillance over the 1990s because of the constraints posed by its internal culture and the discretion provided by its mandate. Change has materialised slowly, with old facilities redirected to new purposes (i.e., conversion) and new surveillance instruments added on top of existing ones (i.e., layering). In what follows, the article traces and explains this pattern of change over the 1990s in order to obtain some insights into the changes in IMF surveillance in the aftermath of the 2007–08 global financial crisis.

The Evolution of IMF Surveillance: The Incorporation of Financial Sector Issues

Although initially focused on macroeconomic issues, today's IMF surveillance also covers the financial sector policies of its members. That is to say, the Fund's assessments of national economies are usually based on the analysis of both macroeconomic and financial sector policies, including domestic regulatory and

---

25. Sven Steinmo, Kathleen Thelen, and Frank Longstreth (eds), *Structuring Politics: Historical Institutionalism in Comparative Analysis* (Cambridge: Cambridge University Press, 1992), pp. 251–267; Paul Pierson, "Increasing Returns, Path Dependence, and the Study of Politics", *American Political Science Review*, Vol. 94, No. 2 (2000), pp. 251–267; and Paul Pierson, *Politics in Time: History, Institutions, and Social Analysis* (Princeton, NJ: Princeton University Press, 2004).

26. James Mahoney and Kathleen Thelen (eds), *Explaining Institutional Change. Ambiguity, Agency, and Power* (Cambridge: Cambridge University Press, 2010), p. 16. See also Streeck and Thelen (eds), *op. cit.*

27. Schickler, *op. cit.*

supervisory frameworks.[28] The incorporation of financial sector issues within the scope of IMF surveillance has taken place over time and has accelerated in response to the emerging market crises of the 1990s. In particular, it was only in the aftermath of the 1994–95 Mexican crisis and the 1997–98 Asian crisis that the Fund began to devote systematic attention to financial sector issues.[29] Indeed, the fact that financial sector vulnerabilities played a prominent role in the 1990s crises and their contagion forcefully brought home the lesson that financial sector stability is key to macroeconomic stability. Furthermore, the fact that the IMF failed to appreciate the risks coming from the domestic financial sector in both the Mexican and Asian crises laid bare the need to reform its surveillance.[30]

For instance, in the aftermath of the Mexican and Asian crises, the internal reviews on IMF surveillance emphasised that Fund staff had not sufficiently focused on financial sector developments, including developments in the banking and financial sector.[31] Interestingly, then, the shortcomings in the oversight activity of the Fund were attributed to the fact that Fund surveillance had traditionally been mostly concerned with macroeconomic policy mix, leading the Fund to conclude that "Fund missions were sometimes not fully aware of the scale of these financial sector problems".[32] Furthermore, the limited attention reserved for financial sector issues in the conduct of surveillance was attributed to "the shortage of relevant expertise on some Fund missions".[33] That is to say, IMF staff members were regarded as not having appropriate financial training, being overwhelmingly recruited from the macroeconomics profession.[34]

To remedy the shortcoming deriving from the Fund's macroeconomic culture and limited financial expertise, a number of policy changes were adopted in order to bring financial sector surveillance "up to par" with the Fund's traditional macroeconomics surveillance.[35] These changes materialised slowly and mainly at the informal level, following the pattern of conversion and layering identified above.

Change by conversion is well represented by the adoption of new operational guidance for IMF staff in order to inform their surveillance activity. Whereas previous guidelines had not made explicit reference to the need to cover financial sector issues in surveillance reports, these issues gained prominence in the guidelines prepared following the Mexican crisis. For instance, the 1995 Staff Operational Guidance Note encouraged staff members to undertake, in their Article

---

28. For an overview of the different aspects of financial sector policy, Abdul G. Abiad, Enrica Detragiache, and Thierry Tressel, "A New Database of Financial Reforms", *IMF Staff Papers*, Vol. 57, No. 2 (2010), pp. 281–302.

29. Carlo Gola and Francesco Spadafora, "Financial Sector Surveillance and the IMF", *IMF Working Papers*, WP/09/247 (2009), p. 3. See also Moschella, *Governing Risk, op. cit.*

30. On the lessons that were drawn from the Asian crisis for the governance of international finance see, for instance, Jacqueline Best, "Moralizing Finance: The New Financial Architecture as Ethical Discourse", *Review of International Political Economy*, Vol. 10, No. 3 (2003), pp. 578–603.

31. IMF Archives, SM/97/53, *Biennial Review of the Implementation of the Fund's Surveillance over Members' Exchange Rate Policies, and of the 1977 Surveillance Decision* (Washington, DC: IMF, 19 February 1997), p. 20.

32. IMF Archives, EBS/98/44, *Review of Members' Policies in the Context of Surveillance-Lessons for Surveillance from the Asian Crisis* (Washington, DC: IMF, 9 March 1998), p. 3.

33. *Ibid.*, p. 4.

34. See also Bessma Momani, "Recruiting and Diversifying IMF Technocrats", *Global Society*, Vol. 19, No. 2 (2005), pp. 167–187.

35. Gola and Spadafora, *op. cit.*

IV reports, "assessments of financial market developments and their implications for macroeconomic policies and performance".[36] Along similar lines, the 1997 Staff Operational Guidance Note recommended that Article IV "reports should include assessments of financial market developments and prospects as well as of problems and policy issues in the banking and financial sector where they are of macroeconomic significance".[37]

The content of the new operational guidelines indicates that change to IMF surveillance had taken place through the redressing of existing instruments, namely Article IV surveillance reports, which were now expected to assess not only macroeconomics but also financial sector variables. Furthermore, the operational guidelines reveal a crucial aspect of the evolution of IMF surveillance. Specifically, they reveal that policy changes have mainly occurred at the level of operational practices among IMF staff members rather than through formal changes. Since the terms of delegation allow the IMF to set the procedures for discharging its surveillance responsibilities, there was no need to change surveillance by adopting formal decisions that would have required the expressed consensus of the membership. Rather, change took place by way of redirecting the operational conduct of IMF staff members.

Next to conversion, change in IMF surveillance has also been characterised by layering—that is, change occurs by the grafting of new elements onto an otherwise stable institutional framework.[38] A vivid example of layering is represented by the creation of the Financial Sector Assessment Program (FSAP). Indeed, the FSAP represents an add-on to the Article IV surveillance reports; it rests on the recognition that despite the increasing attention devoted to financial sector issues in Article IV reports, it is not feasible to expect them to make in-depth assessments of member countries' financial systems.[39] As a result, the Program was launched in May 1999 as an instrument through which to identify financial sector vulnerabilities across IMF membership. In particular, similarly to Article IV reports, the reports prepared under the framework of the FSAP aim at monitoring the soundness of members' policies. In contrast to Article IV reports, however, the focus of the FSAP is solely on the financial system.[40]

Although major changes to IMF surveillance were adopted in response to the Mexican and Asian crises, the IMF continued changing its surveillance in order to adapt to the changing economic environment long after the effects of the crises ran out of steam. In particular, the process of change continued to proceed slowly and incrementally, without major legislative changes. This dynamic is most evident in the policy changes that followed the publication of an external evaluation of IMF surveillance conducted by a group of independent experts in 1999—the so-called Crow Report. Similarly to the findings of previous evaluations of Fund surveillance, the Crow Report attributed the slow pace of

---

36. IMF Archives, SM/95/22, Sup. 3, *Reviews of Surveillance—Staff Operational Guidance Note* (Washington, DC: IMF, 17 April 1995), p. 3.

37. IMF Archives, SM/97/178, *Staff Operational Guidance*, 3 July 1997, as reported in IMF Archives, SM/00/40, *Biennial Review of the Implementation of the Fund's Surveillance over Members' Exchange Rate Policies, and of the 1977 Surveillance Decision* (Washington, DC: IMF, 18 February 2000), p. 86.

38. Thelen, *How Institutions Evolve, op. cit*; Schickler, *op. cit.*

39. IMF, *IMF-World Bank Financial Sector Assessment Program* (Washington, DC: IMF, 1999).

40. In contrast to Article IV, however, FSAP reports are not obligatory. That is to say, member countries may voluntarily accept to disclose the relevant financial data to IMF staff teams in order to allow them to make their assessment of the domestic financial sector.

improvement of IMF financial sector surveillance to a shortage of expertise among IMF staff members in the financial area. For instance, the Crow Report noted that, "area departments have tended to treat [financial issues] as another add-on, which they do not have the time and expertise to fulfil in more than a pro forma way, especially if countries drag their heels in providing information".[41] In other words, existing organisational structures and expertise within the Fund had seriously constrained the transformation of IMF surveillance towards a thorough inclusion of financial sector issues.

Despite this severe judgement on the Fund's performance, the Crow Report did not advocate radical changes to the conduct of IMF surveillance to overcome the organisational and cultural barriers that had thus far limited the transformation of the Fund policy. Rather, the Crow Report suggested reforming Fund surveillance according to the principle that came to be known as the "macroeconomic relevance test".[42] That is to say, it was suggested that IMF staff incorporate non-core issues in the conduct of surveillance to "the extent to which they actively and directly impinge upon the effective conduct of macroeconomic policy".[43] In other words, the inclusion of financial sector issues in IMF surveillance reports was conceived as acceptable within the limits set by traditional practices of Fund surveillance and within the parameters set by the Fund's mandate. The influence of these factors on the scope and direction of IMF reforms is also evident in the conclusions reached by the Executive Board after discussing the March 2000 Surveillance Review. In particular, among the principles meant to guide IMF surveillance, Executive Directors agreed that non-core issues would have been covered in discussions with members "only when these have a direct and sizeable influence on macroeconomic developments".[44] This conclusion rests in part on the analysis of the Fund's organisational structure. Indeed, as the 2002 review of surveillance acknowledged, the Fund's limited expertise and organisational resources had constituted a serious constraint for an in-depth treatment of the new areas of surveillance, including financial sector issues.[45]

Building on these insights, some of the changes to the Fund surveillance adopted over the past decade have aimed at creating an adequate financial expertise inside the IMF. For instance, in 2001 the International Capital Market Department (ICMD) was created to strengthen "the Fund's conceptual work related to the international financial system and to capital market",[46] an aim that has been further pursued via the internal reorganisation that led to the creation of a new department—the Monetary and Capital Markets Department—in August 2006 by merging the Monetary and Financial Systems Department (MFD) and the International Capital Markets Department (ICM). The Department produces research and provides technical assistance on issues related to financial system

41. IMF Archives, EBAP/99/86, *External Evaluation of Fund Surveillance* (Washington, DC: IMF, 15 June 1999), p. 95.

42. Gola and Spadafora, *op. cit.*, p. 45.

43. IMF Archives, EBAP/99/86, *op. cit.*, p. 88.

44. IMF Archives, EBM/00/24, *Biennial Review of the Implementation of the Fund's Surveillance over Members' Exchange Rate Policies, and of the 1977 Surveillance Decision. Summing up by the Chairman* (Washington, DC: IMF, 10 March 2000), p. 102.

45. IMF, *Biennial Review of the Implementation of the Fund's Surveillance and of the 1977 Surveillance Decision—Overview* (Washington, DC: IMF, 2002).

46. IMF, *Establishing International Capital Markets Department*, News Brief No. 01/24, 1 March 2001.

surveillance, banking supervision and crisis resolution, monetary and exchange infrastructure and operations. Furthermore, the launch of the Global Financial Stability Report in March 2002 offers another illustration of the slow and incremental pattern of policy change of Fund surveillance, as shaped by the need to equip the organisation with appropriate financial expertise. Indeed, the Report builds on the existing IMF flagship publication, the World Economic Outlook, extending IMF research from global economic developments to financial issues. In particular, the Global Financial Stability Report provides an evaluation of the international financial system focusing "on current market conditions, highlighting systemic issues that could pose a risk to financial stability and sustained market access by emerging market borrowers".[47]

In short, the evolution of IMF surveillance has been shaped both by its organisational culture, as constructivists argue, and by the terms of delegation, as PA theorists would predict. These factors contributed to the emergence of a distinct dynamic of institutional development that has been slow and informal, characterised by the creation of new facilities alongside existing ones, the conversion of existing programmes to new ends, and changes at the level of staff operational practices. As a result, before the global financial crisis burst, despite the two decades of reforms, IMF surveillance showed significant continuities rather than discontinuities with the past. As the Managing Director concedes, before 2007–08, "we [the IMF] did things pretty much as we always did ... Even the format of our reports has barely changed over the decades, limiting their effectiveness".[48]

The Global Financial Crisis and the Reform to IMF Financial Sector Surveillance

Similarly to what happened in the run-up to the Mexican and Asian crises, in the years that preceded the 2007–09 financial crisis IMF surveillance failed to clearly identify the signs of the incipient risks to global financial stability and to elicit action from global policy-makers. For instance, the IMF has not been able to fully understand the implications deriving from the global search for high yields or to clearly identify the risks building up in the US housing and financial sector, including the securitisation of mortgages and the reliance on the shadow banking system. Likewise, the IMF has been unable to appreciate the degree of global financial interconnectedness and its implications for the real economy. In short, as a recent report prepared by the Independent Evaluation Office (IEO) critically notes, "the IMF did not anticipate the crisis, its timing, or its magnitude, and, therefore, could not have warned the membership".[49]

The IMF's limited appreciation of the incipient risks is well illustrated by the reaction to a talk given by Nouriel Roubini, an economics professor at New York University, at the IMF headquarters on 7 September 2006. On that occasion, Roubini announced that a crisis was bubbling. Specifically, he identified the sequence of the crisis, starting from the burst of the US housing sector leading to homeowners defaulting on mortgages, the devaluation of trillions of dollars of

47. IMF website, "About the Global Financial Stability Report", available: <http://www.imf.org/external/pubs/ft/gfsr/about.htm > (accessed 1 September 2010).

48. Strauss-Kahn, *op. cit.*

49. IEO, *op. cit.*, p. 4.

mortgage-backed securities and the freeze in the global financial system.[50] Faced with such a scenario, which was about to become real, the IMF was sceptical at best. The *New York Times* reconstructed the reaction to Roubini's talk: "As Roubini stepped down from the lectern after his talk, the moderator of the event quipped, 'I think perhaps we will need a stiff drink after that.' People laughed". In the same article, the IMF economist Prakash Loungani noted that Roubini "sounded like a madman in 2006".[51] While we now know that Roubini's views were vindicated by the events that led to the burst of the subprime bubble, this episode illustrates how the Fund's surveillance was well "behind the curve".[52] Although the IMF was not the only observer that failed to appreciate the accumulation of risk in the financial sector and its explosive potential, the Fund's failure blew up in the face of the past decade of reforms aimed at strengthening the IMF's ability to discern financial risks and vulnerabilities .

To remedy the shortcomings brought to the surface by the global financial crisis, a number of proposals have been advanced to reform the system of international financial surveillance in general and IMF surveillance in particular. As far as the latter is concerned, the debate on reform has been conducted both within and outside the organisation. For instance, a significant input into IMF surveillance reform has come from the G20 leaders, who launched a "framework for strong, sustainable, and balanced growth".[53] Specifically, the G20 committed to develop a process through which to set out objectives to achieve economic growth while assessing progress towards their common end—the so-called mutual assessment programme (MAP). The Fund, together with other international bodies, was asked to assist this process. Specifically, the 2009 G20 Communiqué asks the Fund to provide "analysis of how the G-20's respective national and regional policy frameworks fit together" and "develop a forward-looking analysis of whether policies pursued by individual G-20 countries are collectively consistent with more sustainable and balanced trajectories for the global economy". In short, the mutual assessment programme complements traditional IMF surveillance and offers the Fund a way to strengthen its engagement with G-20 members.[54]

Whereas the MAP surveillance exercise is confined to the members of the G20, several proposals have also been advanced in order to allow the IMF to continue discharging its surveillance activity at the global level, that is to say, to conduct surveillance for each of its 187 member countries. In particular, since early 2008 the IMF has produced a number of policy discussion documents in which the organisation reflects on its mandate and future role.

---

50. The link to the speech Roubini gave to the IMF can be found in its blog EconoMonitor, "2006 and 2007 IMF Speeches by Roubini Predicting the Recession and the Financial Crisis", available : <http://www.roubini.com/roubini-monitor/253448/2006_and_2007_imf_speeches_by_roubini_predicting_the_recession_and_the_financial_crisis___and_the_five_stages_of_grief___> (accessed 6 August 2010).

51. Stephen Mihm, "Dr. Doom. Two Years Ago, Nouriel Roubini Predicted the Current Economic Crisis. Now He Sees Things Becoming Far Worse", *New York Times Sunday Magazine*, 15 August 2008.

52. Indeed, this anecdote is also illustrative of the "blinkering" effects of dominant ideational frameworks in global financial governance, as reflected on elsewhere in this special issue. See Lena Rethel, "Each Time is Different! The Shifting Boundaries of Emerging Market Debt", this issue.

53. G20, Communiqué from the Pittsburg Summit, 24–25 September 2009.

54. IMF, *Modernizing the Surveillance Mandate and Modalities*, Prepared by the Strategy, Policy, and Review Department and the Legal Department (Washington, DC: IMF, 26 March 2010), p. 4.

Analysing IMF in-house documents, it is possible to identify two major sets of reform proposals.[55] First, the IMF has been advocating for upgrading the assessment of financial sector policies in the conduct of its bilateral and multilateral surveillance. That is to say, similarly to the recent past, the Fund suggests an expansion of IMF surveillance to bring financial sector surveillance up to par with macroeconomic surveillance. This line of reform is well illustrated in the content of the Statement on Surveillance Priorities (SSP) for the period 2008–2011, as adopted by the IMF Executive Board at the height of the crisis in October 2008. Indeed, according to this document, staff members are encouraged to pay increasing attention to financial sector issues and real economy–financial sector linkages in the conduct of surveillance.[56] Furthermore, in 2009 an initiative was launched to better integrate the analyses conducted within the framework of the FSAP with those conducted within the framework of the traditional IMF macroeconomic surveillance.[57]

Second, and probably in a more innovative fashion, the IMF has been supporting the proposal to redress its bilateral surveillance towards a systemic approach. Indeed, IMF bilateral surveillance is conducted on the assumption that the Fund should oversee each member's domestic economic choices in order to assess the implication of these choices for the member's own stability. In the most recent documents, however, the IMF is suggesting that IMF bilateral surveillance is given a systemic focus. For instance, the already mentioned Statement on Surveillance Priorities suggests that bilateral surveillance should be informed by the analysis of outward spillovers caused by domestic policies. Following this reform objective, the IMF is planning to introduce new "spillover reports", starting with five systemic economies (China, the Euro area, Japan, the UK, and the US), to assess how their policies might affect regional and global stability. The shift towards systemic supervision is also evident from some of the initiatives launched to enhance the quality of financial sector surveillance in response to the subprime crisis, such as the joint IMF-FSB Early Warning Exercise (EWE). Indeed, the aim of the EWE is to identify "tail" risks, that is to say, low probability risks that nonetheless may have systemic impact. The financial sector surveillance note issued in April 2009 has further specified how to assess potential risks, including qualitative and quantitative diagnostic tools and market-based indicators (i.e., equity prices, credit spreads and credit ratings).[58]

In short, what the post-crisis initiatives reveal is that the Fund is moving towards a significant transformation of its surveillance practices. Since domestic policies should be assessed not only against the standard of domestic economic and financial stability but also against the standard of international stability, the proposed transformation of IMF surveillance is staked on the notion that bilateral and multilateral surveillance should be integrated more closely than has been the case so far. As one of the IMF documents puts it, "for the Fund to be able to promote global stability ... it needs to pay much more attention to outward spill-overs from country policies that impact the system".[59]

---

55. See also Moschella, "Lagged Learning", *op. cit.*

56. IMF, *IMF Executive Board Adopts Surveillance Priorities, op. cit.*; and IMF, *Statement of Surveillance Priorities: Revisions of Economic Priorities and Progress on Operational Priorities* (Washington, DC: IMF, 24 September 2009).

57. IMF, *Financial Sector and Bilateral Surveillance—Toward Further Integration* (Washington, DC: IMF, 28 August 2009).

58. *Ibid.*

59. IMF, *Modernizing the Surveillance Mandate and Modalities, op. cit.*, p. 5.

Comparing the reform proposals to IMF surveillance that have emerged thus far with the reform path of IMF surveillance in the 1990s, a number of observations can be made. To start with, in line with the reform process that has been recounted in the previous section, the ongoing round of reforms is strictly linked with existing surveillance instruments. In other words, rather than being a significant transformation of IMF surveillance, the proposal to transform the IMF into a systemic supervisor relies on the efficacy of existing instruments and expertise—i.e., the analyses conducted by IMF staff members within Article IV and FSAP reports, and the multilateral analysis contained in the Global Financial Stability Report. That is to say, current reform proposals are staked on the assumption that existing instruments and practices can be converted to new ends—that Article IV reports and the Global Financial Stability Report can be converted to the task of identifying outward spillovers and cross-financial linkages. While a reform approach based on the past is certainly desirable in order to maximise the lessons learned from previous experiences, the history of the evolution of IMF surveillance raises a number of concerns. In particular, a question can be raised of whether the Fund's macroeconomic culture and organisational structure are ready for the conduct of systemic surveillance.[60] Indeed, as seen in the previous section, most of the reforms of IMF surveillance adopted during the 1990s were aimed at improving the Fund's skills—that is, the ability of staff members to collect and interpret financial sector data. Having appropriate organisational skills and resources is one of the most relevant issues for the current round of reforms given the demanding task that systemic surveillance entails. Seen from this perspective, a couple of shortcomings can be identified.

Starting with the issue of data collection, the proposals floated thus far fall short of suggesting a way to expand the database on which to draw in order to exercise not only financial sector surveillance but also surveillance of a systemic type. Indeed, if financial sector surveillance requires extending the collection of data from macroeconomic data to financial sector data, including data on domestic financial institutions, this effort is most pronounced if the aim is that of giving the Fund the task of exercising systemic surveillance. Indeed, systemic surveillance entails taking into consideration not only government policies but the activities of those actors that form the financial system, including large financial institutions, counterparties and asset managers. In this connection, an effective systemic surveillance would require the Fund to collect information regarding their activities. However, this entails access to information that the Fund is not currently allowed to demand from its members. Although under Article IV, Section 3b member countries have an obligation to provide the Fund with the information needed to conduct bilateral surveillance over exchange rate policies, Article VIII, Section 5 clarifies that members are under no obligation to provide information "in such detail that the affairs of individuals or corporations are disclosed". The IMF is well aware of these shortcomings. For instance, in a background paper to the proposal to give the Fund the role of a systemic supervisor, the Fund acknowledges that "although financial network analysis is increasingly recognized as a priority, the limited availability of data is a major challenge. Progress in mapping the international financial network is most advanced in banking, based on data collected by the BIS. ... But in other areas, there are substantial

---

60. On these issues see the findings of the 2011 report prepared by the IEO, *op. cit.*

data gaps".[61] In particular, the most serious gaps concern data related to exposures and maturities in debt securities and derivatives markets, foreign exchange markets and international equity markets. Not only are data missing; in some cases data do exist but not in a useable form. This is the case, in particular, for networks involving decentralised over-the-counter (OTC) markets where intermediaries typically know their own exposures but not those of counterparties.[62]

As far as the interpretation of available data is concerned, the proposals advanced thus far do not expressly address this issue but take for granted that the Fund possesses the analytical tool kit to carry out the job. For instance, in one of the papers that sets out the rationale for making IMF surveillance systemic, IMF staff members justify their proposal by noting that, "first and foremost, by virtue of its universal membership, the Fund is uniquely placed to monitor and assess economic and policy spillovers across countries, advise on how to achieve global economic and financial stability (a global public good), and serve as a forum where members discuss each others' policies and collaborate".[63] Interestingly, however, the fact that IMF expertise may not be up to the complexities of systemic surveillance in spite of its universal membership is not even raised—although it has been authoritatively noted that, in the run-up to the crisis, the Fund was not able to spot systemic risks.[64] The problem is that such complexities are difficult to avoid. The IMF had already put great effort into traditional surveillance. To give a measure of the centrality of such an activity for the Fund, consider that about 60% of Board meeting time is devoted to surveillance.[65] Along with the surveillance task, then, the IMF is pre-eminently occupied with the key function of providing financial assistance to member countries facing balance of payments problems, an activity that has peaked as a consequence of the financial crisis of 2007–09.[66] Combining these observations with the number of IMF employees (about 2400), a question can thereby be raised of whether the IMF can effectively undertake the analysis of global financial networks. This is not to suggest that the IMF has not developed—and is not able to develop—the analytical skills to undertake a thorough surveillance of the global financial system, as some commentators imply.[67] The problem is more simply that IMF organisational resources are limited and currently strained. As a result, embarking on a demanding reform process such as the one suggested by the proposal to transform the Fund into a systemic supervisor risks overstretching IMF resources.

Finally, what the current reform proposals indicate is that the Fund is continuing its process of adaptation at the level of organisational practices rather than through formal legislative changes. Exploiting the discretion accorded to the

---

61. IMF, *Financial Sector Surveillance and the Mandate of the Fund* (Washington, DC: IMF, 19 March 2010), p. 9.

62. *Ibid.*

63. IMF, *Modernizing the Surveillance Mandate and Modalities, op. cit.,* p. 4.

64. IEO, *op. cit.*

65. Leo Van Houtven, *Governance of the IMF. Decision Making, Institutional Oversight, Transparency and Accountability* (Washington, DC: IMF, 2002), p. 15.

66. André Broome, "The International Monetary Fund, Crisis Management and the Credit Crunch", *Australian Journal of International Affairs*, Vol. 64, No. 1 (2010), pp. 37–54.

67. Biagio Bossone, *The IMF, the U.S. Subprime Crisis, and Global Financial Governance*, 3 February 2009, available: <http://www.voxeu.org/index.php?q=node/2973> (accessed 3 June 2010).

Fund in the conduct of surveillance, the Fund is suggesting that it incorporate systemic surveillance in its mandate by changing IMF staff operational practices and adjusting existing instruments. In other words, no formal change to the Fund's Articles of Agreement is envisaged and the discussion on a Multilateral Surveillance Decision (MSD), which would help clarify the scope and modalities of the new surveillance, is staked on the premise that such a decision is not proposed for adoption—at this stage, at least.[68] Nevertheless, as already noted with regard to the 1990s evolution of IMF financial sector surveillance, the lack of legalisation of IMF reform risks compromising the legitimacy of the organisation.[69] This would risk undermining the effectiveness of the proposed reform. Indeed, developing an approach to financial supervision that is staked on the assumption that domestic policies should be judged in terms of their spillover effects for other countries requires significant political support since members, at least in principle, would have to agree to adjust their financial policies not for the sake of their domestic economy but for the well-being of the international system. Hence, absent the necessary political support, a change in the Fund surveillance is unlikely to be fully implemented.

In conclusion, reading the current proposals for reform of IMF surveillance in light of the past trajectory of surveillance reforms, a number of questions can be raised regarding the efficacy and legitimacy of the suggested reforms. In particular, the proposal to make the Fund a systemic supervisor raises the issue of whether the Fund possesses the in-house organisational skills and resources to collect relevant financial sector data and interpret them. Furthermore, the proposed change, which is planned to occur at the level of IMF staff operational practices, raises concerns about the legitimacy of the reform in that the Fund lacks an explicit mandate to do undertake systemic surveillance.

Conclusions

While in the aftermath of the global financial crisis of 2007–09 a large part of public and scholarly attention has been focused on the reform to financial regulation, including capital and liquidity requirements, and caps on compensation, this article has drawn attention to financial supervision and its flaws. Indeed, in the run-up to the crisis, domestic and international supervision failed to appreciate the risks that were building up in the markets and failed to urge corrective action. "Implementation and enforcement of existing regulation was ... too lax, reflecting a steady drift toward a more hands-off supervisory style, where the belief that the private sector 'knows best' was permitted to take hold".[70]

Among the supervisory failures brought to the surface by the latest financial crisis, the failure of IMF surveillance cannot go easily unnoticed. The Fund is the international organisation explicitly mandated with the task of promoting financial stability by alerting the institution's member countries to potential risks and vulnerabilities, and advising them of required policy adjustments.[71]

---

68. IMF, *Review of the Fund's Mandate, op. cit.*, p. 6.

69. See footnote 9.

70. Laura Kodres and Aditya Narain, "Redesigning the Contours of the Future Financial System", IMFspn1010 (Washington, DC: IMF, 2010), p. 4.

71. IMF, *Bilateral Surveillance over Members' Policies, op. cit.*

The Fund has carried out this job since the time of its creation in 1944 within the framework of its bilateral Article IV reports and the semi-annual global analyses contained in the World Economic Outlook and Global Financial Stability Report. In spite of its mandate and longstanding expertise, the Fund, as most international observers, has nonetheless failed to recognise the signs of the risks to global financial stability and to activate policy-makers' responses to prevent what has largely been described as the worst crisis since the Great Depression.

This article has reflected on the failures of IMF surveillance by putting it into a historical perspective. In particular, the article has investigated the process through which IMF surveillance has been expanded from its original macroeconomic scope to the coverage of financial sector issues. The historical analysis has revealed a number of important insights that can be of help in speculating about the current round of reforms. In particular, the article has found that, in spite of grand claims of reforms, IMF surveillance has slowly incorporated financial sector issues. This has taken place through small, incremental changes such as conversion and layering. That is to say, existing surveillance instruments were never completely discarded but have been redirected to new ends or complemented by new tools and facilities. For instance, Article IV surveillance reports were redirected towards financial sector surveillance and the reports prepared under the framework of the FSAP were created as a complement to Article IV reports. Furthermore, the historical analysis reveals that most of the changes to the Fund surveillance had taken place below the surface, that is to say, they materialised in the operational conduct of surveillance among staff members rather than in formal changes to the Fund's Articles or by-laws.

The article has explained the dynamics of small and informal changes to IMF surveillance during the 1990s by relying on the factors highlighted by the two leading explanations of organisational change—the constructivist and the principal-agent explanations. On the one hand, the findings of the article indicate that the Fund's macroeconomic culture and expertise have shaped the speed of change to IMF surveillance, by making it slow and incremental. Since the Fund did not possess fully fledged financial expertise, the bulk of the reforms adopted over the 1990s aimed to develop such expertise in order to equip the organisation with the tools to collect and interpret financial data. On the other hand, the terms of delegation help explain the prevalence of informal changes to IMF surveillance over time. Rather than seeking the approval of its members, the IMF adapted its surveillance by exploiting the discretion enshrined in its mandate. By combining the influence of organisational culture with that exerted by the terms of delegation on the process of change, the findings of the article contribute to the literature that aims at bridging the divide between constructivist and PA explanations of change.[72] Nevertheless, the findings of the article also enrich the existing literature because organisational culture and the terms of delegation are explicitly used not solely to explain the causes of organisational change but also its dynamics—i.e., speed and magnitude.[73]

The lessons drawn from the process of change of IMF surveillance during the 1990s have been used to assess some of the reform proposals that have been

---

72. Nielson *et al.*, *op. cit.*; Weaver, "The World's Bank and the Bank's World", *op. cit.*; Clegg, "In the Loop", *op. cit.*

73. On this point see also Moschella, "Lagged Learning", *op. cit.*

advanced in the aftermath of the global financial crisis. In particular, the article has concentrated on the proposal to make the Fund a systemic supervisor by redirecting its surveillance towards outward spillovers of domestic policies and linkages among markets and actors in the global financial system. Reading this proposal in light of the historical record, the article has argued that severe problems risk undermining the reform efforts and current optimism regarding the shift to macroprudential regulation. On the efficacy front, the fact that the systemic surveillance proposal is based on the assumption that it is possible to give a systemic focus to existing surveillance instruments—i.e., the FSAP and Article IV reports—raises the question of whether the Fund's macroeconomic culture will be able to address the complexities of the global financial system. In particular, major concerns remain over the ability of the IMF to collect and interpret data on systemically important financial intermediaries and on cross-border financial linkages. On the legitimacy front, the fact that the proposal to make the Fund a systemic supervisor seems set to be implemented through transformation at the level of operational practices raises serious concerns about the legitimacy of such a reform. Indeed, absent a formal mandate to the conduct of systemic surveillance, the political support and the active collaboration of member countries with the Fund is likely to limited at best.

Post-crisis Reform at the IMF: Learning to be (Seen to be) a Long-term Development Partner

LIAM CLEGG

It is by now clear that for the International Monetary Fund (IMF) the global financial crisis has been spectacularly good for business. And whilst the recently announced doubling of the Fund's concessional lending resources and renewed commitment to "poverty reduction" are intrinsically important developments, they also serve to shed light on the politics of change within the organisation. By placing recent developments in their historical context, this article outlines the evolution of competing views amongst key internal actors over how and when the Fund should lend to low-income countries, and highlights the limited ability of US representatives to achieve their aims in this policy area. In line with a series of historical precedents, advocates of a "developmentalist" IMF have again drawn upon a period of crisis to overcome the more "minimalist" views of the US. By doing so, space has been opened up for the IMF to gain traction over "poverty reduction" through the use of ring-fenced spending. With these changes the IMF is gradually learning to become a development partner.

Introduction

It is almost a decade since Paul Mosley sought to assess the 'merits and limitations of the IMF's long-term development partner role'.[1] For the International Monetary Fund (IMF), the intervening years have been something of a rollercoaster ride. Following the Asian financial crisis—the event that acted as the prompt for Mosley's review—this most heavily criticised of international organisations (IOs) endured a period of what at the time appeared to be terminal decline. With private sources of finance relatively plentiful, and currency reserves growing, lending to emerging market economies all but seized up.[2] To the irritation of many staff, the

*This article draws upon archival and interview research undertaken during two research trips to Washington, DC. The majority of the work was carried out during three months spent as a Research Scholar at American University (AU) from November 2008, and follow-up work done during a two-week period as a Visiting Scholar at the American Political Science Association (APSA) Centennial Centre in June 2010. I owe particular thanks to Tamar Gutner of AU, Alison Desrosiers of APSA, and Premela Isaac and Dorota Wyganowska of the IMF Archives. I also acknowledge the financial support of the Economic and Social Research Council (ESRC) (Project No. PTA-026-27-2807).

[1] Paul Mosley, "The IMF after the Asian Crisis: The Merits and Limitations of the 'Long Term Development' Role", *The World Economy*, Vol. 25, No. 5 (2001), p. 597.

[2] See also Lena Rethel, "Each Time is Different. The Shifting Boundaries of Emerging Market Debt", *Global Society*, Vol. 26, No. 1 (2012), pp. 123–143, for a more general discussion of the transformation of emerging market lending and borrowing.

preponderance of "unglamorous" low-income country arrangements in the Fund's overall lending portfolio continued to increase.[3] This was not only a problem for the self-esteem of the staff who felt "frozen out" from the high table of international monetary policy; it was also a problem in terms of job security. Owing to the IMF's funding structure, the lack of interest payments coming in from big loans meant a lack of money to pay staff's wages. Indeed, during 2007 the IMF embarked upon a process of laying off some 300 personnel, around 10% of its total workforce.[4] With the post-crisis lending surge, these dark days seem to be long gone.

Within this sweeping history, the evolution of the IMF's lending to low-income member states deserves special attention. During the past decade there have been deep divisions within the Fund over how the organisation should operationalise its mandate in its interactions with low-income members. At Board level, there has been a clear split between developmentally minded Europeans and the more minimalist US. This article explores the evolution of these cleavages, and reflects upon the "development" trajectory on which the most recent post-crisis reforms have set the IMF. These contemporary reforms fit into an established pattern: periodically, at times of crisis, "coalitions of the willing" have emerged to push the Fund's concessional lending in a direction contrary to the wishes of the US, the organisation's largest quota-holding member. With the recently reiterated commitment to poverty reduction and the use of monitored "social spending" targets, the Fund's movement in this direction will, in the medium term, continue to deepen.

In exploring these dynamics, the article proceeds according to the following structure. In the opening section of the article I situate my work within existing literature on the politics of change in IOs. To highlight the overall contributions made by the article, analyses dealing with the linked themes of state (in-)ability to control IOs, and with the evolution of the "standards of appropriateness" against which IO performance is measured, are drawn upon. In the second section, in order to shed light on more recent contests over the Fund's concessional lending activities, I outline the evolution of the organisation's approach to balance of payments management during its opening decades. The initial movement of the Fund into concessional lending, which occurred during the oil crises of the 1970s and provides early evidence of coalitions acting in opposition to the stated goals of the US, are reviewed in section three. In section four I focus on the movement of the Fund into structural adjustment lending. Although initially lukewarm rather than outright hostile, over time US opposition to the Fund's low-income country lending has crystallised to the extent that such activities are now considered to be "outside of the Fund's mandate". However, in keeping with historical precedents, these views have been overridden with the most recent post-crisis reforms. These reforms, as the final section demonstrates, have served to open up the space for the Fund to demonstrate its impact on poverty reduction, in particular through the planned expansion in the use of social spending targets. In spite of its increased capacity to demonstrate its effectiveness as a development partner, the deep disputes surrounding the appropriateness

---

[3]IMF, *Annual Report 2009* (Washington, DC: IMF, 2009), Annex II.

[4]André Broome, "The International Monetary Fund, Crisis Management, and the Credit Crunch", *Australian Journal of International Affairs*, Vol. 64, No. 1 (2010), pp. 37–38.

of the IMF's low-income country operations will, for the foreseeable future, remain.

The Politics of Ideas at the IMF

The conventional wisdom in international relations is that, for good or ill, the United States occupies a "special position" in key arenas of global governance.[5] In support of this position, quantitatively based analyses have been presented suggesting that US influence in international economic organisations continues to be used, in a wholesale manner, in order to ensure easy access to loans for its allies.[6] However, the methodological weaknesses of such approaches mean that it is imperative that their claims be re-examined.[7] In examining the limited ability of the US to shape the evolution of IMF concessional lending practices, this article contributes to this overall project of reassessing the impact of the Fund's largest quota-holder on the organisation's day-to-day workings.

Recent literature on IOs provides us with a range of conceptual tools with which to explore the dynamics of power in the world of global governance. In the place of past conceptualisations of power as a somewhat amorphous asset, readily transferable between different arenas of world politics, a more context-specific approach has enhanced our capacity to gain traction over developments at individual institutions. In particular, works drawing on rationalist and constructivist models have helped enhance our understanding of the conditions under which states can—and perhaps more importantly cannot—effectively control the operations of international organisations. These literatures are drawn upon in this article to shed light on the symbiotic linkage between key states' attempts to monitor and control IOs and the mechanics of ideational change.

In broad terms, rationalist analyses of IOs focus on the intricacies of the relationship between state "principals" and IO "agents", paying particular attention to the patterns of knowledge- and incentive-based games in a given situation. The starting assumption is that states stand to benefit from delegating functions to international organisations through the locking-in of particular sets of policies and governance arrangements, and through IOs' utility in overcoming collective action problems. However, in order to fully accrue these potential benefits, significant barriers stand in the way of the would-be state masters. Ever-present "information asymmetries" limit the extent to which states are able to monitor the activities of their IOs. In the case of complex IOs like the IMF, whose impact on the "real world" can at best be traced in a highly imperfect manner, this lack of knowledge is of particular significance. In addition, disagreements among principals over the precise goals with which to task IOs can serve to inhibit state control. A combination of these and other factors can enhance IOs' room for "agency

---

[5]For a more extensive discussion of the role of the US in global governance, see Alexandra Homolar, "Multilateralism in Crisis? The Character of US International Engagement under Obama", *Global Society*, Vol. 26, No. 1 (2012), pp. 103–122.

[6]Thomas Andersen, Henrik Hansen and Thomas Markussen, "US Politics and World Bank IDA Lending", *Journal of Development Studies*, Vol. 42, No. 5 (2006), pp. 772–794; Strom Thacker, "The High Politics of IMF Lending", *World Politics*, Vol. 52, No. 1 (1999), pp. 38–75.

[7]N. Woods, "The United States and the International Financial Institutions: Power and Influence within the World Bank and IMF", in R. Foot, S. MacFarlane and M. Mastanduno (eds), *US Hegemony and International Organizations* (Oxford: Oxford University Press, 2003), pp. 92–114.

slack"—to shirk tasks or engage in activities that more directly contravene states' aims.[8]

According to the rationalist approach, there are two sets of tools at the disposal of principals to keep their agents "on task". On the one hand, states can attempt to put in place incentive structures to induce IO staff to pursue particular objectives.[9] This can be done either at the micro level, with rewards going to individual "conforming" staff,[10] or at the institutional level, with additional resources being tied to the achievement of particular tasks.[11] On the other hand, states can act to improve the quality of information they hold about the activities of IOs. Establishing external oversight committees and internal monitoring frameworks are key ways in which this can be achieved, as is the setting up of proxy-indicators with which to keep track of the success (or otherwise) of an IO in relation to a given issue.[12]

International organisations are, by definition, institutions with multiple state-principals. The IMF, for instance, has 187 member states, all of whom are directly represented at plenary meetings of the Board of Governors (the Fund's highest decision-making authority).[13] Although oversight of the day-to-day operations of the Fund is conducted by the Executive Board, with its more manageable 24 Executive Directors, inter-principal disagreements remain a salient fact of life. Rationalist analyses have contributed to our understanding of the various ways in which such disagreements can impact on principals' abilities to control their agents. Put simply, if principals cannot reach agreement among themselves upon a desired course of action, then their capacity to direct and redirect the activities of their agent will be considerably reduced.[14] In addition, attention has been placed on the importance of coalition formation in pushing through a particular agenda. Through effective processes of alliance building, it becomes possible for less powerful members to collectively determine outcomes in a given situation, at times against the opposition of more formally powerful members.[15]

---

[8]D. Hawkins, David Lake, Daniel Nielson, and Michael Tierney, "Delegation under Anarchy: States, International Organizations, and Principal-agent Theory", in D. Hawkins, David Lake, Daniel Nielson, and Michael Tierney (eds), *Delegation and Agency in International Organizations* (Cambridge: Cambridge University Press, 2006); Daniel Nielsen and Michael Tierney, "Delegation to International Organizations: Agency Theory and World Bank Environmental Reform", *International Organization*, Vol. 57, No. 1 (2003), pp. 241–276.

[9]D. Lake and M. McCubbins, "The Logic of Delegation to International Organizations", in D. Hawkins *et al.* (eds), *op. cit.*

[10]Nielsen, Tierney and Weaver demonstrate that "parachuting in" personnel to promote the Comprehensive Development Framework was an important means of achieving operational change at the World Bank in the mid- to late 1990s. Daniel Nielsen, Michael Tierney and Catherine Weaver, "Bridging the Rationalist-Constructivist Divide: Re-engineering the Culture of the World Bank", *Journal of International Relations and Development*, Vol. 9, No. 1 (2006), pp. 107–139.

[11]André Broome, "The Importance of Being Earnest: The IMF as a Reputational Intermediary", *New Political Economy*, Vol. 13, No. 2 (2008), pp. 125–151.

[12]For an account of how the Millennium Development Goals have become important proxy-indicators of success at the World Bank, see Liam Clegg, "Our Dream is a World Full of Poverty Indicators: The US, the World Bank, and the Power of Numbers", *New Political Economy*, Vol. 15, No. 4 (2010), pp. 473–492.

[13]See IMF official website, available: <http://www.imf.org/external/about/govstruct.htm> (accessed 22 September 2010), pp. 125–151.

[14]4. M. Lyne, D. Nielson and M. Tierney, "Who Delegates? Alternate Models of Principals in Development Aid", in D. Hawkins *et al.* (eds.), *op. cit.*, p. 44.

Although the approach generates many useful insights into the world of international organisations, the criticism has been levelled against rationalist works that they fail to take sufficient account of the social dynamics of behaviour and change.[16] By bracketing out questions of *why* states come to see particular courses of action as desirable, and *how* the mechanics of ideational change occur over time, a significant piece of the IO puzzle is left unexamined. In order to overcome this shortcoming, a number of studies have advocated supplementing the rationalist approach with the focus on ideas within constructivist scholarship.[17]

With a lineage going back, via Barnett and Finnemore,[18] to the work of Max Weber, constructivist scholarship has sought to explore the more subtle forms of power at the disposal of IOs. In particular, significant focus has been placed upon the capacity of IOs to frame the way in which a global policy-making community "sees" a given issue. By drawing on their established position as a source of authority on a given issue, IOs are able to shape dominant ideas regarding both the key features of a policy problem and the most efficacious means of addressing the problem. In the case of the IMF, for example, its widely recognised institutional expertise enabled the organisation to shape important aspects of how state actors understand (appropriate responses to) balance of payments emergencies.[19]

In order to maintain and bolster their capacity to exert this subtle but significant form of influence, it is important that IOs retain the confidence of key constituent groups within their "social environment".[20] Developing an ability to show evidence of the successful execution of their mission is a central component of this process. In its recent history, the IMF has been relatively ineffective in putting forward evidence of its success, especially in relation to its low-income country operations.[21] This shortcoming, combined with deep-seated uneasiness over the appropriateness of the organisation's foray into the world of structural adjustment, has contributed to the disagreements at Board level as to how the Fund should operationalise its mandate in its interactions with low-income country member states. However, the establishment by an IO of simplified

---

[15]*Ibid.*, pp. 58–59.

[16]Liam Clegg, "In the Loop: Multilevel Feedback and the Politics of Change at the World Bank and IMF", *Journal of International Relations and Development*, Vol. 13, No. 1 (2010), p. 65; E. Gould, "Delegating IMF Conditionality: Understanding Variations in Control and Conformity", in D. Hawkins *et al.* (eds), *op. cit.*, p. 310. See also Manuela Moschella, "IMF Surveillance in Crisis. The Past, Present and Future of the Reform Process", *Global Society*, Vol. 26, No. 1 (2012), pp. 43–60.

[17]Clegg, "In the Loop", *op. cit.*; Catherine Weaver, "The World's Bank and the Bank's World", *Global Governance*, Vol. 13, No. 4 (2007), pp. 493–512; Catherine Weaver and Susan Park, "The Role of the World Bank in Poverty Alleviation and Human Development in the Twenty-first Century", *Global Governance*, Vol. 13, No. 4 (2007), pp. 461–468;

[18]Michael Barnett and Martha Finnemore, *Rules for the World: International Organizations in World Politics* (Ithaca, NY: Cornell University Press, 2004). The recent edited volume of Abdelal, Blyth and Parsons serves to establish the "state of the art" of the constructivist research agenda in International Political Economy (IPE). See R. Abdelal, M. Blyth and C. Parsons, "Introduction: Constructing the International Economy", in R. Abdelal, M. Blyth and C. Parsons (eds), *Constructing the International Economy* (Ithaca, NY: Cornell University Press, 2010), pp. 1–19.

[19]Ralf Leiteritz, "Explaining Organizational Outcomes: The IMF and Capital Account Liberalization", *Journal of International Relations and Development*, Vol. 8, No. 1 (2005), p. 2; Barnett and Finnemore, *op. cit.*, p. 46.

[20]Manuela Moschella, *Governing Risk: The IMF and Global Financial Crises* (Basingstoke: Palgrave, 2010); Alastair Johnston, "Treating International Institutions as Social Environments", *International Studies Quarterly*, Vol. 45, No. 4 (2001), p. 488.

[21]See final section below.

proxy-indicators of its impact can greatly enhance their ability to re-establish their status as "an authority". Indeed, such indicators can serve to shape understandings of an IO's mission to the extent that not only does "what gets measured gets done", but that "what gets measured shapes underlying beliefs about what should get done". The tying of World Bank lending to the Millennium Development Goals (MDGs) in recent years provides a strong example of this process; the Fund's dalliance with social spending targets provides a comparatively nascent example.

For constructivists, ideas surrounding key concepts at the centre of an IO's mandate are inherently flexible. Recent works have sought to highlight that IOs themselves are rarely homogenous beasts, and that different internal sub-groupings commonly hold competing understandings of how the organisation's mission should best be approached. In relation to the Fund, for example, Chwieroth has shown that staff educational background significantly shaped battles over the desirability of capital account liberalisation;[22] in relation to the World Bank, Weaver has shown that getting key veto-players on board has been central to the foregrounding of the "governance agenda".[23] Building on these insights, I show that such ideational contests also take place upstairs, in the boardroom. Opposing understandings among key Executive Directorates of how the Fund should operationalise its mandate in low-income countries have been a central feature of life in the recent history of the organisation.

Both rationalist and constructivist approaches contribute valuable insights into the emergence and evolution of these Board-level contests. On the constructivist side of the fence, ideas clearly matter. The emergence of competing understandings among key actors about what constitutes appropriate action in the Fund's low-income country lending is a core component of the recent history of the Fund. In addition, through the emergent practice of employing social spending floors in its arrangements and making the links between such spending and the MDGs explicit, the IMF is beginning to establish a means of indicating its commitment—and contribution—to poverty reduction. This shift will enhance the capacity of the Fund to communicate its success in this area, and to convince doubters within its social environment of the appropriateness of its engagement in the realm of poverty reduction. From the rationalist side of the fence, we can see that although intra-principal disputes have been a consistent feature of debates over the IMF's concessional lending activities, at times of crisis "coalitions of the willing" have been formed to push through reforms in opposition to the expressed wishes of US authorities.[24] In addition, the increasing use of social spending targets can be understood as a useful tool with which developmentally minded principals can more effectively monitor the IO's poverty reduction performance.

Figure 1 provides a schematic overview of the evolution of low-income country lending at the IMF. Initially, the Fund was relatively successful in establishing the

---

[22]Jeffrey Chwieroth, *Capital Ideas: The IMF and the Rise of Financial Liberalization* (Princeton: Princeton University Press, 2010).

[23]Catherine Weaver, *Hypocrisy Trap: The Poverty of Reform at the World Bank* (Ithaca, NY: Cornell University Press, 2008).

[24]See also Donna Lee, "Global Trade Governance and the Challenges of African Activism in the Doha Development Agenda Negotiations", *Global Society*, Vol. 26, No. 1 (2012), pp. 83–101, for a discussion of how coalitions of smaller states can contest the viewpoints of dominant players in the field of trade.

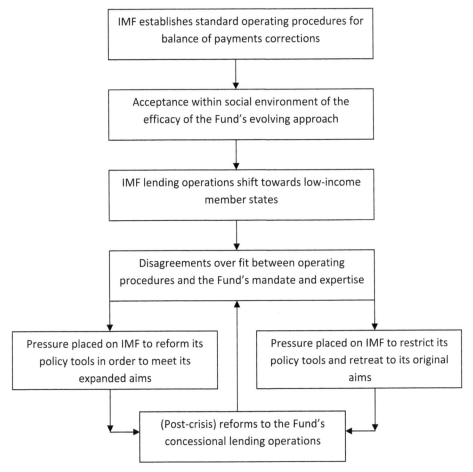

Figure 1. IMF's Negative Feedback Cycle.

authority of its expertise in the field of balance of payments corrections. However, as the organisation's lending operations increasingly came to incorporate low-income member states, disagreements began to emerge over the appropriateness of its standard operating procedures for this constituent group. From the time of the oil crises, opposing pressures have been placed on the Fund and, with the ramping-up of structural adjustment lending, disagreement over the fit between the Fund's operations and its mandate and expertise has in recent times widened. By the late 2000s US hostility to the Fund's low-income country lending operations was openly acknowledged within the organisation. However, with the response to the 2008–09 financial crisis we see that again reforms have gone against the grain of US wishes. Although disagreements remain, the Fund has—with the aid of minor shifts in operational practices—enhanced its ability to demonstrate its efficacy as a development partner. Although these reforms will not settle longstanding disputes, they will nonetheless enhance the capacity of the organisation to incrementally reshape the understanding of key actors in its social environment as to what constitutes appropriate behaviour by the IMF.

Constructing Balance of Payments Expertise

Ideas about what an international organisation should do, and how it should go about doing it, are inherently flexible. Networks of external and internal actors are commonly forged within and around an IO in order to advance a particular understanding of the core aspects of its mission. Over time these networks can effect dramatic changes to how the organisation's primary goals are both defined and met. There is, however, an overarching "stickiness" that limits the range of possible outcomes. In this regard, the formal mandate of an IO and the *modus operandi* that becomes established in the opening stages of its existence are of particular importance.[25] At the IMF, initial patterns that emerged regarding the organisation's operationalisation of its balance of payments remit have cast a long shadow, which has served to shape actors' differing interpretations of how the Fund's interactions with low-income countries should be structured. The disagreements that have emerged between the US and other representatives (particularly the Europeans) have revolved around how far the "original" basis of the Fund's expertise should be allowed to stretch. Over time, the conservativeness of the US has been consistently matched by the more permissive attitudes of European and other member states.[26]

When its Articles of Agreement came into force in 1945, the core task with which the IMF was charged was maintaining the stability of the international monetary system. In Article 1 of the Fund's mandate, a stable monetary system was laid out as *the* foundation upon which the balanced growth of international trade could occur, which, it was hoped, would in turn raise rates of productivity, growth and employment across member states. A central mechanism through which monetary stability was to be achieved was the Fund's provision of financial resources to members with external imbalances.[27] By allowing members access to a collective pool of offsetting finance, the IMF was designed to "shorten the duration and lessen the degree of disequilibrium in the international balances of payments of members".[28]

As is well known, there was initially a great deal of debate as to what shape the rules governing access to Fund resources should take. In the 1944 discussions at Bretton Woods, John Maynard Keynes, negotiating on behalf of the UK government, fought for a light approach to be taken regarding access rules. Keynes cautioned in particular against the dangers of the IMF "being grandmotherly"—

---

[25] A. Vetterlein, "Change in International Organizations: Innovation or Adaptation? A Comparison of the World Bank and the International Monetary Fund", in D. Stone and C. Wright (eds), *The World Bank and Governance: A Decade of Reform and Reaction* (London: Routledge, 2006), pp. 125–144.

[26] Although evident in this issue area, this US–Europe division is by no means a persistent feature of life at the IMF. On the promotion of capital account liberalisation, for example, as many pressures came from Europe as from the US. See Rawi Abdelal, *Capital Rules: The Construction of Global Finance* (Cambridge, MA: Harvard University Press, 2007).

[27] Article I, Section V. See IMF official website, available: <http://www.imf.org/external/pubs/ft/aa/aa01.htm> (accessed 22 September 2010).

[28] 8. Article I, Section VI. See IMF official website, available <http://www.imf.org/external/pubs/ft/aa/aa01.htm> (accessed 22 September 2010).

behaving as a hectoring matriarch, forcing her wisdom onto family members in return for handing out money.[29] However, as during the early years of its operations the Fund acquired an unparalleled level of expertise on balance of payments problems, the "Old Lady of 19th Street" began to become distinctly grandmotherly. From the late 1950s onwards, the practice of attaching monitored policy conditionality to loans became increasingly commonplace.[30]

The key analytic advances that provided the intellectual underpinnings to the Fund's use of conditionality were made in the early to mid-1950s, and were centred on the absorption and monetary approaches to understanding balance of payments issues.[31] The absorption approach to solving balance of payments shortfalls, notably expounded in IMF Working Papers by Tsiang and Alexander,[32] focused on the role played by domestic spending in aggravating a country's balance of payments position. Advances around this model led Fund staff to encourage countries with disequilibria to institute policies to dampen aggregate demand as part of a correctional policy package. Regarding the monetary approach, the contribution of Polak, highlighting credit expansion as the primary causal factor in determining balance of payments imbalances,[33] influenced the inclusion of policies to restrict domestic credit creation in Fund-supported programmes. In addition, further down the line—after the breakdown of the Bretton Woods system of fixed exchange rates in 1973—currency devaluation also increasingly became integrated into IMF policy conditionality.[34] Although refinements and changes occurred in the Fund's modelling of balance of payments problems in later years, by the early 1960s the die of IMF conditionality had been cast. In particular, the burgeoning Fund expertise on balance of payments was of an avowedly macroeconomic form, concentrating on the "big" fiscal and monetary policy levers available to states rather than the supply side structural reforms that could potentially have addressed balance of payments disequilibria, albeit over a longer timeframe.[35]

By the mid-1970s there was a broad consensus among member states that the "tough love" of IMF conditionality was a necessary and effective means of overcoming balance of payments disequilibria. Indeed, in their 1978 review of conditionality the Executive Board made a call for members with significant external imbalances to turn to the expertise of Fund staff sooner rather than later in

---

[29]Harold James, *International Monetary Cooperation since Bretton Woods* (Washington, DC: IMF, 1996), p. 78. It should be noted that Harry Dexter White, the chief US negotiator, was a staunch advocate of a more interventionist IMF.

[30]James Boughton, *The Silent Revolution: Global Finance and Development in the 1980s* (Washington, DC: IMF, 2001), p. 558.

[31]For an overview of the evolution of conditionality, see Barnett and Finnemore, *op. cit.*, pp. 51–60; Boughton, *op. cit.*, pp. 557–636, and references therein.

[32]Sydney Alexander, "Effects of Devaluation of a Trade Balance", *IMF Working Paper* (1952); S.C. Tsiang, "Balance of Payments and Domestic Flow of Income and Expenditure", *IMF Working Paper* (1950).

[33]Jacques Polak, "Monetary Analysis of Income Formation and Payments Problems", *IMF Working Paper* (1957).

[34]Andrew Sumner, "In Search of the Post-Washington (Dis)consensus", *Third World Quarterly*, Vol. 27, No. 8 (2006), pp. 1401–1412; Tony Killick, *IMF Programmes in Developing Countries* (London: Routledge, 1995), p. 135; S. Dell, "Stabilization: The Political Economy of Overkill", in J. Williamson (ed.), *IMF Conditionality* (Washington, DC: Institute for International Economics, 1983), p. 35.

[35]D. Finch, "Adjustment Policies and Conditionality", in Williamson (ed.), *IMF Conditionality, op. cit.*, p. 78.

order to improve the chances of an orderly resolution of these problems.[36] However, as the Fund increasingly began to lend to low-income members, questions began to emerge about the efficacy of its established prescriptions in these new contexts.

During the opening decades of the IMF's existence, low-income countries did not figure prominently on the organisation's agenda. Owing to the relatively low number of politically independent developing countries, the existence of colonial currency blocs, and their minimal engagement in networks of international trade, the question of how the Fund would operationalise its mandate with this constituency remained largely unasked. It was not until the 1970s that these countries became engaged in the Fund's lending operations to a significant extent.[37] However, once attempts began to be made to systematically arrange the terms of engagement between the IMF and low-income members, conflicting views on what constituted appropriate behaviour began to emerge.

The IMF Steps into Concessional Lending

From the mid-1970s the centre of gravity in the use of Fund resources shifted dramatically towards the developing world. This shift represented a major reorientation in the work of the IMF, and through to the contemporary era lending arrangements with developing countries have generally outnumbered those with industrialised members.[38] This shift has been accompanied by rising disagreements among the Fund's major quota-holders as to the parameters that should be set regarding the Fund's engagements with this new group of constituents. Indeed, this contest has been referred to as "a battle for the soul of the institution".[39] US resistance to the formation of the Oil Facility Subsidy Account and early criticism of the "light touch" approach of the Enhanced Fund Facility (EFF), alongside the contrasting position of European Executive Directors, demonstrates that the current divisions at the IMF have deep historical roots. In addition, these early disagreements illustrate that crises and coalition formation have consistently played an important role in the politics of change at the organisation.

The beginning of what became a major refocusing of the lending activities of the IMF came in 1973. Over the course of the year, sanctions by the Organisation of Petroleum Exporting Countries (OPEC) in response to the Yom Kippur War, alongside more general supply limitations, saw the price of crude rocket.[40] Owing to the difficulty faced by importing countries in switching consumption away from such a vital commodity, current account deficits rapidly began to widen. The Fund's response was to create an Oil Facility, through which offsetting finance could be provided to countries with balance of payments problems. In order to make the Facility accessible to low-income countries, a Subsidy Account was appended to the Facility. Through the Subsidy Account,

---

[36]Boughton, *op. cit.*, p. 559.

[37]Margaret de Vries, *The IMF in a Changing World* (Washington, DC: IMF, 1986), pp. 118–120.

[38]IMF, *Annual Report 2009, op. cit.*, Annex II.

[39]Boughton, *op. cit.*, p. 644.

[40]Edward Morse, "A New Political Economy of Oil", *Journal of International Affairs*, Vol. 53, No. 1 (1999), pp. 1–29.

contributions from a group of 25 industrialised countries reduced the rate of inter-est charged to developing country borrowers from the standard Oil Facility rate of 7.7% to 2.7%.[41] The US government was openly opposed to the formation of the Subsidy Account, arguing that it served both to grant legitimacy to the OPEC action (which had specifically targeted the US) and to enhance the sustainability of the shifted terms of trade that it had brought about.[42] However, in spite of this US opposition, the successful formation of a coalition of 25 member states who were willing to provide the necessary resources to establish the Account led to its creation. Counter to common understandings of how the IMF functions, here we see the strategic interests of the US being overridden by a grouping of less materially powerful states seeking to establish a resource transfer mechanism to low-income members. Unsurprisingly, the US chose not to contribute to the Subsidy Account.[43]

At the same time that the Oil Facility (and also, from 1977, the IMF's Trust Fund) were acting to normalise the idea of the IMF as a provider of concessional resources to low-income countries with no monitored conditionality,[44] a confron-tation arose over the functioning of its parallel "strings attached" lending. An Enhanced Fund Facility had been launched in 1974, in response to the growing belief among the Fund staff and Board that, rather than being a temporary "shock", the oil price rise (and consequent balance of payments deficits) in fact represented a long-term change in the world economy. In order to promote the heavy reforms that adjustment by developing countries would entail, it was decided that, in place of the standard one-year stand-by arrangement, EFF arrangements would have a three-year lifespan. In terms of the content of the conditionality, EFF agreements largely represented a continuation of "business as usual", with the macroeconomic expertise of staff informing performance criteria.[45] However, in rigorously applying its existing expertise regarding the correction of balance of payments problems to the new group of developing country borrowers, Fund staff inadvertently provoked a confrontation with a coalition of its European member states.

Partly owing to its low take-up rate, the EFF initially proved relatively uncon-troversial. However, it was in 1979, with the second oil shock, that disagreements over its operations began to come out into the open. Immediately after the 1979 oil price hike, the French and British representatives pushed for the IMF to ensure that resources were available to assist low-income members through the inevitable period of balance of payments stress. Moreover, at the 1979 annual meeting the French and British governments called for Fund conditionality to be relaxed so as to ensure that the organisation's potential to help developing countries was not stymied through the imposition of programmes that developing countries

---

[41]Boughton, *op. cit.*, p. 639; James, *op. cit.*, pp. 253–254, 317.

[42]James, *op. cit.*, p. 316.

[43]See IMF, *Annual Report 1981* (Washington, DC: IMF, 1981), p. 102.

[44]The IMF's Trust Fund, opened in 1977, also served to deepen this practice. For reasons of space I will not go into the interesting history of the Trust Fund, but for further information see Boughton, *op. cit.*, p. 639; de Vries, *op. cit.*, p. 119.

[45]James, *op. cit.*, pp. 328–335; Susan Schadler, Adam Bennet, Maria Carkovik, Louis Dicks-Mireaux, Mauro Mecagni, James Morsink, and Miguel Savastano, *IMF Conditionality: Experience under Stand-by and Extended Arrangements* (Washington, DC: IMF, 1995), p. 3; Stephan Haggard, "The Politics of Adjust-ment: Lessons from the IMF's Extended Fund Facility", *International Organization*, Vol. 39, No. 3 (1985), p. 506.

were unwilling or unable to submit to.[46] Following this public pressure from major quota-holding member states, from 1979 there was a marked increase in IMF lending to low-income countries, and a concurrent easing of conditionality.[47]

With these events, we see the emergence for the first time of a concern on the part of European members that the established expertise and *modus operandi* of the Fund might not be appropriate for the needs of low-income countries. In reaction, we also see the emergence of a US concern that, in its attempts to accommodate these new borrowers, the Fund was diluting its effectiveness. As early as 1981, the US Executive Director called for a return to tough conditionality to counteract what was seen as the tendency towards "more and more financing for less and less adjustment" in the Fund's engagements with developing countries. The US Executive Director also added his voting weight to the matter, withholding support for Fund arrangements with Grenada, India and Pakistan on the grounds that an insufficient focus was being placed on conditionality.[48]

The events around the Oil Facility Subsidy Account and the EFF illustrate that, from the outset, the Fund's increasing engagement with developing countries was marked by controversy. Although the US hostility to the Oil Facility Subsidy Account was informed by geo-strategic concerns as much as beliefs about what constituted appropriate activity on the part of the Fund, the success of the 25-country coalition demonstrates the inability of the US to dictate processes of change within the organisation. The US resistance to the "watering down" of EFF conditionality, in contrast, provides an early example of the US view that the efforts of the Fund, in its engagements with low-income countries, must be tightly focused on the resolution of balance of payments problems. Meanwhile, European permissiveness on this issue presages a willingness to view low-income countries as something of a special case, and to consequently rethink the standards of appropriateness with which to judge the activities of the IMF. As is demonstrated below, these ideational contests, combined with the provision of supplementary material resources to the Fund, have continued to shape the more recent history of the organisation's low-income country operations. And as with the Oil Facility and EFF, times of crisis have continued to play a catalytic role in fermenting both inter-principal disputes and operational change.

The Fund Steps into Structural Adjustment, and Steps out of its Mandate?

The Structural Adjustment Facility (SAF), which was established in 1986, served to secure the position of the IMF as a provider of concessional loans to its low-income members and to widen the practice of making longer-term (i.e. three-year) arrangements. In 1987 the SAF was 'Enhanced' to become the ESAF, and in 1999 was converted into the Poverty Reduction and Growth Facility (PRGF). Early optimism about the SAF was quickly replaced by a re-emergence of disputes between Board members as to the fit between the new lending modalities and the IMF's expertise and mandate, with again a clear US–European division emerging. The creation of the PRGF and the expansion in 2009 of its lending resources demonstrate

---

[46]Boughton, *op. cit.*, pp. 561–562, 637.

[47]James, *op. cit.*, p. 340; J. Williamson, "On Judging the Success of IMF Policy Advice", in Williamson (ed.), *IMF Conditionality, op. cit.*, pp. 640–646.

[48]James, *op. cit.*, p. 565.

that the coalition of developmentally minded states is currently winning the "battle for the soul" of the IMF. With the continuing existence of sharply differing views of how the Fund should act, however, the war is not yet over.

Unusually for a major policy development at the IMF, the proposal to establish the SAF came directly from member state governments, with no prompting from the Executive Board agenda or preliminary staff papers. At a meeting of the Interim Committee in the spring of 1985,[49] the Finance Ministers and Central Bankers present noted that over the next few years the IMF would be receiving substantial repayments of loans made under the Trust Fund, in total some SDR 3 billion.[50] It was agreed that these resources should be made available to the organisation's lowest-income members. Accordingly, the Interim Committee sent instructions to the Executive Board to consider the options available for such a new concessional lending window.[51]

The blueprints of the SAF that were laid out by the Board later that year served to consolidate significant trends within the Fund's engagements with low-income countries. Through the SAF, the Fund was given the capacity to provide loans at a 0.5% rate of interest, and it was agreed that arrangements under the SAF would be over a three-year period, with semi-annual benchmarks used to determine whether an agreement would remain active.[52] Perhaps most significantly, the SAF marked the confirmation of the departure by the IMF from the "clean" world of macroeconomics into the realm of structural adjustment. Through their recent Trust Fund and EFF engagements with developing countries, Fund staff and management had begun to realise that the external imbalances in such countries could not be corrected with the use of fiscal and monetary levers alone. Rather, it was agreed that the specific barriers to growth that had precluded the attainment of a stable external position would need to be targeted. Such reforms included reducing the power of state-run monopoly industries and marketing boards to allow for producer prices to be determined freely, and a series of micro-level regulatory reforms intended to stimulate domestic enterprise and enhance prospects for (export-led) growth.[53]

At the time of the launch of the SAF, Executive Directors exhibited a general sense of optimism during Board discussions of its structure and operations. However, even at this time there is a recurrent theme from the US authorities that the SAF must be tightly focused on rectifying (rather than simply ameliorating) balance of payments disequilibria,[54] and that conditionality must be used rigorously. In order to strengthen the effectiveness of conditionality, the wider use of "prior

---

[49]The Interim Committee was created in 1974, when the growth in Fund membership made the plenary Board of Governors meetings impracticably large. The Committee provided policy advice to the Board, and communicated feedback and guidance to the Executive Directors and senior staff. The forum was renamed the International Monetary and Financial Committee in 1999. It contains 24 members, all of whom are IMF Governors, and reflects the constituency groupings of the Executive Board. See IMF Independent Evaluation Office, *Governance of the IMF* (Washington, DC: IMF, 2008), pp. 10–11.

[50]Special Drawing Rights (SDRs) are the unit of account used by the IMF.

[51]Boughton, *op. cit.*, p. 637.

[52]*Ibid.*, p. 649; Gopal Garuda, "The Distributional Effects of IMF Programmes: A Cross-country Analysis", *World Development*, Vol. 28, No. 6 (2000), p. 1046.

[53]For a detailed discussion of the content of "structural adjustment", see IMF Exchange and Trade Relations Department, "Monitoring of Structural Adjustment in Fund-supported Adjustment Programs" (Washington, DC: IMF Staff Paper, 1987). Archive reference EBS/87/254.

actions"—conditions that had to be met before any increments of a loan were disbursed—was strongly advocated. In addition, calls were made for SAF arrangements to shift from having imprecise qualitative criteria to having more quantitative conditions, in order that targets could be more readily monitored.[55]

Such concerns were by no means unique to the US representatives.[56] However, when attention began to shift to the enhancement of the SAF, a current of discontent began to become evident. Reflecting on the Fund's early experiences with the SAF, the US Executive Director stated that:

> In certain cases ... there appears to have been a tendency to focus structural reforms and structural benchmarks on areas where the potential for early progress seems to be greatest, rather than on areas where the need for reforms is greatest ... In the view of my authorities, [it is important] that we face up to the need to push hard on some doors which are not very easy to open—in the interest of achieving the objectives of the policy frameworks.[57]

When the SAF was enhanced in 1987 the relative coolness of the US authorities can be seen by the low level of their contribution to the ESAF Subsidy Account. At a little over SDR 100 million, the US contribution was dwarfed by the amounts provided by France (SDR 1.2 billion), Germany (SDR 830 million), the UK (SDR 400 million) and others.[58]

There is strong evidence that, through the 1990s, the IMF's concessional lending was carried out in a manner that reflected the concerns voiced by the US. According to a later IMF review, SAF and ESAF arrangements tended to have relatively low levels of "hard" conditionality (prior actions and performance criteria that had to be met in order to secure the disbursal of a loan) and high levels of "soft" conditionality (benchmarks with a less automatic link to resource distribution).[59] In addition to the relatively low level of hard conditionality, low-income borrowers were also granted waivers to allow for continued loan disbursement in spite of missed targets more often than other categories of Fund borrowers.[60] Whatever the reasons for these tendencies,[61] they served to harden the attitude of the US authorities against the Fund's low-income country lending.

---

[54]IMF Executive Board Minutes (Informal Session), 20 November 1987, pp. 21–22. Archive reference EBMIS/87/7.

[55]IMF Executive Board Minutes, 18 December 1987, pp. 44–45. Archive reference EBM/87/175.

[56]Indeed, other Executive Directors raised concerns about the incompatibility between the legal requirement that Fund resources remain "revolving" and the rolling out of medium-term arrangements with low-income members. IMF Executive Board Minutes, 18 December 1987, p. 3. Archive reference EBM/87/175.

[57]IMF Executive Board Minutes, 20 November 1987, p. 22. Archive reference EBMIS/87/7.

[58]Boughton, *op. cit.*, p. 670.

[59]IMF Independent Evaluation Office, *Evaluation of the Prolonged Use of Fund Resources* (Washington, DC: IMF, 2002), p. 44.

[60]*Ibid.*, pp. 44–48. See also Michel Camdessus and Moses Naim, "A Talk with Michel Camdessus about God, Globalization, and His Years Running the IMF", *Foreign Policy*, Vol. 120 (2000), p. 41.

[61]After the initial pressure to recycle resources from the Trust Fund had passed, the growing need for "defensive lending", alongside the danger of "cross conditionality" magnifying the impact of the failure of an arrangement, were undoubtedly significant factors underlying these trends.

The growing cacophony of "anti-IMF" voices provided a resonant background noise to this hardening of attitudes. Through the 1990s a steady stream of reports, whether from outside of the Fund[62] or from the internal actors,[63] flagged up a concern that, rather than helping low-income countries, IMF-supported programmes were in fact serving to harm their development prospects. In addition, from the middle of the decade high-profile Non-Governmental Organisation (NGO) campaigns, particularly focused around the "drop the debt" campaigns, put increasing efforts into lobbying both Executive Directors and US domestic politicians.[64] A major problem for the Fund was its inability to communicate a positive narrative around its concessional lending activities. Although a number of staff assessments did indeed find evidence of a positive correlation between IMF programmes and economic growth and the correction of balance of payments disequilibria,[65] such reports were never effectively "spun" for non-expert consumption.[66] Consequently, the dominant "story" of the Fund's low-income lending was one of frustration and failure.

Criticism of the IMF began to reach fever pitch in the late 1990s as campaigns in favour of debt relief were joined by widespread anger at the perceived mishandling of the 1997–98 East Asian financial crisis. It is at this time that the US view, that the Fund's concessional lending activities had become too ineffective to justify their continuation, began to emerge into the open. As the "legitimacy crisis" of the IMF was reaching its zenith, the International Financial Institution Advisory Commission of the US Congress released its damning verdict on the IMF in 2000 (known as the Meltzer Report). In the light of what the Meltzer Report saw as more than a decade of ineffective lending to low-income countries, it called in no uncertain terms for the termination of the IMF's concessional lending operations.[67] Although the Meltzer Report represented the findings of a Congressional Commission, and as such illustrates the views of only one of the branches of US government, it reflected the general frustration on the part of the US representatives at the Fund that the organisation had strayed well beyond its area of expertise.[68]

---

[62]See, for example, J. Sachs, "Strengthening IMF Programs in Highly Indebted Countries", in C. Gwin and R. Feinberg (eds), *Pulling Together: The IMF in a Multipolar World* (New Jersey: Transaction, 1989); Graham Bird, *IMF Lending to Developing Countries* (London: Routledge, 1995); Killick, *op. cit.*

[63]See, for example, IMF, "Fund-Supported Programs, Fiscal Policy, and Income Distribution", *IMF Occasional Paper*, No. 46 (1986).

[64]André Broome, "When Do NGOs Matter?", *Global Society*, Vol. 23, No. 1 (2009), pp. 59–78; Joshua Busby, "Bono Made Jesse Helms Cry: Jubilee 2000, Debt Relief, and Moral Action in International Politics", *International Studies Quarterly*, Vol. 51, No. 2 (2006), pp. 247–275.

[65]Susan Schadler, Franek Rozwadowski, Siddharth Tiwari and David Robinson, "Economic Adjustment in Low-income Countries", *IMF Occasional Paper*, No. 106 (1993).

[66]This shortcoming continues to dog the IMF. In the words of a senior member of the External Relations Department, it is "not in economists' genes" to communicate evidence of operational success in accessible terms. Interview with author, November 2008.

[67]*Report of the International Financial Institution Advisory Panel*, March 2000, p. iv. See US House of Representatives official website, available: <http://www.house.gov/jec/imf/ifiac.htm> (accessed 22 September 2010).

[68]An anecdote from a former Executive Director (in place at the time of the Meltzer Report) hints at this closeness, which is corroborated in the accounts and Executive Board Minutes noted in the following paragraphs. The Executive Director told of an informal office game whereby points were awarded to staff within the Directorate for convincingly matching statements by the US Executive Director to recommendations from the Meltzer Report. Interview with author, November 2008.

Although there was a slight reduction in the volume of PRGF lending during the mid-2000s, with new approvals dipping below SDR 0.5 billion from 2005–08,[69] US opposition to the Fund's concessional lending continued to crystallise. There is widespread acceptance within the IMF, for example, that the US support for the creation of the Policy Support Instrument (PSI) in 2005 was intimately tied in to its position on PRGF lending. The PSI is a non-lending facility through which the IMF places its "stamp of approval" on the policy programmes of PRGF-eligible countries, but with no financial resources attached. The dominant "insider interpretation" of the emergence of the PSI was that US support shifted in favour of its creation in 2004, when the authorities began to view it as a potentially useful mechanism for "weaning off" low-income countries from concessional lending.[70]

In addition to the PSI issue, internal evaluations of the Fund's low-income country activities through the 2000s served to highlight a growing dissatisfaction of the US with PRGF lending. Several Independent Evaluation Office (IEO) reports provide hints of Board-level tension[71]—hints that are more than confirmed by the Board's discussions of these reports. In July 2004 the US Executive Director used the discussion of the *IEO Evaluation Report on PRSPs and the PRGF* to voice deep concerns over the Fund's low-income country operations:

> The IEO report issues a clear "danger" warning. [The PRGF] has blurred distinct forms of IMF support ... into a single function—lending—which is increasingly being made to serve a development role. The Fund's unique role and therefore special contribution to enhancing growth in low-income countries is in jeopardy.[72]

In the same meeting the UK Executive Director issued a rather more measured response to the IEO report,[73] while the German Executive Director in fact offered a defence of the Fund's performance by shifting the blame for poor outcomes to low-income country governments.[74]

By the late 2000s the US Executive Director's office at the Fund had come to see a fundamental disjuncture between the type of long-term, structural adjustment-focused lending of the Fund's PRGF and the balance of payments remit of the organisation's Articles of Agreement. In the words of a very senior member of

---

[69]IMF, *Annual Report 2009, op. cit.*, Annex II.

[70]Staff within several Executive Directors' offices (including the US office) provided this interpretation of events, as did other senior management within the Fund. Interviews with author, November and December 2008.

[71]A 2007 IEO report concluded that Fund staff "lack[ed] clarity on what they should do on the mobilisation of aid, alternative scenarios, and the application of poverty reduction and social impact analysis", and that Executive Directors had expressed a range of views on these issues. See IMF Independent Evaluation Office, *The IMF and Aid to Sub-Saharan Africa* (Washington, DC: IMF, 2007), pp. vii, 87–89.

[72]IMF Executive Board Minutes, 21 July 2004, p. 73. Archive Reference EBM/04/71.

[73]The UK statement noted that "the Fund needs to decide how the PRGF will evolve so that it can best provide assistance", and that "the IEO report provides a useful set of principles for developments in this area". *Ibid.*, p. 91.

[74]The German statement noted that "the many problems the [PRGF] is facing are not due to insufficient staff resources being devoted to it. Rather, we think that low-income countries themselves could, in some instances, have done more to make the [PRGF] more successful—a question that has not received sufficient attention in the evaluation". *Ibid.*, p. 97.

the US Executive Director's office, spoken as the global financial crisis was unfolding:

> The IMF is outside its mandate with the PRGF. Nobody, certainly not the Fund, knows how to "do" development. The PRGF has not been a success. If you listen to others, such as the French or Gordon Brown [the then UK Prime Minister], you'd get a different impression ...[75]

In a close parallel with the findings of the Meltzer Report, an understanding had evolved according to which the external imbalances of many low-income countries were of a developmental nature, the proper responsibility of the World Bank and far outside of the expertise of the Fund. Whereas in the US office an ideational framework had formed according to which a line in the sand could be drawn between balance of payments problems (within the Fund's mandate) and developmental issues (outside the Fund's mandate), other important actors within the organisation held competing views. A senior member of staff within the UK Executive Director's office, for example, outlined the following understanding of the Fund's role:

> If the US had its own way, there wouldn't even be the PSI, certainly not the PRGF. They want the Fund to be involved in emergency stabilisation, away from anything growth and poverty reduction orientated. This is not possible: the two are inseparable.[76]

The use of the US position as a foil around which to present the view within the UK office is telling.

By the late 2000s, then, the US opposition to PRGF lending was very firmly established, was common knowledge inside the institution and was increasingly well known on the outside as well. The more supportive (though by no means uncritical) attitude of other Executive Directors—including the Europeans—to the Fund's concessional lending activities was also internally acknowledged. In keeping with past precedent, in 2009 the European-led "coalition of the willing" drew upon the opportunities opened up by the financial crisis to further bolster the IMF's "developmental turn" by massively expanding the organisation's concessional lending base. Again, the provision of supplementary resources was a key mechanism through which operational change was secured, in this case through the sale of SDR 500 million of the Fund's gold stocks, and the bilateral commitment of some SDR 200–400 million.[77] A very senior member of staff in the US Executive Directorate provided a succinct explanation of how such a significant reform could have gone through that led to operational changes anathema to the expressed wishes of the one member state with an effective veto:

---

[75]Interview with author, December 2008.

[76]Interview with author, December 2008.

[77]The size of bilateral contributions will ultimately be dependent on the level of demand for concessional loans. In July 2010 the Norwegian government agreed an SDR 300 million loan-based package, and if sufficient demand is demonstrated the UK government will consider committing additional resources. Interview with senior member of staff at the UK Department for International Development, August 2010.

We acquiesce. The PRGF isn't about balance of payments, it's more about budget support. We think the IMF should stay closer to its mandate, whereas others, such as the French and UK, think it should be more involved in development-type activities.[78]

In a "consensus-based" international organisation such as the IMF, so long as a broad, purse-string-holding alliance can be formed, even reforms that go against the expressed wishes of the organisation's formally most powerful member can be accomplished; and especially so in times of generalised crisis.

Learning to Be a Long-term Development Partner?

The history of the IMF's concessional lending facilities has been marked by disagreements between Executive Directors over the fit between these novel operations and the mandate and established expertise of the organisation. The US has consistently advocated a restricted role for the Fund, tightly focused on emergency balance of payments support; the more flexible Europeans have come to view an inextricable crossover between "developmental" and "balance of payments" problems, and have accordingly adopted a more permissive understanding. Through the control of supplementary resources during periods of crisis, this latter understanding has come to shape recent reforms at the organisation. These deep disagreements flow, in part, from the ineffectiveness of the IMF at demonstrating success in its low-income country operations. Contemporary operational changes will enhance the Fund's capacity to communicate evidence of success, although this limited evidence of the IMF "learning to be (seen to be) a development partner" is unlikely to provide a reputational panacea.

The roots of the IMF's ineffective communications run deep. Fundamentally, the "real" impact of IMF-supported programmes on low-income countries has never been comprehensively established. Indeed, the Fund itself is disarmingly candid about the lack of knowledge about how to enhance growth and poverty reduction.[79] In this context of uncertainty, the impossibility of generating precise counterfactuals (i.e., what would have happened in lieu of a Fund programme), and the ever-present "problem of attribution" (i.e., how praise or blame is apportioned between the IMF and domestic authorities for a programme that is formally agreed between both parties), mean that debates about the impact of Fund programmes will remain open. This lack of an accepted performance yardstick has allowed both for differing interpretations of the Fund's efficacy to be formed among Board members and for vocal critics of the Fund to become established. Two features of the Fund in particular have served to hamper its capacity to advance its "side of the story". Although there is evidence of movement in both characteristics, these shifts are unlikely to resolve the deep disputes

---

[78]Interview with author, December 2008.

[79]The IEO's review of the PRGF, for example, contains the following assessment: "Since the evaluation is about how the IMF can help countries improve their prospects for growth and poverty reduction, it is worth emphasising at the outset that knowledge of the links between policies and growth remains limited and understanding of the links between policies and poverty reduction even less so". IMF Independent Evaluation Office, *Evaluation of the IMF's Role in the Poverty Reduction Strategy Papers and the Poverty Reduction and Growth Facility* (Washington, DC: IMF, 2004), p. 17.

within the organisation. Consequently, disagreements between key internal actors are likely to remain a salient feature of life at the IMF.

Historically, the Fund has been hampered by its proclivity for secrecy and its lack of attention to the distributional impact of the programmes it has supported. First, the IMF is an institution that, throughout its existence, has been used to acting "behind the scenes". For many years, key policy documents routinely remained classified; indeed, up until the late 1990s several categories of report—including Article IV and Use of Fund Resources Reports—could not be published even if the relevant country authorities so wished.[80] With such a low-profile approach, "public relations" was very far down the organisation's agenda. Second, as an institution, the Fund has traditionally not collected the type of data that could be drawn upon to effectively bolster its developmental credentials. Despite its recent discursive turn towards "poverty reduction",[81] the IMF has generally focused on establishing a macro-environment in which external equilibrium and growth could occur; distributional issues tended to be seen as a matter for domestic politics, not recorded or monitored in Fund programmes.[82] However, establishing a paper trail of its impact on the domestic distribution of resources is a *sine qua non* of demonstrating its poverty reduction track record. Shifts in both of these characteristics are underway.

On secrecy, there has been a minor revolution at the Fund. The IMF now operates a policy of presumed disclosure of Board documents and the minutes of most Board discussions are available following a five-year embargo. In addition, the Asian financial crisis acted as a catalyst for reforms to the Fund's External Relations Department (EXR). The first ever Board discussion of EXR came in the aftermath of the crisis, in July 1998, and since then significant focus has been placed on improving the effectiveness of the organisation's image management. Not only has the budget of the central EXR been increased;[83] guidance has also been issued to in-country staff to help enhance the effectiveness of their outreach activities.[84] Under the ebullient leadership of Managing Director Dominique Strauss Kahn, this focus on getting a "positive message" out has further increased, and has specifically been focused on the organisation's low-income country operations. Indeed, the IMF-sponsored *Changes* conference, held in Tanzania in March 2009, was designed to "reset" common perceptions of the IMF's relations with African states and highlight success stories on the continent.[85]

In order to more successfully embed the idea in the minds of key actors within its social environment of the IMF as an effective partner to low-income countries, simplified proxy-indicators provide a potentially powerful tool. From the early years of the PRGF, arrangements have included a "priority spending" category, which set out areas of expenditure to be protected from general cuts and commonly included categories of health and education spending. Recently this

---

[80]IMF, *Signalling by the Fund: A Historic Review* (Washington, DC: IMF, 2004), pp. 25–26.

[81]Jacqueline Best, "Why the Economy is Often the Exception to Politics as Usual", *Theory, Culture, and Society,* Vol. 24, No. 4. (2007), p. 89.

[82]Garuda, *op. cit.*; Giavanni Cornia, Richard Jolly and Frances Stewart, *Adjustment with a Human Face* (Oxford: Oxford University Press, 1987).

[83]IMF External Relations Department, "Strengthening the Fund's External Communications: Plans and Resource Implications" (Washington, DC: IMF Staff Paper, 2000), p. 2. Archive reference SM/00/14.

[84]IMF, "Guide for Staff Relations with Civil Society Organizations" (Washington, DC: IMF, 2003).

[85]Interview with senior External Relations Department staff, December 2008.

category has been relabelled as "social spending" and the Fund has sought to draw upon the increases in social spending listed in a number of active PRGF arrangements as evidence of its contribution to protecting the poor through the global financial crisis.[86]

As of yet, priority spending and social spending have not been included in PRGF programmes as monitored conditionality; their inclusion has come in the form of voluntary additional information about policy intentions. However, the IMF has recently committed itself to setting explicit targets for such spending in low-income country arrangements. In the words of a current member of EXR:

> With this new practice, the IMF reinforces the linkage between the pro-grams it supports and the goal of poverty reduction and growth, and acknowledges the importance of taking exceptional measures to protect the poor during the current crisis.[87]

Furthermore, the online Monitoring of Fund Arrangements (MONA) database provides a ready-made mechanism through which to collate these data on social spending. With the aid of MONA, the IMF's commitment to the protection of pro-poor spending in low-income countries can be unambiguously demonstrated in an 'objective', quantitative manner. With the pressure that the Fund is putting on low-income borrowers to justify items of "social expenditure" in terms of their contribution to poverty reduction (as measured primarily by the MDGs),[88] the links between the IMF and effective poverty reduction stand to become even more closely demonstrated.

It is possible that the IMF's attempts to construct closer links to poverty reduction may rebound, as a failure to meet the MDGs could potentially become a stick for critics (perhaps including the US) to beat the organisation with.[89] However, providing that such blame is avoided,[90] the increasing pro-duction of data to support claims that the IMF is acting to protect the interests of the global poor will become a positive asset. In an analogous manner to the World Bank's successful use of poverty reduction as a legitimation device over the past decade,[91] by increasingly setting social spending floors in its low-income country arrangements, and by highlighting the links between such spending and the MDGs, the IMF's capacity to reshape understandings of its performance in its social environment will be significantly enhanced. The Fund has begun to utilise these data even before their systematic collection has begun;[92] once this process is underway, this instrumental use will only increase.

---

[86]See Maureen Burke, "Despite Crisis, Poor Countries Try to Maintain Social Spending", *IMF Survey Magazine* (2010), pp. 1–3. Burke's heavily trailed article was itself an attempt by EXR to highlight a 2009 report covering this trend.

[87]Burke, *op. cit.*, p. 1

[88]*Ibid.*

[89]T. Gutner, "When 'Doing Good' Does Not: The IMF and the Millennium Development Goals", in M. Finnemore and S. Sell (eds), *Governing the Globe* (Cambridge: Cambridge University Press, 2010), pp. 266–291.

[90]On the mechanics of "blame-shifting" in global governance, see David Bailey and André Broome, "The Blame Game: From Blame Avoidance to Multi-level Blame Displacement", Paper presented at the International Studies Association Annual Conference, New Orleans, 17 February 2010.

[91]See Clegg, "Our Dream is a World Full of Poverty Indicators", *op. cit.*

[92]Burke, *op. cit.*

Conclusion

The global financial crisis of 2008–09 breathed new life—and new resources—into the IMF. In addition, the period of post-crisis reforms has served to highlight the ongoing disputes within the organisation over the appropriateness of its low-income country lending operations. In line with a position that can be traced back to the early 1980s, the US representatives at the IMF continue to view the Fund's engagement with these countries as at best problematic and outside its institutional expertise, and at worst outside of the organisation's balance of payments-focused mandate. In contrast, shifting coalitions of actors, led in particular by the British and French Executive Directors, have adopted a more flexible understanding. By viewing any division between balance of payments and broader development as essentially arbitrary, these actors have been more accommodating of the Fund's expanded engagement with low-income countries, and at key junctures in the organisation's recent history have stepped in with supplementary finances with which to bolster its concessional lending capacity.

The discursive shift by the Fund into the world of poverty reduction and the MDGs over recent years has been consolidated by recent post-crisis operational reforms. The commitment to using monitored social spending floors in future arrangements, and the efforts to make explicit the links between such spending and the MDGs, will significantly enhance the Fund's ability to communicate evidence of its success as a development partner. Providing the organisation is able to avoid blame in the (likely) event that the MDGs are not met by 2015, this enhanced capacity will allow for the understanding among key actors in the organisation's social environment to be re-formed. However, in view of the historical depths of the contemporary disputes over the Fund's appropriate role, this process will be neither rapid nor complete.

Global Trade Governance and the Challenges of African Activism in the Doha Development Agenda Negotiations

DONNA LEE

This article develops a bottom-up approach to global trade governance and explains how subordinate states are able to develop resistance strategies to top-down processes in the World Trade Organisation (WTO). It highlights the growing activism and influence of African states in the global governance of international trade through a case study of the involvement of African states in the current Doha Development Agenda (DDA) negotiations. In so doing, it presents new evidence of the role played by non-dominant states in shaping and contesting the rules and practices of contemporary global trade governance. The article also provides theoretical insights into the source of African resistance in the WTO by drawing attention to the role of discourse in contemporary global trade governance. In this case study the analysis focuses in particular on how subordinate African actors make use of prevailing discourses of development to hold major powers and the WTO to account for their public commitment to negotiate new trade rules that will deliver development. It underlines the extent to which subordinate actors tend to use what is available to them—in this case the discourses of dominant actors—to challenge existing power structures. The conclusion reached is that African resistance creates an African dilemma; while resistance to existing power processes means that African member states can no longer be ignored in WTO negotiations, it also means that the WTO as a forum for global governance is less effective since consensus-based agreement becomes more difficult to achieve. And the less effective the WTO is in multilateral trade governance, the more member states—and in particular dominant states—ignore the WTO and seek bilateral and regional alternatives in order to secure market opening.

Introduction

There is no real crisis in world trade of the macro and micro economic sort that is evident in the global financial system, as discussed in several of the articles in this special issue.[1] Recently released world trade figures demonstrate that throughout

*Thanks to the Department of Politics & International Studies, University of Birmingham for funds to support the research for this article. Thanks also to Nicki Smith, Lena Rethel and the two anonymous reviewers for their extremely helpful comments on an earlier version. Finally, I would like to thank Heidi Ullrich for help with arranging and conducting the interviews in Geneva and Brussels, as well as Hisham Sabbagh and Isabel de Quieroz Nazare for help with the research of WTO documents and African news sources.

the first half of 2010 the value of international trade grew at a healthy rate, some 25% higher than in 2009. Developing countries in Asia, Africa and the Middle East experienced growth in the value of their exports of around 35% or more, as a result of both increased demand and a rise in commodity prices.[2]

This growth, however, has taken place in a context in which multilateral governance of world trade is fragile, if not in some sort of crisis—particularly the processes of global governance that create market opening. In contrast to the surge in international cooperation and renewed efforts at global financial governance that followed the financial crisis in 2008, the relatively healthy state of global trade has induced a state of growing apathy with regard to global trade governance in many states—particularly the developed states. Moreover, other forms of trade governance, notably bilateral free trade agreements, have proliferated, and as World Trade Organisation (WTO) multilateral talks in Geneva have continued to stall, this has created a sense of, at best, irrelevance of the multilateral process in member state capitols and, at worst, a sense of a systemic failure of multilateral trade governance in the WTO's headquarters and member state trade missions in Geneva. In sum, the recent growth in world trade has taken place largely as a result of growing bilateralism and regionalism rather than effective multilateralism and it would appear that the WTO has become less relevant to the major trading states than the General Agreement on Tariffs and Trade (GATT) system it replaced. This article offers some thoughts on the extent of this crisis of multilateral governance in world trade by focusing on the role that new players in the multilateral trade negotiations process have played in the continued delay of the current Doha Development Agenda (DDA) round of talks. In particular, the article focuses on the emergence of African states as key protagonists in the DDA talks. While attention has been paid to the challenges to the WTO system from the shift in power in the global political economy, and especially the impact of the rise of Brazil, India and China—the so-called "BICs"[3]—few have considered the impact of the increased activism of African states in the organisation and global trade governance.[4] This focus on the BICs is understandable given the increasing market power that these rising powers now enjoy in the global economy. But the BICs are not the only new kids on the block in Geneva. The African states—most of which are least-developed countries—have also become more active and embedded in the WTO negotiating process. Yet this

---

1. James Brassett and Nick Vaughan-Williams, "Crisis *is* Governance: Sub-prime, the Traumatic Event, and Bare Life", *Global Society*, Vol. 26, No. 1 (2012), pp. 19–42; Liam Clegg, "Post-crisis Reforms at the IMF: Learning to be (Seen to be) a Development Partner?", *Ibid.*, pp. 61–81; Manuela Moschella, "IMF Surveillance in Crisis. The Past, Present, and Future of the Reform Process", *Ibid.*, pp. 43–60; Lena Rethel, "This Time is Different! The Shifting Boundaries of Emerging Market Debt", *Ibid.*, pp. 123–143.

2. WTO, "Trade Value Still up by about 25% in the First Half of 2010", Press Release, 1 September 2010, available: <http://www.wto.org/english/news_e/pres10_e/pr614_e.htm> (accessed 9 September 2010).

3. Russia is not a member of the WTO and so I use "BICs" rather than the more recognised "BRICs". For detailed analysis of the role of the BICs see Amrita Narlikar, "New Powers in the Club: The Challenges of Global Trade Governance", *International Affairs*, Vol. 86, No. 3 (2010), pp. 717–728.

4. For detailed analysis of Africa in the WTO see Michael F. Jensen and Peter Gibbon, "Africa and the WTO Doha Round: An Overview", *Development Policy Review*, Vol. 25, No. 1 (2007), pp. 5–24; Donna Lee, "Bringing an Elephant into the Room: Small African State Diplomacy in the WTO", in Andrew F. Cooper and Tim M. Shaw (eds.), *The Diplomacies of Small States: Between Vulnerability and Resilience* (Basingstoke: Palgrave, 2009), pp. 195–206; Richard E. Mshomba, *Africa and the World Trade Organization* (Cambridge: Cambridge University Press, 2009).

has not been fully captured by the literature on global trade governance. Indeed, as Ian Taylor points out, there is too little attention being paid to Africa in the more general international political economy (IPE) literature.[5] When Africa is included in global governance and IPE debates, the analysis tends to focus almost exclusively on the impact of global governance and the international political economy on African countries and the continent.[6] Here I offer an alternative, inverse analysis that focuses instead on how African states, concerned about the increasing unequal distribution of the benefits of market opening, can shape the processes and outcomes of global trade governance.

The global trade governance literature has also failed to fully explore the use of discourses by subordinate actors to resist dominant players in international organisations like the WTO. Social constructivist approaches remind us of the crucial role discourses can play in international relations, though they tend to suppose that prevailing discourses serve dominant state purposes only.[7] Recently, Rorden Wilkinson has discussed the role of discourse in the WTO as a tool of the dominant powers and non-state elites within the global trade system as a way of illustrating the social processes at work in securing top-down, asymmetrical agreements in global trade.[8] In this article, however, I invert the predominant method used by others. Rather than seeing agency and dominant discourses as the exclusive weapons of the strong, I highlight instead how dominant discourses can become "weapons of the weak".[9] My purpose is to explore how subordinate actors (in this case least-developed African states) have made use of the discourse of the dominant states (in this case a discourse of development) in the WTO as a means of challenging and resisting the power of the dominant states. The central point I wish to make is that the contestation process does not entail challenging the dominant development discourse in search of a counter-hegemonic discourse, but rather it involves weak actors (in a structural sense) using the discourse to hold powerful states accountable for their trade behaviour. I develop this bottom-up approach to the role of discourse in global governance from earlier work by Jason Sharman on peripheral states in the system of tax havens.[10] By deploying Sharman's methodology, I can highlight the ways in which African states are able to make use of the prevailing discourse of development in the DDA—a discourse initiated and advanced by the major states—to resist a multilateral trade agreement that falls short of their expectations of what is promised in the

---

5. Ian Taylor, "Globalisation Studies and the Developing World: Making International Political Economy Truly Global", *Third World Quarterly*, Vol. 26, No. 7 (2005), pp. 1025–1042.

6. For a full discussion of this point see Will Brown, Sophie Harmon, Stephen Hurt, Donna Lee and Karen Smith, "New Directions in International Relations in Africa", *Roundtable: Commonwealth Journal of International Studies*, Vol. 98. No. 402 (2009), pp. 263–267.

7. For an excellent review of these literatures see Jeffrey T. Checkel, "Social Constructivisms in Global and European Politics: A Review Essay", *Review of International Studies*, Vol. 30, No. 2 (2004), pp. 229–244.

8. Rorden Wilkinson, "Language, Power and Multilateral Trade Negotiations", *Review of International Political Economy*, Vol. 16, No. 4 (2009), pp. 597–619.

9. A phrase I borrow from James C. Scott's *Weapons of the Weak: Everyday Forms of Peasant Resistance* (New Haven: Yale University Press, 1985). See also Jason C. Sharman, "The Agency of Peripheral Actors: Small State Tax Havens and International Regimes as Weapons of the Weak", in John M. Hobson and Leonard Seabrooke (eds.), *The Everyday Politics of the World Economy* (Cambridge: Cambridge University Press, 2007), pp. 45–62.

10. Sharman, *op. cit.*

development discourse. Thus the dominant discourse of development becomes a source of subordinate state resistance in the DDA and a key factor explaining the delay and deadlock in the negotiations. Thus, while states such as Kenya, Burkina Faso, Uganda and Egypt may may lack market power, they make up for this structural subordination by using discursive power in their attempts to resist dominant states in the WTO.

Since the launch of the DDA, African states have insisted that major powers deliver on their public commitment to development. When development issues have been sidelined in, for example, the market access (NAMA) negotiations or by European and Japanese attempts early in the negotiations to place the so called "Singapore issues" onto the agenda,[11] African states (along with other developing and least-developed countries) have vetoed agreement.[12] I provide new qualitative evidence to support the argument that the resistance was triggered and aided by discursive factors. I use WTO documentation as well as data from a series of interviews with African missions in Geneva and Brussels, and non-state actors based in Geneva who work with, and support, African WTO member states from organisations such as the South Centre and the International Centre for Trade and Sustainable Development (ICTSD), as well as officials from the WTO, the African Union, and the United Nations Conference on Trade and Development (UNCTAD).[13] My purpose is to demonstrate growing least-developed country activism in the WTO and suggest that it is a significant, though certainly not the only, factor in the continuing delay and frequent deadlock in the Doha Round. I limit my analysis to an explanation of why it is that these subordinate states have become participants in the WTO system in the last decade. It is too premature to examine the effectiveness of this activism until we know the details of the endgame.

The article is structured as follows. I begin by analysing the DDA deadlock and the ways in which scholars have sought to explain this deadlock, before going on to suggest an alternative approach, one based on a focus upon the agency of non-dominant actors, as another way of explaining the impasse in the DDA. I then highlight evidence of growing African agency in the DDA, focusing on the factors that explain the emergence and development of an enhanced willingness and capacity of some African states to engage with and contest current global trade governance processes in the WTO. Having highlighted African agency as a key element of the current DDA talks and why the talks are in stalemate, I then explore the significance of this activism to current global trade governance. The conclusion reached in the final section is that African resistance creates a dilemma for these subordinate states. While resistance to existing power processes means that African member states *can no longer be ignored* in WTO negotiations, it means that the WTO as a forum for global governance is less effective since

---

11. There are four trade-related issues that are referred to as the "Singapore Issues": government procurement, investment, competition and facilitation.

12. For a detailed discussion of the diplomatic strategies of African states in the DDA see Donna Lee and Nicki Smith, "Small State Discourses in the International Political Economy", *Third World Quarterly*, Vol. 31, No. 7 (2010), pp. 1091–1105; Lee, "Bringing an Elephant into the Room", *op. cit.*

13. The author held 24 open-ended interviews during March 2010, June 2010 and July 2011 with various officials based in African missions in Geneva and Brussels, as well as officials from the African Union, the WTO, UNCTAD and key non-governmental organisations who work with the Africa Group in the WTO. These interviews were conducted on the basis that interviewees would remain anonymous and quotes would not be directly attributed, as is customary practice.

consensus-based agreement becomes more difficult to achieve. And the less effective the WTO is in multilateral trade governance, the more member states—and in particular dominant states—*ignore the WTO* and seek bilateral and regional alternatives in order to secure market opening, leading to what Sharman calls "institutional Darwinism" in global governance. That is, competition between various forms of trade governance—bilateralism, regionalism and multilateralism—with the prospect that only the fittest (most effective) will survive.

Deadlock in the DDA

It is not possible in an article of this size to provide a detailed account of the course of the negotiations and a blow by blow narrative on the occasions when the talks have stalled. Instead I simply highlight that most high-level meetings of the Doha talks have ended in deadlock and, as a result, even though the member states have been negotiating for 10 years, a DDA agreement is far from completion. We should not underestimate the task in hand. The membership is large (over 150) and the trade and trade-related issues under discussion are broad and contentious; members have been trying to reach a multilateral agreement to create market opening for agricultural and manufacturing goods, trade in services (GATS) and trade-related aspects of intellectual property. It is not an exaggeration to say that the Doha Round has chiefly been in deadlock and has been marred by a series of failed WTO ministerial meetings, some very spectacular such as the so-called "Collapse of Cancun" in 2003.[14] And while others produced some progress, for example the December 2005 Hong Kong Ministerial, they were quickly followed by impasse in the DDA negotiating committees as delegates sought to unpack the details of the Hong Kong Declaration on ending agricultural subsidies by 2013.[15] The negotiations following the Hong Kong meeting proved hugely difficult and it was not long before further deadlock in the talks, mainly over agricultural subsidies, arose at the July 2006 Geneva meeting after which the Director General of the WTO, Pascal Lamy, called for a suspension of the talks. A further high-level meeting in Potsdam in June 2007 also ended in deadlock, with the issue of developed country agricultural subsidies again the main sticking point. Although Doha meetings resumed in Geneva in July 2008 (as a result of discussions among elite nations at the 2007 meeting of the World Economic Forum), these talks lasted only nine days and collapsed in the absence of meaningful progress on the issue of developed country agricultural subsidies as well as conflict over special safeguard measures.[16] The subsequent failure to

14. For detailed analysis of the Cancun ministerial meeting see Amrita Narlikar and Rorden Wilkinson, "Collapse at the WTO: A Cancun Post-mortem", *Third World Quarterly*, Vol. 25, No. 3 (2004), pp. 447–460.

15. For a detailed analysis of the negotiations up to and including the Hong Kong Ministerial see Donna Lee and Rorden Wilkinson (eds.), *The WTO after Hong Kong: Prospects for, and Progress in, the Doha Development Agenda* (London: Routledge, 2007).

16. Special safeguard measures are a tariff mechanism that protects poor farmers by allowing some developing countries and least-developed countries to set a tariff when prices fall or when imports surge. For details see James Scott and Rorden Wilkinson, "What Have the Poorest Countries to Gain from the Doha Development Agenda (DDA)?", Paper presented at the conference "Ten Years of the 'War against Poverty': What Have We Learned since 2000; What Should We Do 2010–2020?" Chronic Poverty Research Centre, University of Manchester, 8–10 September 2010.

break the Doha impasse at a meeting in Geneva in December 2009, when once again developing and least-developed countries continued to insist on a meaningful development content to any DDA agreement, highlighted once again the difficulties in reaching a multilateral trade deal.[17]

Despite the fact that the Doha Ministerial Declaration, setting out the content of DDA, makes explicit mention of the need to give special consideration to the needs of developing countries,[18] James Scott and Rorden Wilkinson, in a detailed analysis of the Doha Round from a development perspective, argue that the "development content of the Round has been whittled away over the course of the negotiations".[19] At a meeting of trade ministers in late January 2011, Pascal Lamy was able to obtain agreement that the Doha Round would be completed in 2011. The likelihood of this seems remote. With the United States demanding more market access to developing countries at that meeting, and developing countries responding that the US should offer more in special safeguards in agricultural trade to protect their poor farmers, the North–South stand-off in the DDA continues.[20] Given the resistance of developing and least-developed countries to an agreement without significant development content, there seems little prospect of an endgame to the Round as it enters its second decade of negotiations.[21]

Certainly the view often expressed by officials working in and around the WTO in Geneva when asked about the likelihood of completion of Doha is a pessimistic one. Many of the government and WTO officials interviewed in the summer of 2010 spoke repeatedly of their frustrations with the negotiating process and the social impact of the continued failure of the DDA talks. Some described the city as something of a ghost town and lamented, "there is nothing going on here". Mission officials talked of trade delegates returning to their capital cities to "renew their careers" and "find more significant trade policy work". WTO officials talked about the need to move on to work in other organisations "where there was more happening". Not that the WTO as an institution can do much about the current deadlock. As a member-driven institution with a relatively small secretariat, it lacks the political, judicial and administrative means to compel the member states to complete the Round. Instead it is reduced to repeated appeals by the Director General for re-engagement and renewed political will from member states.[22]

---

17. For detailed discussion of the development content of the DDA negotiations see Scott and Wilkinson, "What Have the Poorest Countries to Gain", *op. cit.*

18. "Ministerial Declaration. Adopted on 14 November, 2001", WTO, WT/MIN(01)/Dec/1, 20 November 2001.

19. Scott and Wilkinson, "What Have the Poorest Countries to Gain", *op. cit.*, p. 12.

20. *The Hindu*, "WTO Members for Concluding the Round 2011", 9 January 2011, available: <http://www.thehindu.com/business/Economy/article1137855.ece> (accessed 11 February 2011).

21. The WTO website provides a useful timeline of the DDA negotiations, available: <http://www.wto.org/english/tratop_e/dda_e/negotiations_summary_e.htm>. For more detailed discussion of the course of the DDA negotiations from a developing country perspective written by the head of the South African trade delegation in Geneva, see Faisal Ismail, *Reforming the World Trade Organisation: Developing Countries in the Doha Round* (Jaipur: CUTS International and Friederich Ebert Stiftung, 2009). See also James Scott and Rorden Wilkinson, "What Happened to Doha in Geneva? Re-engineering the WTO's Image while Missing Key Opportunities", *European Journal of Development Research*, Vol. 22, No. 2 (2010), pp. 141–153.

22. Most of Pascal Lamy's recent speeches are attempts to create new momentum in the negotiations. See <http://www.wto.org/english/news_e/sppl_e/sppl_e.htm> (accessed 28 March 2011).

When asked about the causes of the impasse, African officials unsurprisingly talked repeatedly of the need for major states to "deliver on their development promises" in the DDA negotiations. This sense of expectation of, or even entitlement to, development is also evident in many formal submissions to the WTO by African states and the Africa Group. In 2006, for example, following the release of the Draft Ministerial Text (more commonly referred to as the "Derbez Text") at the Cancun ministerial meeting in September 2003,[23] the Kenyan delegation to the WTO Committee on Trade and Development submitted a detailed critique of the proposals outlined in the Text on behalf of the Africa Group. It concluded that "the proposed decisions will not confer any economic benefits on developing countries, much less facilitate their integration into the multilateral trading system. They are framed in language which would not oblige developed countries to take positive measures to increase market access opportunities for developing countries."[24]

Some of the African officials working in Geneva talked repeatedly, when interviewed, of a reluctance to complete the Round without significant development commitments. One official stated: "We are not unreasonable negotiators. All we have been insisting on in the committees is that others keep to the development agenda we all agreed to when we launched the new Round in 2001. Even when commitments on issues related to our development are agreed during the negotiations, they get forgotten later on." Formal communiqués submitted to the WTO by the Africa Group during the negotiations support these views. For example, in 2006 the Africa Group issued a communiqué to a special session of the WTO Committee on Agriculture which quoted Paragraph 55 of the Hong Kong Ministerial Declaration, a section containing an explicit commitment that members would address the "particular trade-related concerns of developing and least-developed countries related to commodities in the course of the agriculture and NAMA negotiations".[25] A common theme of the interviews was that African officials believed that developing countries had a "legitimate right" to expect a Doha agreement to deliver development; "Why call it a development round otherwise?", one asked. Clearly, African hopes were raised by the language and norms of development written into the Doha Declaration.

Explaining the DDA Deadlock

Deadlock in multilateral trade negotiations is nothing new. The GATT had long been a venue for stalemate in multilateralism before it was replaced by the WTO.[26] Although scholarly attention has been paid to the continuing deadlock

---

23. The "Derbez Text" is available on the WTO website: <http://www.wto.org/english/thewto_e/minist_e/min03_e/draft_decl_rev2_e.htm>.

24. "Analysis of the Twenty Eight Specific Proposals, Communication by Kenya on Behalf of the Africa Group", WTO, TN/CTD/W/29, 9 June 2006, p. 25.

25. "Modalities for Negotiations on Agricultural Commodity Issues. Proposal Submitted by the Africa Group to the Special Session of the Committee on Agriculture", WTO, TN/AG/GEN/18, 8 June 2006.

26. See Rorden Wilkinson, *The WTO: Crisis and the Governance of Global Trade* (London: Routledge, 2006). See also John W. Evans, *The Kennedy Trade Round in American Trade Policy: The Twilight of the GATT?* (Cambridge, MA: Harvard University Press, 1971) for further details of deadlock in the GATT in the 1960s.

in the current DDA talks,[27] no-one has yet concluded that the challenges this poses for the WTO are fatal. Most analysis sees the continued breakdown as either an opportunity for reform of the WTO system—particularly its decision-making process[28]—or as a diplomatic mechanism for agreeing a series of minor concessions that generally satisfies most member states, but fails to produce substantive changes to international trade regulation.[29]

Almost without exception, explanations of the deadlock use a top-down approach, highlighting the shifting structural factors and in particular the emergence of new major powers in the international trade system. These positivist approaches frame the problem using familiar global governance themes such as order and disorder, balances of power and fragmentation, hierarchy and chaos.[30] The new global trade governance landscape is presented as a complex and numerous set of strategic alliances that includes perhaps a dozen or so states as major powers with diverse, often conflicting trade interests in the WTO. This disordered and fragmented system replaced the more ordered and balanced system of the early GATT regime that was dominated by a small number of developed states whose trade interests and ideas were fundamentally compatible, and who were able to impose a multilateral agreement on an essentially compliant and relatively small GATT membership.[31] In contrast to this hierarchical early GATT system, the WTO has, since its inception in 1995, generally lacked these ordering and cohesive structural mechanisms. Instead it hosts a larger and more unwieldy number of powers in the global economy such as China, India and Brazil,[32] as well as a host of powerful coalitions of states such as the Group of Twenty developing countries (G20).[33] Central to this argument

27. Peter Collier, "Why the WTO is Deadlocked and What Can Be Done about It', *The World Economy*, Vol. 29, No. 10 (2006), pp. 1423–1449; Lee and Wilkinson, *op. cit.*; Amrita Narlikar and Peter Van Houten, "Know the Enemy: Uncertainty and Deadlock in the WTO", in Amrita Narlikar (ed.), *Deadlocks in Multilateral Negotiations: Causes and Solutions* (Cambridge: Cambridge University Press, 2010), pp. 142–163; John Odell, "Breaking Deadlocks in International Institutional Negotiations: The WTO, Seattle and Doha", *International Studies Quarterly*, Vol. 53, No. 2 (2009), pp. 273–299; Wilkinson, *The WTO, op. cit.*; The Warwick Commission, *The Multilateral Trade Regime: Which Way Forward?* (Coventry: University of Warwick, 2007); Alasdair R. Young, "Transatlantic Intransigence in the Doha Round: Domestic Politics and the Difficulty of Compromise", in Narlikar, *Deadlocks in Multilateral Negotiations, op. cit.*

28. See in particular Narlikar, "New Powers in the Club", *op. cit.*; The Warwick Commission, *op. cit.*; Ismail, *Reforming the World Trade Organisation, op. cit.*

29. See Wilkinson, *The WTO, op. cit.*

30. See, for example, Jennifer Clapp, "The WTO Agriculture Negotiations and the Global South", in Lee and Wilkinson, *op. cit.*, pp. 37–55; Thomas Cottier and Satoko Takenoshita, "The Balance of Power in WTO Decision-making: Towards Weighted Voting in Legislative Response", *Aussenwirtshaft*, Vol. 59, No. 2 (2003), pp. 171–214; Joost Pauwelyn, "The Transformation of World Trade", *Michigan Law Review*, Vol. 104, No. 1 (2005), pp. 1–69; Amrita Narlikar, "The Ministerial Process and Power Dynamics in the World Trade Organisation: Understanding Failure from Seattle to Cancun", *New Political Economy*, Vol. 9, No. 3 (2004), pp. 413–428; Amrita Narlikar, "New Powers in the Club", *op. cit.*; Robert Hunter Wade, "The Ring Master of Doha", *New Left Review*, Vol. 25, January–February 2004, pp. 146–152. For more general discussion of the role of power politics in WTO negotiations, see also Peter Drahos, "When the Weak Bargain with the Strong: Negotiations in the WTO", *International Negotiation*, Vol. 8, No. 1 (2003), pp. 79–109; Jeffrey J. Scott (ed.), *The WTO after Seattle* (Washington, DC: Institute for International Economics, 2000); Richard Steinberg, "In the Shadow of Law or Power? Consensus-based Bargaining and Outcomes in the GATT/WTO", *International Organization*, Vol. 56, No. 2 (2002), pp. 339–374.

31. For full discussion of this see Bernard. M Hoekman and Micheal M. Kosteki, *The Political Economy of the World Trading System: From GATT to WTO* (Oxford: Oxford University Press, 1995).

is that WTO deadlock results from a lack of order and authority in the deliberative process; no one member, or duopoly of members, or strategic coalition has sufficient power and authority to impose an agreement. Put simply, authority and market power in the contemporary global economy is now too dispersed to enable a member state-driven institution such as the WTO to effectively govern multilateral trade. Moreover, in this more anarchic structure, the major powers—including the fast developing states—have conflicting views on the priorities of trade liberalisation. Positivist approaches focus on this ideational contestation and structural anarchy to explain the fractious DDA negotiations.[34]

Critical approaches have long highlighted the diversification of interests and unequal power structures in the WTO and, using an equally top-down approach to deadlock, point to the emergence of developing country coalitions that have embedded a North–South dynamic into the WTO and the DDA.[35] This North–South conflict pits previously dominant developed member states such as the US and members of the European Union (EU) against increasingly assertive and active alliances of developing countries such as the G20. At the heart of this North–South conflict are the differing demands of the US and EU for liberalising measures to open up access to developing country markets in new areas such as services and government procurement, and the resistance of increasingly assertive developing countries who use their emerging market power to forefront their chief concerns with implementation issues.[36] Thus the emergence of a North–South fault line as the central conflict in the DDA negotiations is seen as the key factor explaining the continued impasse in the global governance of multilateral market opening.[37]

While structural shifts are important factors in explaining the problems of achieving agreement in the DDA negotiations, an exclusive structural approach, whether from a critical or liberal perspective, loses sight of significant questions in global governance such as how we understand the growing influence of non-compliant least-developed states like Benin and Chad in, for example, the DDA cotton negotiations—a trade issue that has been a headline topic in the talks since the tabling of the Cotton Initiative in 2003.[38] Chad and Benin have almost no market power and thus no structural power in the international political economy compared to other resistant developing country member states in the

---

32. For detailed discussion of these new developing country powers in the WTO see Narlikar, "New Powers in the Club", *op. cit.*

33. For details of the G20 in the WTO see Ian Taylor, "The Periphery Strikes Back: The G20 at the WTO", in Lee and Wilkinson, *op. cit.*, pp. 155–168.

34. Andrew Hurrell and Amrita Narlikar, "The New Politics of Confrontation: Developing Countries at Cancun and Beyond", *Global Society*, Vol. 20, No. 4 (2006), pp. 415–433; Amrita Narlikar and Brendan Vickers (eds.), *Leadership and Change in the Multilateral Trading System* (Leiden: Martinus Nijhoff, 2009).

35. See Clapp, *op. cit.*; Ian Taylor, "The Periphery Strikes Back", *op. cit.*; Amrita Narlikar and Diana Tussie, "The G20 at the Cancun Ministerial: Developing Countries and their Evolving Coalitions in the WTO", *The World Economy*, Vol. 27, No. 27 (2004), pp. 947–966.

36. Lee and Smith, "Small State Discourses", *op. cit.*

37. See Faisal Ismail, *Reforming the World Trade Organisation*, *op. cit.*; Bhagirath Lal Das, *The Current Negotiations in the WTO: Options, Opportunities and Risks for Developing Countries* (London: Zed Books, 2005); Kevin P. Gallagher, "Understanding Developing Country Resistance to the Doha Round", *Review of International Political Economy*, Vol. 15, No. 1 (2008), pp. 62–85.

38. Donna Lee, "The Cotton Club: The Africa Group in the WTO", in Lee and Wilkinson, *op. cit.*, pp. 137–154. See also Elinor L. Heinisch, "West Africa versus the United States on Cotton Subsidies: How, Why and What Next?", *Journal of Modern African Studies*, Vol. 44, No. 2 (2006), pp. 251–274.

WTO such as India and South Africa, and yet they are able to resist attempts by major powers to impose a DDA. The Cotton Initiative is one example of how states, considered by structural approaches as weak and subordinate, contest and construct WTO processes. Such examples show that in not addressing the agency of some of the least-developed states, structural approaches are missing interesting and significant elements of global trade governance and perhaps fail to fully explain deadlock in the DDA.

Not all positivist approaches focus on structure at the expense of agency in explaining the DDA impasse. Drawing on rational choice theory, and in particular game theoretic approaches to negotiations, Amrita Narlikar and Peter van Houten argue that the continued deadlock in the DDA negotiations is best explained by uncertainty (caused by imperfect information) between the developed countries and the developing countries regarding the claims made by each in the negotiations, as well as uncertainty about the "true" and the "revealed" preferences of each. Game theoretic approaches argue that agency-level informational and signalling issues stifle the negotiations and create deadlock which cannot be broken until "uncertainty about mutual goals and bottom-lines" is overcome.[39]

The emergence of strategic coalitions compounds the "signalling of interests" problem in the DDA since their unstable nature multiplies the uncertainty problem for negotiating partners who must try to judge the legitimacy and strength of the claims and preferences signalled by the leaders of the coalition. Thus, Narlikar and van Houten argue, the deadlock in the DDA is best explained by uncertainty over the economic preferences of the "unknown South"— unknown because coalitions of the South such as the G20 have, at different periods in the negotiations, been weak (at the Geneva Ministerial in 2006) and strong (at the Cancun Ministerial in 2003); they have been cohesive on some issues (such as cotton) but also divided on others (non-agricultural market access).[40] Central to rational theory approaches is the assertion that agency in negotiations is individualistic and that activism in the WTO—whether by weak or dominant actors—is driven by utility-maximising values and rational motives alone. Deadlock in the DDA, according to this approach, is assumed as a rational response by member states to the information available to them about possible welfare gains and costs before, and during, the negotiations.

Game theoretic approaches suppose rather than demonstrate that states always behave in utility-maximising ways in the WTO system on the basis that the economic interests of states are self-evident. Yet as constructivist scholars of international relations remind us, interests are themselves constructed more broadly by social, political and cultural conditions as well as by economic conditions.[41] We should not suppose that agency in WTO negotiations always involves utility-maximising actors. It can include, as I demonstrate below, norms and discursive practices that inform the expectations of member states about the WTO regime, multilateral trade negotiations and the actual trade behaviour of states. My argument is that African resistance to dominant states' market opening demands in the DDA may well be a normative and principled

---

39. Narlikar and van Houten, *op. cit.* See also John Odell, *Negotiating the World Economy* (Ithaca, NY: Cornell University Press, 2000); John Odell (ed.), *Negotiating Trade: Developing Countries in the WTO and NAFTA* (Cambridge: Cambridge University Press, 2006).

40. Narlikar and Van Houten, *op. cit.*, p. 148.

41. Again, see Checkel, *op. cit.* for a summary analysis of these literatures.

response to dominant powers that is informed by their (African) social, economic and political expectations of how they can secure development in the WTO regime. In sum, agency has normative, discursive and social elements and we should not suppose that it is always driven by rational economic motives.

In what follows, I argue that deadlock and delay in the DDA agreement are explained, in part, by discursive practices in the WTO. Discursive practices in the DDA around development and global economic governance led by dominant states served to raise African expectations of an entitlement to development, and a collective African anticipation that the global economic institutions such as the WTO would deliver the developed countries' promise of development. In the Doha Round, African agency is not exclusively utility maximising or individualistic. Neither, I argue, are least-developed and developing African states entirely weak and vulnerable (as structural approaches argue), or purely utility maximising (as game theoretic approaches suppose). Rather, they are "won't do" countries, to use a phrase coined by Robert Zoellick, the US trade representative at the WTO Cancun ministerial meeting.[42] These countries have used the discourse of development championed by dominant states, as well as their experiences of negotiations with these states, to better "resist on the red letter issues" as one interviewee in Geneva stated, even if this means that agreement will not be reached. This *collective* resistance of subordinate states to dominant states based on discourses of development has been a significant factor in a prolonged period of institutional deadlock in multilateral trade governance.

Africa in Global Trade Governance

We have learnt to ask why, we have learnt to ask how, and we have learnt to say "No".

(Interview with an African delegate to the WTO in Geneva, June 2010)

Traditionally, African states, when considered at all, are seen as a problem to be addressed by global economic governance and as recipients of global economic governance rather than the shapers of global economic policies and processes. This is particularly the case with small African states whose least-developed economies and scant market power, it is assumed, leaves them unable to meaningfully contribute to a decision-making environment like the WTO where large market power matters. Prevailing conceptualisations of global governance see African and other least-developed countries as marginal actors in global economic governance regimes such as the WTO, the International Monetary Fund (IMF), the World Bank, the G20 Finance Ministers and the World Economic Forum.[43] Indeed, the experience of most African countries as they engage with these institutions is

---

42. Robert B. Zoellick, "America Will Not Wait for the Won't Do Countries", *Financial Times*, London, 22 September 2003, p. 15. For a previous detailed analysis of the "won't do" strategy of developing and least-developed countries in the DDA, see Lee and Smith, "Small State Discourses", *op. cit.* Note that this Lee and Smith article focuses on the discourses of smallness rather than the discourses of development in order to analyse the influence of small states in the international political economy.

43. See, for example, Roman Grynberg (ed.), *WTO at the Margins: Small States and the Multilateral Trade System* (Cambridge: Cambridge University Press, 2006).

one of economic dependence and political marginalisation. In the case of the WTO, however, African engagement is now direct and central to the current Doha Round of negotiations.[44]

Before the establishment of the WTO, African countries enjoyed very little, if any, influence in multilateral trade governance. Although most African countries were members of the GATT,[45] histories of the eight multilateral trade rounds conducted during the GATT period (1948–1995) indicate that African member states were largely absent from these negotiations. Although recent work by Wilkinson and Scott argues that developing countries such as India, Cuba, Chile, South Africa and Brazil were active participants in the GATT, their analysis does not include least-developed African countries, so we can assume that they were not active participants.[46]

In contrast to their relative passivity in the GATT, African countries have become active in the WTO. There is much evidence of the active involvement of African states in the WTO, including the large number of proposals submitted by African states and the Africa Group,[47] the appointment of African delegates as Chairs of negotiating committees, the regular meetings of the Africa Group in Geneva, and the leadership of other coalition groups by African states (such as Mauritius's position as coordinator of the Africa, Caribbean and Pacific Countries [ACP] group and Zambia as coordinator of the Least Developed Countries [LDC] group).

How is it that African states have become more active in the WTO during the Doha Round negotiations? There are at least three reasons that explain this activism. First there is the "weapon of resistance" provided by the discursive turn that prioritises "development" and "fairness" in the context of market opening objectives. Second is the consensus-based decision-making process in the WTO that provides a mechanism for resistance by enabling African states to say "no". Third are the various ways in which the deliberative capacity of African states has been enhanced during the DDA so that they are better able to "ask why" and "ask how" in the DDA process. This is most striking in the more developed states such as Kenya and Egypt, but it also includes several least-developed states such as Burkina Faso and Rwanda.[48]

Development Discourses and African Activism

While least-developed countries may lack market power due to the small size and scale of their economies, they have discursive power as a result of a decisive discursive turn in global economic governance at the beginning of the new century. This

44. Lee, "Bringing an Elephant into the Room", *op. cit.* For an alternative view that sees low levels of African engagement in the Doha Round see Jensen and Gibbon, *op. cit.*

45. Most African countries became members of the GATT as colonies of the signatory states. Membership simply entailed the extension of GATT rights and obligations to African countries rather than any active participation in GATT negotiations. For details see Mshomba, *op. cit.*

46. Rorden Wilkinson and James Scott, "Developing Country Participation in the GATT: A Reassessment", *World Trade Review*, Vol. 7, No. 3 (2008), pp. 473–510.

47. See Joseph Senona, *Compilation of the Formal African Proposals to the WTO* (Harare: SEATINI; Midrand, South Africa: Institute for Global Dialogue, 2005).

48. It should, however, be remembered that many least-developed states still have inadequate capacity to engage in WTO processes in any meaningful way.

discursive turn placed development firmly at the top of the agenda of various global governance regimes. A series of events beginning with the November 1999 WTO ministerial meeting in Seattle, and including the United Nations Millennium Summit in September 2000 which adopted a set of "Development Goals", provided a very powerful development steer for the WTO that found its way into the Doha Ministerial Declaration in November 2001. Cumulatively they created what Michael F. Jensen and Peter Gibbon call a "heightened role of moral argument".[49] These developments heralded a collective global responsibility for development to reduce poverty in the least-developed states of the world.[50] Developing countries, including African states, have been able to challenge the major powers in the WTO to deliver on development throughout the DDA negotiations on the basis of this collective steer on development. The dominant discourse of development opened up opportunities for African states to say "no" to any agreement that did not include meaningful development outcomes. This is seen particularly in the cotton negotiations, which quickly became an acid test of the commitment of the US in particular to advance the interests of the poorest farming communities in West and Central Africa by reducing domestic subsidies to American farmers. Given the symbolism of the cotton issue in the DDA, the Africa Group has stated more than once that there will be no completion of the DDA without an agreement on cotton.[51] Having signalled that the current Doha Round would place the needs of the developing countries at the centre of the work programme, the legitimacy of the WTO system of global governance, as well as the reputation of the powerful states that dominate the regime, now rests on a meaningful development outcome. Previously, the legitimacy of the global governance of trade rested on its remarkable success at reducing tariffs and generating growth in global trade. Few contest the effectiveness of global trade governance in achieving this, but trade liberalisation as an end in itself is no longer sufficient. Since the emergence of the discourse of development, the success of the WTO now rests on its ability to govern trade in a more equitable and fair way to create development for the poorest countries in the international system and reduce poverty among the poor communities in the world. The prevalence of a development discourse, with its normative appeals to fairness, has been a key factor in facilitating the activism of least-developed African countries during the DDA.

Jason Sharman notes that weak states can appropriate the rhetoric of strong states to even up the imbalance of structural power between them.[52] The WTO development discourse provides opportunities for least-developed states to challenge the powerful states by using the language and vocabulary of fairness that the dominant states have directly introduced into the WTO. For example, the Marrakesh Agreement establishing the WTO in 1995 placed the development needs of the least-developed states at the forefront of the new organisation. The development language in the Agreement was often quoted in the formal submissions by African states to the various negotiating committees in the two months just before the suspension of the DDA negotiations in July

---

49. Jensen and Gibbon, *op. cit.*, p. 5.

50. Joseph E. Stiglitz and Andrew Charlton, *Fair Trade for All: How Trade Can Promote Development* (Oxford: Oxford University Press, 2005).

51. Lee, "The Cotton Club", *op. cit.*

52. Sharman, *op cit.*

2006.[53] As discussed above, African officials use the language of development when talking about their expectations and experiences of the DDA.

Consensus Decision Making and African Activism

It is customary in the WTO to make decisions by consensus even though, in theory, a voting system is in place. This means that, in practice, weaker states can, if they are willing, veto multilateral agreement. Each formal WTO negotiating body reaches agreement by unanimity and as such "no-one's objections can be ignored".[54] Even though the practice of so-called "Green Room" meetings continues, and is evidence of the importance of market power in the WTO,[55] this is seen as "irrelevant if an elite negotiated and drafted the text as long as every member can express his consent or dissent regarding the draft".[56] Non-objection, however, is not the same as setting the agenda and while Africans have become more active in the WTO and successful in resisting the top-down imposition of an agreement, they have also been frustrated in their attempts to obtain agreement on substantive policy changes in many areas and especially in the agriculture committee and sub-committees.

While it is important that African states can veto Green Room decisions because of the existence of the consensus rule, it does mean that the specific policy interests of those not in Green Room are placed on the DDA agenda without other forms of intervention. Furthermore, African absence in the formal negotiating committees (as opposed to the informal Green Room process that cannot claim legitimate decision-making powers) amounts to non-objection in the way that the consensus rule is applied; this is because member states have to be present at the negotiating committee meeting, council meeting or ministerial meeting to veto decisions. To take full advantage and to develop engagement strategies beyond saying "no" from the openings provided by the "development" discursive turn and consensual decision-making processes at the WTO, African states have had to enhance their deliberative capacities during the Doha Round to ensure they have enough "bums on seats" at formal meetings, and to ensure that those present have some technical expertise and knowledge of trade issues. Some—though by no means all—African states have met this challenge. And in this process of capacity building, the development of the Africa Group coalition has facilitated the sharing of limited resources to ensure an African presence in the WTO meeting rooms.

---

53. See, for example, the following Africa Group submissions: "Analysis of the Twenty Eight Agreement Specific Proposals. Submission by Kenya on behalf of the Africa Group", WTO, TN/CTD/W/29, 9 June 2006; "Communication from the Africa Group. Operationalizing Technical Assistance and Capacity Building in Trade Facilitation", WTO TN/TF/W/56, 22 July 2005; "Review and Clarification on the Green Box. Communication by the Africa Group", WTO TN/AG/GEN/15, 6 April 2006; "Communication from Benin on behalf of the Africa Group. Implementation the Technical Assistance and Capacity Building and Special and Differential Treatment (SDT) Mandates of Annex D of the July 2004 Framework", WTO TN/TF/W/95, 9 May 2006.

54. James Tijmes-Lhl, "Consenus and Majority Voting in the WTO", *World Trade Review*, Vol. 8, No. 3 (2009), p. 420.

55. For details of the Green Room process see Fatoumata Jawara and Aileen Kwa, *Behind the Scenes at the WTO: The Real World on International Trade Negotiations; The Lessons of Cancun*, updated ed. (London: Zed Books, 2004).

56. Tijmes-Lhl, *op. cit.*, p. 421.

Enhanced Negotiating Capacity as a Source of African Activism

African members' more effective involvement in the Doha Round negotiations has been augmented as a result of a combination of a number of capacity-building factors. Providers of training and technical assistance have included traditional state-based organisations such as the WTO, UNCTAD, the African Union, and the United Nations Economic Commission for Africa (UNECA), as well as non-governmental organisations (NGOs) such as the ICTSD, Oxfam, the Advisory Centre in WTO Law (ACWL), and South Centre.[57]

Although some of the African Mission officials interviewed in Geneva in March and June of 2010 seemed wary of WTO support, the take-up of WTO training programmes for African delegates is high, especially among least-developed countries. The Development Division of the WTO spends 30% of its budget on training courses for African member states, and also provides interns to African missions to enhance their capacity in Geneva, as well as a full-time staff African Group coordinator who organises meetings and retreats for African States.[58]

African states have been quite shrewd in exploiting the support offered by other trade-related international and NGOs based in Geneva. There is an extensive range of supportive organisations that share and champion the development goals of least-developed countries, creating a widespread social and political network in Geneva to enhance the deliberative capacity of some of the most resource-starved missions. It is important to recognise the way in which African states use this non-elite network to empower themselves in the DDA negotiations. African officials in Geneva spoke of the practice of seeking technical information and intelligence from these organisations as a starting point. They also mentioned that they often seek advice on writing WTO submissions and proposals. One interviewer claimed, for example, that UNCTAD had assisted African states in drafting Africa Group proposals on agriculture and NAMA, and that Oxfam had assisted African states in drafting Trade Related Intellectual Property Rights (TRIPs) proposals. NGO staff who work with African missions in Geneva claimed that the 2003 Cotton Initiative submitted by the so-called Cotton Four (Benin, Burkina Faso, Chad and Mali) was authored by a leading member of staff from a partner NGO also based in Geneva. It is an open secret in Geneva that the ACWL writes African and other developing country proposals—largely because it has spare capacity due to the limited engagement of developing countries in the Dispute Settlement Mechanism (DSM).[59]

Not only have African states used these organisations to enhance their capacity, they have also made normative use of them in their discursive practices in the negotiations. Oxfam, for example, is used by African states according to some African delegates in order to develop what they called the "Crying Game" strategy in the cotton negotiations. Oxfam's detailed research into the relationship between US cotton subsidies and poverty in African cotton-farming communities was a key document that informed the Cotton Initiative and helped the Cotton

---

57. Interviews with African officials in African missions, the African Union, as well as staff from the ICTSD, South Centre, UNCTAD, Geneva, March and June 2010.

58. Interview with WTO officials, Geneva, March 2010.

59. Interviews with African officials in African missions, the African Union Mission as well as staff from the ICTSD, South Centre, UNCTAD, Geneva, March and June 2010.

Four gain normative traction in the ensuing cotton negotiations.[60] Oxfam was also instrumental in influencing the publication of editorials in major US newspapers supporting African positions in the cotton negotiations.[61]

African states have also helped themselves by developing means of collective coordination and the sharing of resources to enhance their capacity to engage in the DDA, most notably through the development of a so-called "Focal Point" system in the Africa Group and the LDC Group in the WTO.[62] This involves a large number and wide range of African states including Kenya, Nigeria, Morocco, Egypt, Burkina Faso, Lesotho, Zambia and Rwanda, who each take a lead in each of the negotiating committees and ensure that Africa has a presence and influence across the DDA negotiations. This system is seen as a particularly effective way of making the best use of limited capacity within the Africa Group and the LDC Group, where most least-developed states have very small missions in Geneva.[63] The focal system is, however, more than a simple resource-sharing process. It is also, according to several participants I interviewed, an important social system where officials meet with each other and share experiences of the negotiating process. It is an "African space" in Geneva where they can celebrate the successful interventions some may have had in committees, or discuss their failures with each other. The focal point system provides shared African opportunities for understanding the negotiating process and sharing ideas about how they might better influence that process.

Another development in capacity building, one that is mission based rather than collectively based, has been the tendency among most African states since 2006 to increase the number of officials working in their missions in Geneva. Using the 2006 and 2009 WTO Staff Directories as a guide, we can see that states such as Burkina Faso and Kenya have more than doubled the size of their Missions.[64] That said, enhanced capacity in Geneva is often achieved by simply shifting staff from capitols or Brussels to work at the WTO.[65] It was interesting to experience first-hand the very stark contrast in the relatively high staffing levels of some African missions in Geneva compared to the low staffing levels found in the same country missions in Brussels. Clearly some least-developed African countries have been forced to prioritise engagement in the multilateral negotiations in the DDA over bilateral or regional trade negotiations with the EU. Despite most African missions enjoying enhanced resources, staffing levels are still at a minimum in a number of least-developed countries such as Zambia. Continuing capacity issues seem to be a particular problem for francophone states, according to some WTO officials, and these states struggle to engage effectively in the DDA according to a number of delegates and officials interviewed on this subject in Geneva.

---

60. Oxfam, "Cultivating Poverty: The Impact of US Subsidies on Africa", Briefing paper No. 30 (London: Oxfam, 2002).

61. Lee and Smith, "Small State Discourses", *op. cit.*

62. Interviews with officials from African missions, Geneva, March and June 2010.

63. For example, Cape Verde, Namibia and Tunisia have just one representative in Geneva. Data from *WTO Directory*, March 2009.

64. In the Kenyan Mission, the staffing levels rose from four in 2006 to eleven in 2009. In the Burkina Faso Mission, staffing levels also rose from four in 2006 to eleven in 2009, making their Geneva Mission the same size at that of Brazil and South Korea. See *WTO Directory*, 2006 and 2009 (Geneva: WTO).

65. Interviews with officials from African missions, Geneva and Brussels, June 2010.

Finally, a further way in which African states have enhanced their capacity to effectively engage in the Doha Round talks has been through coordination with other developing country coalitions such as the G20, the G33, the NAMA 11, the ACP, and the Like Minded Group, using the development discourse as a way of building collective action among members. Coordination with these groups has enabled the Africa Group to focus its more limited resources on issues not covered by these groups (such as cotton) or piggy back on the proposals submitted by these groups, such as NAMA. According to some commentators and delegates, coordination with other groups has generally proved quite easy. This is because the very size of the Africa Group—one of the largest coalitions in the WTO—makes it an attractive strategic partner in negotiations.

The added value of all this capacity-building activity is that previously invisible African states have become more important to the process and form of current WTO negotiations and thus global trade governance as a whole. This has been well documented in recent research into, for example, the cotton and TRIPs negotiations.[66] Africa has learnt to say "no" and enhanced its capacity to effectively engage in the DDA negotiations. In July 2008, when the prospects for completion of the DDA were as promising as they had ever been, the African issue of cotton was one of only two issues (the other being the special safeguard mechanism) from a list of 20 so-called "critical issues" not resolved at the ministerial meeting.[67] The Africa Group have repeatedly stated that without an agreement on cotton there will be no final DDA deal though, as others have pointed out, the negotiations could have also floundered on a number of key issues for least-developed countries, including the special safeguard mechanism, market access for less developed countries, geographic indicators, tropical products and bananas.[68]

A focus on the role that African states have played in the continued deadlock in the DDA negotiations tells us many things, not least that African activism *can no longer be ignored*. The problem, however, is no longer one of ensuring that African voices are heard in the WTO, but whether anyone is there to listen. Perhaps the crisis of multilateral trade governance is that the WTO *can be, and is being, ignored* and in the last decade has seemingly become less relevant to major trading nations.

The Dilemma of African Activism

The Doha Round is already the longest multilateral trade round in the history of multilateral trade governance. The delay in completing the DDA seems to have increased the appetite of some member states to pursue bilateral and regional alternatives to trade governance. For the US, Australia and the EU in particular, the WTO is not the "only game in town". And what Sharman refers to as "institutional Darwinism"[69] now seems to characterise trade governance in the

---

66. Lee, "Bringing an Elephant into the Room", *op. cit.*; Mshomba, *op. cit.*

67. Scott and Wilkinson, "What Have the Poorest Countries to Gain", *op. cit.*, pp. 13–14.

68. See Faisal Ismail, "An Assessment of the WTO Doha Round July–December 2008 Collapse", *World Trade Review*, Vol. 8, No. 4 (2009), pp. 579–605; Scott and Wilkinson, "What Have the Poorest Countries to Gain", *op. cit.*

69. Sharman, *op. cit.*, p. 52.

international system. That is, the WTO is competing with regional trade agreements and bilateral trade agreements in international trade rule-making. Major developed country governments—who account for a majority of the value of world trade—have been actively pursuing bilateral and regional free trade and investment agreements in order to open up existing and new markets for some time.[70] In an environment where suitable alternatives to multilateral trade agreements exist and are more quickly achieved, the political commitment of developed countries to the Doha Round is, not surprisingly, somewhat diluted.

Although African states are also increasingly involved in bilateral and regional trade agreements with major markets, particularly Europe and increasingly China,[71] these are less likely to produce the level of development possible in multilateral trade agreements. This is because the negotiations usually involve classic structural conditions of weak states trying to negotiate with the strong (conditions that I have argued are mitigated by the existence of a prevailing development discourse in the WTO), and outcomes rarely exact the kinds of concessions that African countries are demanding in the current Doha Round. In fact, the concessions are often termed "WTO Plus" since they go beyond the WTO's market opening agenda.[72]

The dilemma for African states is that their increased activism, along with that of other developing countries, has raised the level of North–South contestation over the trade rules and processes governing global trade policy and has failed to generate sufficient agreement in areas of trade policy to complete the DDA. The continued deadlock in the DDA has frustrated everyone, including major trading states such as the US, the EU and China, who now seem less inclined to be as active in pursuing multilateral solutions to market opening as they are bilateral and regional solutions. The surge in developing country engagement with global trade governance in the last decade has, it could be argued, created a counter-surge in bilateral and regional efforts at trade governance, and as a result the WTO appears to be less significant to contemporary international trade governance.

Conclusion

By highlighting new forms of African governance with an analysis of the Africa Group as a major protagonist in the current WTO multilateral trade talks, this article has demonstrated that African states can impact global economic governance (even in instances where they lack structural power relative to developed states). This raises interesting epistemological and ontological questions about our approach to studying Africa, global governance and the international

---

70. For details and analysis of the growth in bilateral and regional trade agreements, see Ann Capling and Patrick Low (eds.), *Governments, Non-state Actors and Trade Policy Making: Negotiating Preferentially or Multilaterally?* (Cambridge: Cambridge University Press, 2010); Jo-Ann Crawford and Roberto V. Fiorentino, "The Changing Landscape of Regional Trade Agreements", WTO Discussion Paper No. 8 (Geneva: WTO, 2005); Adrian G. Flint "The End of a 'Special Relationship'? The New EU-ACP Economic Partnership Agreements", *Review of African Political Economy*, Vol. 36, No. 119 (2009), pp. 79–92.

71. Crawford and Fiorentino, *op. cit.*; Denis M. Tull, "China's Engagements in Africa: Scope, Significance and Consequences", *The Journal of Modern African Studies*, Vol. 44, No. 3 (2006), pp. 459–479.

72. See, in particular, Flint, *op. cit*

organisations that are meant to do the global governing. Shining a light on African activism in the WTO and the key role discourse plays in the emergence of this activism shows the intellectual value to be gained by adopting a bottom-up approach to global trade governance. Such an approach can first recognise and then analyse the impact of non-elite actors such as least-developed African states on global trade governance processes. In the case of the WTO the impact has been considerable, perhaps even critical, since it has added to the mechanics of deadlock in the negotiations and this in turn has encouraged states to seek alternatives to multilateral trade governance. The deadlock in the DDA has highlighted the institutional weaknesses of the WTO, the weak political commitment to development among the developed countries, and the continuing absence of a collective commitment to fairness in global trade governance. African and other developing country activism during the Doha Round negotiations has made deadlock the standard rather than the exceptional circumstance in the WTO over the last 10 years. Although deadlock was a feature of the GATT system, it was never the default condition. As a result, Washington and other developed country capitals appear to be shifting their political commitment to diplomatic alternatives to secure trade growth. Global trade governance is thus in something of a crisis, even at a time of growth in the value of global trade.

Multilateralism in Crisis? The Character of US International Engagement under Obama

With the end of the George W. Bush presidency and the inauguration of the Obama administration, observers and policymakers around the world hailed the potential for the United States to engage in a new era of multilateralism on issues ranging from nuclear proliferation to climate change to humanitarian intervention. In contrast to the perceived unilateralism of the Bush era, the Obama presidency raised expectations of international cooperation and increasing interdependence between countries, as well as promising to usher in a more diplomatic and consultative approach by the US to the challenges of global governance. This article disaggregates the concept of "multilateralism", and generates a set of indicators that are used to examine the character of US engagement in multilateralism in the "Age of Obama". It focuses in particular on analysing the Obama administration's response to international crises in the area of global security governance.

Introduction

How has America engaged the world in the "Age of Obama"? Barack Obama's election to the highest office in the United States was celebrated as a "major victory for progressive forces"[1] in the US domestic sphere, and it also raised expectations both at home and abroad for greater US *multilateral* engagement in the international arena. After a presidential election campaign during which America's global role and responsibilities were subject to sustained public debate and represented a clear point of disagreement between the two major party candidates, the inauguration of the Obama presidency signalled an approach to American foreign and security policy that would significantly depart from the character of US international engagement under former President George W. Bush. While US foreign policy under Bush spurred debates about a new form of US imperialism, Obama's "mandate for change" was connected to the expectation that, with his election, the US would reinterpret its national interests as well as the means to achieve them.

Chief among these means was a restoration of US multilateralism and US engagement in international institutions that would replace the ingrained preference of the George W. Bush administration for a unilateralist approach and its

---

1. Jerry Harris and Carl Davidson, "Obama: The New Contours of Power", *Perspectives on Global Development and Technology*, Vol. 9, No. 1–2 (2009), p. 211.

reliance on military force and *ad hoc* alliances. Support for greater US engagement in multilateral decision-making processes under Obama was shared by both global public opinion and international elites. For example, United Nations (UN) Secretary-General Ban Ki-moon anticipated the dawn of "a new multilateralism", based on statements Obama made during his campaign regarding "a new era of global partnership" and building "bridges of cooperation with the UN and other nations".[2] In particular, the early award of the Nobel Peace Prize to Obama can be regarded as the clearest expression of these widespread hopes for a more diplomatic and multilateral character of US international engagement.

In order to evaluate how the character of US international engagement has evolved under the Obama administration in practice, this article is divided into four sections. First, the article unpacks the term multilateralism, which is conceived here as a process, and clarifies how multilateralism relates to questions about hegemony and dominance. The article then presents different forms of multilateralism and develops a set of indicators for assessing US multilateralism. In the final two sections, the article briefly explores the character of US international engagement in response to two different forms of (actual and potential) crises in global security governance: nuclear proliferation and humanitarian emergencies. This focus on security rather than political economy issues is to complement the emphasis of this special issue on the global financial crisis and its effects,[3] in particular because the realm of (international) security is generally regarded as least responsive to multilateral cooperation.[4] The article argues that while it has been repeatedly suggested that multilateralism *is* in crisis, in particular through America's limited international engagement in multilateral global governance processes, this is not the case. Rather, multilateralism is a dynamic process that shifts over time, and this article shows how the pendulum may swing between unilateral, bilateral and multilateral US approaches to global governance problems under Obama.

1. Multilateralism as a Hegemonic Leadership Strategy

Interactions between states in order to find solutions to mutual problems, to respond to supranational crises and to pursue national interests *vis-à-vis* other states can take many forms. As Martin observes, "states can reach decisions through genuinely multilateral discussions, a series of bilateral agreements or the imposition of decisions on a unilateral basis".[5] Generally, "multilateralism"

---

2. Quoted in Wolfgang Kerler, "U.N. Hopes for 'New Multilateralism' under Obama", *IPS* (5 November 2009), available: <http://ipsnews.net/print.asp?idnews=44590> (accessed 3 October 2010).

3. James Brassett and Nick Vaughan-Williams, "Crisis *is* Governance: Sub-prime, the Traumatic Event, and Bare Life", *Global Society*, Vol. 26, No. 1 (2012), pp. 19–42; and Lena Rethel, "Each Time is Different! The Shifting Boundaries of Emerging Market Debt", *ibid.*, pp. 123–143.

4. Indeed, other contributors to this special issue demonstrate that even in functional areas of global governance "below" the level of security, the financial crisis has been a less powerful driver of change than is commonly assumed. See, in particular, Liam Clegg, "Post-crisis Reform at the IMF: Learning to be (Seen to be) a Long-term Development Partner", *Global Society*, Vol. 26, No. 1 (2012), pp. 61–81; Manuela Moschella, "IMF Surveillance in Crisis: The Past, the Present, and the Future of Reforms", *ibid.*, pp. 43–60; Donna Lee, "Global Trade Governance and the Challenges of African Activism in the Doha Development Agenda Negotiations", *ibid.*, pp. 83–101.

5. Lisa Martin, "Interests, Power, and Multilateralism", *International Organization*, Vol. 46, No. 4 (1992), p. 768.

has enjoyed a normative advantage over other forms of interaction between states as the "good" way of achieving international cooperation, and it has been used prolifically both in the theory and the practice of international relations in order to describe a diverse range of forms and types of international cooperation.[6] At the same time, however, multilateralism remains one of the most underdeveloped concepts in International Relations (IR) scholarship, and has tended to be defined through stating what multilateralism is not (unilateralism, bilateralism and imperialism are notable examples), rather than through clarifying what it actually is.

Multilateralism is commonly defined as either: (1) the coordination of state policies through institutionalised or *ad hoc* international cooperation (multilateralism as policy coordination); or (2) international cooperation in a specific issue area in accordance with an accepted set of principles (multilateral policy coordination within a normative framework). One basic definition describes multilateralism as "the practice of co-ordinating national policies in groups of three or more states, through *ad hoc* arrangements or by means of institutions".[7] Building on this definition, Ruggie emphasises that the concept of multilateralism should be expanded in order to highlight that multilateralism at its core refers to "coordinating relations among three or more states in accordance with certain principles", and that multilateralism therefore represents a "generic institutional form".[8] "Very simply", Ruggie argues, "the term 'multilateral' is an adjective that modifies the noun 'institution'".[9]

These two common examples of how to understand multilateralism are symptomatic of a wider problem connected to the prolific and frequently unspecified use of the term: the failure to distinguish between "multilateral institutions" and the "institution of multilateralism". As Caporaso points out, while the former relates to "formal organizational elements of international life", the latter "is grounded in and appeals to the less formal, less codified habits, practices, ideas, and norms of international society".[10] As a consequence, multilateralism can refer to "an organizing principle, an organization, or simply an activity".[11] This article advances a procedural understanding of US multilateralism as a *cooperative strategy of US international engagement*. In particular, the article distinguishes multilateralism from imperialism as the preferred strategy of the US as the world's predominant power in order to solve supranational problems, shape the international order and bind other states to American leadership.

Scholarly discussions of American leadership have taken many different forms throughout the last three decades. During the 1980s, debates centred on the potential for American decline and hegemonic stability theory, whereas during the 1990s debates shifted to the "unipolar moment" and possible links between polarity and stability as well as the state and character of American

---

6. See, for example, J. Caporaso, "International Relations Theory and Multilateralism: The Search for Foundations", *International Organization*, Vol. 46, No. 3 (1992), pp. 600–603.

7. Robert O. Keohane, "Multilateralism: An Agenda for Research", *International Journal*, Vol. 45, No. 4 (1990), p. 731.

8. John G. Ruggie, "Multilateralism: The Anatomy of an Institution", *International Organization*, Vol. 46, No. 3 (1992), p. 568.

9. *Ibid.*, p. 570.

10. Caporaso, *op. cit.*, p. 602.

11. *Ibid.*, p. 603.

hegemony.[12] Although the United States was neither isolationist nor did it abstain from using its military force to intervene in distant conflicts during the 1990s, the George W. Bush administration's interventionist, autonomous and unilateral approach to US foreign policy in the first decade of the twenty-first century revived the longstanding scholarly debate on the notion of an American empire.[13]

As a consequence of the greater prominence given to the international implications of undisguised American military might by US foreign policy under the George W. Bush administration, much of the recent scholarly debate has concentrated on whether US international engagement represents a "new" or "modern" form of imperialism in the contemporary international system. This is commonly understood as being based less on direct territorial control and economic exploitation, and instead operating through deliberate efforts to induce US-friendly regime change under the guise of democratisation and market-based economic reform, which has often been conflated with the "neocon" agenda.[14] With the election of President Obama, the question of whether US foreign policy is promoting imperialism with a "friendly face" rather than the harder edge of oppression and coercion more commonly associated with earlier forms of colonial imperialism, and, if so, what it should be called, how long it will last and what implications this has for US national security and America's domestic economy, and for the rest of the world, continues to attract a great deal of scholarly attention.

What lies at the core of both old and new debates about US imperialism, American hegemony and American decline are questions about US superiority and power, and how America should (or should not) utilise its global advantages in responding to (inter)national challenges and crises. Yet what exactly differentiates American *hegemony*—defined simply as the predominance of one state that is militarily, economically, politically or culturally superior to other states—from an American *empire* apart from striving for territorial gains, colonisation and economic exploitation remains unclear and under-conceptualised. In addition, the lack of differentiation forms part of the scholarly confusion over the past, present and future of American leadership. For example, without any further qualifications, Cox's definition of empire as a predominant state—which sets "the principal rules for those who live within the imperium and punish and reward in equal measure those who either disobey or play by these rules"—could

12. See, for example, Charles Krauthammer, "The Unipolar Moment", *Foreign Affairs*, Vol. 70, No. 1 (1990/1991), pp. 23–33; G. John Ikenberry, *Liberal Order and Imperial Ambition: Essays on American Power and World Politics* (Cambridge and Malden, MA: Polity, 2006); John Mearsheimer, "Back to the Future: Instability in Europe after the Cold War", *International Security*, Vol. 15, No. 1 (1990), pp. 5–56; William C. Wohlforth, "The Stability of a Unipolar World", *International Security*, Vol. 24, No. 1 (1999), pp. 5–41; cf. Mark Beeson and André Broome, "Hegemonic Instability and East Asia: Contradictions, Crises, and US Power", *Globalizations*, Vol. 7, No. 4 (2010), pp. 479–495.

13. See, for example, Andrew J. Bacevich, *American Empire: The Realities and Consequences of U.S. Diplomacy* (Cambridge, MA: Harvard University Press, 2002); Chalmers Johnson, *The Sorrows of Empire: Militarism, Secrecy, and the End of the Republic* (New York: Metropolitan Books, 2004); Niall Ferguson, *Empire: The Rise and Demise of the British World Order and the Lessons for Global Power* (New York: Basic Books, 2004); Michael Mann, *Incoherent Empire* (New York: Verso, 2003).

14. See Alexandra Homolar-Riechmann, "The Moral Purpose of US Power: Neoconservatism in the Age of Obama", *Contemporary Politics*, Vol. 15, No. 2 (2009), pp. 179–196; cf. Steven Lamy, Robert English and Steve Smith (eds.), "Hegemony and Its Discontents: A Symposium", *International Studies Review*, Vol. 7, No. 4 (2005), pp. 525–529.

equally be applied to describe a hegemon.[15] A country's power to create and sustain an international order that is beneficial to its interests has little explanatory value here, because it cannot account for differences in the style of leadership or character of international engagement of a predominant state over time.

Conceptualising the character of contemporary US international engagement instead requires fleshing out these differences based on two "ideal types" of leadership in the international arena: *hegemony* and *dominance*. As a starting point, both hegemony and dominance can be defined as the predominance of one state that is militarily, economically, politically, culturally or ideologically superior to other states.[16] This implies that a country's power alone—material or otherwise—is meaningless in isolation; it necessarily refers to a relationship between two or more actors, and must therefore be understood as a "relational concept".[17] A country then "has power as a consequence of its interactive relations with other states in the system and its structural positions in the networks of relations",[18] as well as through holding an advantageous position in the distribution of capabilities and possessing an ability "to choose and to shape the structure"[19] of the international order.

Yet even if power is understood in relational terms (in the broadest sense), there is a qualitative distinction in the way that power is exercised differentiating hegemony from dominance, which has frequently been under-appreciated in earlier studies on the character of the international engagement of a predominant state.[20] As a consequence, the core defining feature setting apart these two "ideal types" of predominance is the character of the relationship between a superior power and successive states. Von Triepel argues that hegemony, in contrast to dominance, is characterised by "true leadership" of the predominant power that exercises only "assertive influence" rather than force over successive states; hegemony is "energetic leadership but [self-]restrained power" to which successive states voluntarily subordinate themselves in order for a hegemonic order to emerge.[21] More recently, the mutual and consensus-based nature of the relationship between a predominant power and "lesser" states has been emphasised by Keohane, who argues that "Hegemonic leadership does not begin with a *tabula rasa*, but rather builds on the interests of states. The hegemon seeks to persuade others to conform to its vision of world order and to defer to its leadership".[22] Similarly, Cronin makes the important point that hegemony requires

15. Michael Cox, "Still the American Empire", *Political Studies Review*, Vol. 5, No. 1 (2007), p. 5; cf. Michael Cox, "Martians and Venutians in the New World Order", *International Affairs*, Vol. 79, No. 3 (2003), pp. 523–532; cf. Ruggie, *op. cit.*, pp. 585–586.

16. See Heinrich von Triepel, *Die Hegemonie. Ein Buch von führenden Staaten* (Aalen: Kohlhammer, 1974) (2nd reprint of the Stuttgart edition, 1943), p. 154.

17. David A. Baldwin, *Economic Statecraft* (Princeton, NJ: Princeton University Press, 1985), pp. 18–24.

18. Hyung Min Kim, "Comparing Measures of National Power", *International Political Science Review*, Vol. 31, No. 4 (2010), p. 405.

19. Susan Strange, "The Persistent Myth of Lost Hegemony", *International Organization*, Vol. 41, No. 4 (1987), p. 565.

20. Cf. Joseph S. Nye, *Bound to Lead: The Changing Nature of American Power* (New York: Basic Books, 1990), p. 87; Robert Gilpin, *War and Change in World Politics* (Princeton, NJ: Princeton University Press, 1981), p. 29.

21. von Triepel, *op. cit.*, pp. 32–33, 40–41; cf. Nye, *op. cit.*, p. 176.

22. Robert O. Keohane, *After Hegemony: Cooperation and Discord in the World Political Economy*, 1st Princeton Classic Edition (Princeton, NJ: Princeton University Press, 2005), p. 137.

"an acknowledgement of hegemonic authority", and is thus a form of leadership that "can only develop within a social environment with the consent of the broader community".[23]

Hegemony is then not simply a form of property or a set of material capabilities that are controlled, owned or developed by a powerful state. Hegemony is instead a qualitative attribute which is conferred on a dominant state by others through social relations. Hegemony is international leadership based on the self-restraint of the predominant power, and its attempt to create an international order beneficial to its interests through a power relationship based on the duality of consent and acceptance, rather than coercion and submission. In order to bind successive states to its leadership, a hegemonic state therefore tends to operate through means that favour cultural and ideational power and the projection of norms (leading by example) over military force and economic sanctions, and offers incentives to comply rather than simply punishing non-compliance (domination through force).[24] In short, a hegemonic state seeks to attract support rather than to enforce compliance through coercion, and involves successive states in the process of creating and upholding a beneficial international order rather than merely dictating terms to them (see Table 1 for an illustration of the differences between hegemony and dominance). As a consequence, whereas dominance advances imperialism as the strategy of a predominant state to create an international order beneficial to its interests and goals, as well as to enhance and maintain its position within this order, multilateralism should be understood as a cooperative hegemonic leadership strategy.

2. A Framework for Assessing the Strength of US Multilateralism

Since the clear emergence of the US as a hegemonic power after the Second World War, the US has employed a variety of leadership strategies to pursue its interests—including both cooperative and coercive approaches—and US multilateral actions have appeared in many different forms. As Ruggie observes, "All hegemonies are not alike",[25] and an international order created through hegemonic influence is not necessarily either benign or beneficial to all parties.[26] Yet, as discussed above, hegemony—as distinct from dominance—depends to a large extent on the dominant power's *legitimacy* as it is perceived by other states.

The acceptance of a hegemon, as well as the international order it seeks to build and maintain, therefore hinges upon other states explicitly or implicitly granting their consent to the type of programme proposed by the predominant power, their belief in its feasibility, as well as their agreement with the leadership style of the hegemon.[27] While a hegemon, as the predominant power, has the capabilities to rely primarily upon unilateral action or bilateral agreements to pursue its short-term interests, only multilateralism—understood as a cooperative hegemonic leadership strategy—is able to confer upon a hegemonic state the legitimacy

23. Bruce Cronin, "The Paradox of Hegemony: America's Ambiguous Relationship with the United Nations", *European Journal of International Relations*, Vol. 7, No. 1 (2001), p. 107.

24. G. John Ikenberry and Charles A. Kupchan, "Socialization and Hegemonic Power", *International Organization*, Vol. 44, No. 3 (1990), pp. 283–315.

25. Ruggie, *op. cit.*, pp. 585–586.

26. Mark Beeson and Richard Higgott, "Hegemony, Institutionalism and US Foreign Policy: Theory and Practice in Comparative Historical Perspective", *Third World Quarterly*, Vol. 26, No. 7 (2005), p. 1174.

27. See Cronin, *op. cit.*, p. 108.

Table 1. Hegemony vs. Dominance.

	HEGEMONY	DOMINANCE
POWER	Self-restrained	Unrestrained
RELATIONSHIP	Consent – Acceptance	Coercion – Submission
STRATEGY	Multilateralism	Imperialism
MEANS	Lead • Attract support • Provide incentives to Comply • Involve • Cultural and ideational power ('Lead by example')	Oppress • Coerce support • Punish non-compliance • Dictate • Military power and economic sanctions (Dominate through force)

that is necessary to sustain an international order over time.[28] A predominant power cannot remain a hegemon if it does so "at the expense of the system that they are trying to lead".[29]

Although the character of US international engagement in the post-war international order has varied significantly over time, it is perhaps unsurprising that US hegemony enjoyed more political support (and greater legitimacy) and was subject to relatively less overt political contestation, the more the United States exercised its power multilaterally, indirectly and in a self-restrained fashion.[30] For example, at least with respect to US allies in Europe and Asia, America's multilateral leadership strategy after the end of the Second World War placed a strong emphasis on relatively open access to multilateral institutions, the transparency of domestic and multilateral decision-making processes, visible engagement in multilateral activity, integration in (and self-binding through) multilateral institutions, and a diffusion of power. These processes of "bonding, binding, and voice opportunities" were symptomatic of the "penetrated character" of US hegemony after the Second World War.[31] This helped to make US predominance more open, more predictable and more acceptable to weaker states, and ultimately enabled the US to enjoy a high degree of legitimacy in a substantial part of the international arena.[32] In turn, the unilateral and undisguised application of US power and the apparent lack of multilateral activity in its international engagement under President George W. Bush significantly reduced the perceived legitimacy of US leadership and spurred debates about a new era of US imperialism and about the sources of "anti-Americanism".[33]

28. Cf. Martha Finnemore, "Legitimacy, Hypocrisy, and the Social Structure of Unipolarity", *World Politics*, Vol. 61, No. 1 (2009), pp. 58–85; Ian Hurd, "Breaking and Making Norms: American Revisionism and Crises of Legitimacy", *International Politics*, Vol. 44, No. 2/3 (2007), pp. 194–213.

29. Cronin, *op. cit.*, p. 103.

30. See Beeson and Higgott, *op. cit.*, 2005; G. John Ikenberry, "Is American Multilateralism in Decline?", *Perspectives on Politics*, Vol. 1, No. 3 (2003), pp. 533–550.

31. G. John Ikenberry, "Institutions, Strategic Restraint, and the Persistence of American Postwar Order", *International Security*, Vol. 23, No. 3 (1998/1999), pp. 43–78.

32. *Ibid.*

33. Alexandra Homolar, "The Political Economy of National Security", *Review of International Political Economy*, Vol. 17, No. 2 (2010), p. 418; Hurd, *op. cit.*; Peter J. Katzenstein and Robert O. Keohane (eds.), *Anti-Americanisms in World Politics* (Ithaca, NY: Cornell University Press, 2007).

Following the end of George W. Bush's disastrous second term in office, Barack Obama's emphasis on restoring America's international legitimacy reflected, but also served to generate, increased momentum for the US to assume a more multi-lateral stance in global politics. During the presidential election campaign in 2008, Obama announced that it was time "to renew the trust and faith" in an America that "leads the world once more", and repeatedly underscored the importance of international cooperation in addressing contemporary global threats and challenges and to reform existing alliances, partnerships and institutions, as well as to build new ones.[34] Yet despite Obama's stated objective of restoring America's international legitimacy, it remains a matter of intense debate whether the US under Obama has entered "a bright new age of multilateralism" or has simply returned to the "more concealed form of unilateralism" exercised by George W. Bush's predecessors.[35] As with the definition of the concepts of hegemony and dominance, examining the character of US international engagement under Obama in order to establish the strength of its commitment to multilateral leadership is not a straightforward task. To do so effectively requires careful consideration of the alternative forms of multilateralism the US could potentially pursue, as well as identification of the factors that are indicative of the degree of commitment by the US to multilateralism as a global leadership strategy.

Even if understood in strictly procedural terms, multilateralism in practice can take many forms with respect to the degree of formalisation of multilateral cooperative behaviour, ranging from very informal negotiations and diplomatic practices among states to highly formalised, treaty-based and mutually binding multilateral agreements.[36] Multilateralism can also vary significantly in the scope of its reach in terms of the number of participating states. As illustrated in Table 2, access to multilateral decision-making processes can be open to all or most states (*inclusive multilateralism*), or it can be restricted to states from particular regions and to those that have a particular form of government or attain a certain level of military or economic capabilities (*exclusive multilateralism*). In theory, multilateralism as a US leadership strategy could include involvement in anything from an informal forum for three-state negotiations to a form of world government.[37] Indeed, as Bouchard and Peterson point out, "multilateralism is viewed differently by different American political tribes, and even within them".[38]

Contemporary debates on the character and strength of US international engagement under Obama suggest that the hopes of a revival of the multilateral character of US foreign and security policy remain closely connected to a more formalised and inclusive understanding of multilateral US leadership. US international engagement is perceived as more multilateral (and more legitimate) the greater the number and diversity of countries the US multilateral leadership strategy involves, and the more the US is willing to enter into, renew and

---

34. Barack Obama, "Remarks of Senator Barack Obama to the Chicago Council on Global Affairs" (23 April 2007), available: <http://my.barackobama.com/page/content/fpccga/> (accessed 28 September 2010); Barack Obama, "Renewing American Leadership", *Foreign Affairs*, Vol. 86, No. 4 (2007), pp. 2–16.

35. Allan Watson, "US Hegemony and the Obama Administration: Towards a New World Order?", *Antipode*, Vol. 42, No. 2 (2010), pp. 242–243.

36. See Ikenberry, "Is American Multilateralism in Decline?", *op. cit.*, pp. 533–534.

37. Luis Cabrera, "Review Article: World Government: Renewed Debate, Persistent Challenges", *European Journal of International Relations*, Vol. 6, No. 3 (2010), pp. 511–530.

38. Caroline Bouchard and John Peterson, "Multilateralism: Dead or Alive?", *Mercury Working Paper*, Vol. 1, No. 1 (2010), p. 19.

Table 2. Inclusive vs. Exclusive Multilateralism.

INCLUSIVE MULTILATERALISM	EXCLUSIVE MULTILATERALISM
Wide membership (regions, material capabilities, forms of government)	Restricted membership (regions, material capabilities, forms of government)
'Open' negotiations	'Closed' negotiations
Formal (institutionalised) and informal	Formal (institutionalised) and informal

reform binding agreements and international institutions. This latter point—the greater importance attached to formalised multilateral arrangements rather than *ad hoc* inter-state cooperation—helps to partly explain why the US-led military forces involved in the invasion of Iraq in 2003 (George W. Bush's "coalition of the willing") were widely perceived as lacking legitimacy, despite the relatively high number of countries who voiced public support for the military intervention (although only four besides the US contributed military forces to the actual invasion). A further important determinant of the character of US international engagement is the style of rhetorical action deployed by the executive. In this respect, the "rhetorical presidency"—meaning the narration and interpretation of international or domestic events, the articulation of the "national interest", and setting the agenda in terms of viable political options through presidential discourse—can potentially channel policy debates over the appropriate direction of US international engagement in one direction or another.[39]

In order to assess the strength of the contemporary US commitment to multilateral international engagement, Table 3 provides a set of indicators against which the character of President Obama's approach to US foreign and security policy can be evaluated. These indicators can be divided into three categories:

1. The form and use of executive diplomacy (*style*). This incorporates presidential presence at multilateral fora, presidential rhetoric and symbolic action highlighting the significance of multilateral action in resolving problems of global governance, and presidential appointments that indicate a multilateral commitment.
2. The willingness to spend political capital (*action*). This can include presidential actions that are indicative of a commitment to multilateral solutions to global governance problems such as executive orders, regulations and the submission of relevant legislation to Congress, as well as the level of priority attached to a multilateral policy agenda.
3. Policy achievements (*outcomes*). Examples may include the successful passage of legislation and regulatory changes towards multilateral solutions to international problems, as well as the establishment, reinforcement and reform of global governance institutions.

In addition to these indicators, an assessment of contemporary US multilateralism should also take into account the potential domestic (and international)

39. Wesley W. Widmaier, "Constructing Foreign Policy Crises: Interpretive Leadership in the Cold War and War on Terrorism", *International Studies Quarterly*, Vol. 51, No. 4 (2007), pp. 784–785.

Table 3. Indicators of Multilateral Leadership.

STYLE *Executive diplomacy*	ACTION *Political capital*	OUTCOMES *Policy achievements*	RESTRAINTS *Potential counterfactors*

• Presidential presence at multilateral fora
• Presidential rhetoric
• Symbolic action
• Appointments
	• Presidential action
	• Priority of policy agenda
		• Passage of legislation/ regulatory change
		• Establishment/ reform/ reinforcement of international institutions
		• Cooperative solutions to international problems
			• Path dependence
			• Domestic constraints
			  ○ Constitutional
			  ○ Political
			  ○ Cultural
			  ○ Public opinion

constraints that President Obama faces and which may act as "counter-factors". For example, these constraints can include institutional and ideational path dependence, as well as constitutional, political, cultural and public opinion dynamics that impact upon the Obama administration's freedom of action in pursuing multilateral leadership strategies. The "paradox of hegemony" suggests that US predominance in the international arena might increase domestic pressure on the President to limit US multilateral engagement in favour of unilateral action.[40] There is thus a continual tension between a predominant power's parochial (self-) interests, which domestic political actors might prefer to be pursued on a unilateral basis, and its responsibility to maintain a beneficial international order through acting on behalf of a "common good".[41]

3. US Multilateralism and Nuclear Weapons under Obama

Nuclear proliferation, climate change, humanitarian emergencies and economic crises all highlight the need for collective state action to effectively address problems that are transnational by definition, a point that Barack Obama made repeatedly during the 2008 presidential election campaign. During his speech in Berlin in 2008, for example, Obama argued that "no one nation, no matter how large or powerful, can defeat such challenges alone ... now is the time to join together, through constant cooperation, strong institutions, shared sacrifice, and a global commitment to progress, to meet the challenges of the 21st century".[42] Since assuming office in January 2009, President Obama has made significant efforts to translate his stated preference for the US to engage in multilateral decision-making processes over unilateral actions into official policy discourses. For example, restating his earlier commitment to international engagement and cooperation as a vital means to respond to global and US

---

40. See Cronin, *op. cit.*

41. *Ibid.*, pp. 104–105.

42. Barack Obama, "Senator Obama's Speech in Berlin" (24 July 2008), available: <www.nytimes.com/2008/07/24/us/politics/24text-obama.html> (accessed 5 October 2010); see also Barack Obama, Nobel Lecture (Oslo, 10 December 2009), available: <http://nobelprize.org/nobel_prizes/peace/laureates/2009/obama-lecture_en.html> (accessed 5 October 2010).

national security threats, Obama's National Security Strategy 2010 is centred on five key elements:[43]

- Building "stronger mechanisms of cooperation" with historic allies, emerging powers and multilateral institutions.
- US engagement and leadership through diplomacy.
- The elevation and integration of development in order to improve individuals' material conditions across the globe, which is regarded as the foundation "for greater global cooperation".
- Improving the coordination of civil and military efforts in conflicts.
- The shoring up of "traditional sources of our influence" such as economic strength and "the power of our example".

Nonetheless, as the following discussion of two key challenges in global security governance—nuclear weapons and humanitarian emergencies—demonstrates, halfway into his first term of office Obama's record of US multilateral leadership is mixed at best.

The nuclear weapons debate remains one of the most controversial and complicated issue areas in global governance, where the friction between normative ideals and hard-headed *realpolitik* has a tendency to result in failure to make tangible progress on practical solutions. Since the bombings of Hiroshima and Nagasaki at the end of the Second World War, the destructive power and devastating long-term effects of nuclear weapons have spurred intense political, academic and public debates on the legality of their possession and use, their value both as a deterrent and in combat operations, and the effectiveness of mechanisms that aim at the control of their possession and use as well as at their abolishment. In short, nuclear weapons have posed a central problem in global security governance for more than half a century. During his 2008 election campaign, Obama pledged to take steps towards a radical solution of this problem—the global elimination of nuclear weapons. He argued that, "A world without nuclear weapons is profoundly in America's interest and the world's interest. It is our responsibility to make the commitment, and to do the hard work to make this vision a reality."[44]

In Prague on 5 April 2009, Obama outlined his strategy of how to fulfil the campaign promise of gradually moving toward a nuclear weapons-free world.[45] The agenda consisted of three key components that define the character of Obama's approach to US leadership in the gradual abolition of nuclear weapons. First, the strategy had a unilateral component aimed at reducing the role of nuclear weapons in the US national security strategy. Second, the agenda had a bilateral component that aimed at reducing both the US and Russian arsenals of nuclear weapons through negotiating a new Strategic Arms Reduction Treaty (START) with Russia. Finally, the Prague agenda had a multilateral component aimed at reforming and rebuilding existing international agreements and

43. Barack Obama, "National Security Strategy 2010", available: <www.whitehouse.gov/sites/default/files/rss_viewer/national_security_strategy.pdf> (accessed 5 October 2010).

44. Barack Obama, "Statement on Call for World without Nuclear Weapons" (17 January 2008), available: <www.highbeam.com/doc/1P3-1414725831.html> (accessed 29 November 2011).

45. Barack Obama, "Remarks at Hradcany Square Prague, Czech Republic" (5 April 2009), available: <www.whitehouse.gov/the_press_office/Remarks-By-President-Barack-Obama-In-Prague-As-Delivered/> (accessed 5 October 2010).

institutions as well as establishing new ones. These goals included achieving a global ban on nuclear testing after half a century of talks—with Obama pledging to "immediately and aggressively pursue ratification of the Comprehensive Test Ban Treaty" (CTBT)—and seeking a new treaty that "verifiably ends the production of fissile materials intended for the use in state nuclear weapons". Further aims included the cooperative strengthening of the Nuclear Non-Proliferation Treaty (NPT), building a new framework for civil nuclear cooperation and securing all vulnerable nuclear material within four years through an international effort. In outlining these ambitious aims, Obama emphasised that an effective international institutional structure incorporating binding rules, as well as strict procedures for the punishment of rule violations, would be a prerequisite for moving to a nuclear weapons-free world.

President Obama's style in taking the lead in the abolishment of nuclear weapons is indicative of a strong multilateral element in his approach to US international engagement. Rhetorically, his approach is inclusive rather than exclusive, emphasising the US commitment under his leadership to establish formal multilateral mechanisms to reduce horizontal and vertical nuclear proliferation and initiate nuclear disarmament, involving all countries, to which the US would (conditionally) choose to subordinate itself. In addition, Obama has demonstrated the centrality of the multilateral component of the Prague agenda through his presence at subsequent international gatherings that have dealt with the global governance problem of nuclear weapons. In April 2010, for instance, he convened the Nuclear Security Summit in an effort to foster collective ways to secure the world's nuclear materials. With leaders from nearly 50 countries attending the summit, this was the largest meeting hosted by a US President since 1945. Moreover, in May 2010 Obama attended the NPT Review Conference in New York, where he again reaffirmed his commitment to multilateral solutions "to stop the spread of nuclear weapons around the world, while pursuing the ultimate goal of a world without them", and emphatically underlined the centrality of the NPT in this global effort.[46]

Compared with his predecessor, President Obama has therefore put significant emphasis on a multilateral "style" in finding cooperative solutions to the problems that nuclear weapons pose to governing international security. As yet, however, this has not resulted in concrete US-led multilateral action in the form of spending political capital other than non-committal agreements,[47] nor has it led to actual policy outcomes such as the reform of existing international institutions, the creation of new ones and achieving the passage of legislation (such as the ratification of the CTBT). The more multilateral style of presidential rhetoric by Obama could therefore be criticised for simply "picking the low-hanging fruit" in this issue area, rather than grasping the nettle of designing and implementing formal policy changes. The initial success of Obama's multilateral leadership style in involving a broad range of countries to develop cooperative solutions to the dangers of horizontal nuclear proliferation and unwanted access to nuclear materials by state and non-state actors still needs to be followed by concrete

---

46. Barack Obama, "Statement by the President on the Non-Proliferation Treaty Review Conference" (New York, 28 May 2010), available: <www.whitehouse.gov/the-press-office/statement-president-non-proliferation-treaty-review-conference> (accessed 29 November 2011).

47. See Ian Kearns, "Nuclear Security after the Washington Summit", *The RUSI Journal*, Vol. 155, No. 3 (2010), pp. 48–53.

actions in order to clearly demonstrate a substantive shift towards a more multilateral character of US international engagement.

Where President Obama has been more successful in taking concrete steps toward reducing nuclear arsenals is through a mix of bilateral cooperation and unilateral action. For example, in just over 12 months after taking office the Obama administration successfully negotiated a new Strategic Arms Limitation Treaty with Russia, which was signed in April 2010. In order to reach this agreement, however, Obama appears to have used the prospect of abandoning plans for the "third pillar" of US missile defence to be based in the Czech Republic and Poland as a bargaining chip, without consulting either the two countries directly involved or other NATO members. In this example, Obama's approach can be understood as the exercise of what Young has referred to as "structural leadership",[48] whereby the possession by the United States of substantial material resources (in this case the capacity to sustain a global network of military bases and installations) could be translated into a bargaining chip to achieve agreement on the terms of a new nuclear arms reduction treaty.

Obama also managed to achieve an important change in the official role of nuclear weapons in US security policy through undertaking unilateral action. The 2010 Nuclear Posture Review redefines US nuclear policy in comparison to the Bush administration by renouncing the development of new nuclear weapons and shoring up the importance of the NPT by explicitly ruling out a US nuclear attack against states without nuclear weapons that are compliant with their NPT obligations. While it remains to be seen how effective such unilateral actions are for the development of a stronger multilateral framework for the governance of nuclear weapons technology, deliberate and highly symbolic unilateral acts by the United States can potentially serve to transform the discursive framework as well as the bargaining context within which multilateral negotiations take place.[49]

The above discussion on the contemporary US approach to global security governance with respect to nuclear weapons illustrates how the effectiveness of multilateral decision-making processes often relies upon a symbiotic relationship with bilateral bargaining processes, and may also depend upon a willingness to take unilateral actions with uncertain prospective returns. In pursuing these nuclear policy goals, Obama has been faced with intense domestic political pressure and international counter-factors that significantly limited his potential to implement the agenda set out in Prague through formal and inclusive multilateral means. For example, as Perkovich suggests, there has been a clear lack of international cooperation, because states whose agreement remains vital to implementing Obama's Prague agenda have either been inactive, hesitant or opposed to achieving it. Moreover, in no country, including the US, has public opinion been sufficiently mobilised to make the goal of a nuclear weapons-free world a priority issue to be tackled by governments.[50]

---

48. Oran Young, "Political Leadership and Regime Formation: On the Development of Institutions in International Society", *International Organization*, Vol. 45, No. 3 (1991), p. 288.

49. On the importance of new security narratives for stimulating defence policy change, see Alexandra Homolar, "Rebels without a Conscience: The Concept of Rogue States in US Security Policy", *European Journal of International Relations*, Vol. 17, No. 4 (2011), pp. 705–727.

50. George Perkovich, "The Obama Nuclear Agenda One Year after Prague" (Washington, DC: Carnegie, 2010), available: <www.carnegieendowment.org/files/prague4.pdf> (accessed 5 October 2010).

4. US Multilateralism and Humanitarian Intervention under Obama

Questions about how to best respond to humanitarian emergencies generated by severe government repression and intrastate conflict, as well as questions about the legality of military interventions by external actors in cases of severe human rights violations and humanitarian emergencies, have been a matter of intense debate since the eruption of violent intrastate conflicts after the end of the Cold War. Debates have been spurred by prominent cases of ethnic cleansing and genocide during the 1990s, such as in Somalia, Haiti, Rwanda, East Timor, Bosnia, Kosovo and most recently Darfur, to name only a few. The idea of humanitarian intervention through the use of military force in order to respond to (or prevent) humanitarian emergencies in the form of "widespread and grave violations of fundamental human rights"[51] gained added momentum at the beginning of the twenty-first century. Three developments in particular have contributed to a renewed scholarly and public interest in the question of whether the international community has a moral obligation to intervene—including through the use of military force—to halt severe human rights violations, and thus to violate a core principle of the Westphalian order: state sovereignty. These developments include: (1) the increasing international legitimacy of the idea of the "responsibility to protect"; (2) the *post hoc* attempt by the Bush administration to employ the notion of humanitarian intervention to legitimise the Iraq war; and (3) the drawing of a causal link between the prosecution of the "war on terror" and the problem of "failed states".

First, despite remaining the subject of ongoing political and academic controversy, the notion that states have the "Responsibility to Protect" (R2P) their populations from severe human rights violations—including mass atrocities such as genocide, war crimes, ethnic cleansing and crimes against humanity—has gained a high degree of acceptance from the international community (and Western liberal democracies in particular) since it first surfaced in the early 1990s, even among countries that have strived to defend their national sovereignty and resist external interference.[52] The 2005 UN World Summit Outcome final document, for example, lends its support to the concept of R2P by concluding that "all States ... have the duty to promote and protect all human rights and fundamental freedoms", and "Each individual State has the responsibility to protect its population from genocide, war crimes, ethnic cleansing and crimes against humanity", which explicitly includes the *prevention* of such egregious acts of violence.[53] Should a state fail to do this, the international community, acting through the UN, has a duty to assist the state in question through capacity building but the UN reserves the right to intervene with appropriate means, including resorting to the use of military force.[54] In 2006, the UN Security Council (UNSC), through UNSC resolution 1674, reaffirmed these provisions. Thus, while the debate about humanitarian interventions during the early post-Cold War period

---

51. J.L. Holzgrefe, "The Humanitarian Intervention Debate", in J.L. Holzgrefe and Robert O. Keohane (eds.), *Humanitarian Intervention: Ethical, Legal, and Political Dilemmas* (Cambridge: Cambridge University Press, 2003), p. 18.

52. Alex J. Bellamy and Mark Beeson, "The Responsibility to Protect in Southeast Asia: Can ASEAN Reconcile Humanitarianism and Sovereignty", *Asian Security*, Vol. 6, No. 3 (2010), pp. 262–279.

53. United Nations, "World Summit Outcome: Final Document" (24 October 2005), available: <www.un.org/summit2005/documents.html> (accessed 29 November 2011), pp. 27–28, 30.

54. *Ibid.*, p. 30.

focused primarily on the question of whether violations of human rights constituted a threat to international peace and security, the idea of humanitarian interventions—and how far these represented a "legitimate" exception to the rules of state sovereignty, non-interference in countries' domestic affairs and the principle of the non-use of military force—has become increasingly linked to the protection of (fundamental or universal) human rights.[55]

Second, the George W. Bush administration sought to justify the use of military force in Iraq as a response to an exigent humanitarian emergency, especially after the US administration's principal initial justifications for the Iraq War—the development of weapons of mass destruction and state support for terrorism—lost any force they may have previously had in attracting international support for the invasion of Iraq.[56] Finally, the idea that the "war on terror" requires the restructuring and rebuilding of "failed" states through external intervention has frequently been advanced both by scholars and by political leaders.[57] This emphasises how the idea that states have a clear "responsibility to protect" their domestic population has become more explicitly tied to the concept of state sovereignty. Indeed, the growing legitimacy of R2P as a global norm is gradually transforming the accepted responsibilities that are generally deemed to go hand in hand with the institution of sovereign statehood, and which remain an important source of recognition by other states and a bulwark against external intervention. For instance, Keohane argues that "societies with low capacity for self-governance will have to accept very limited sovereignty".[58] Yet, as Ignatieff points out, "the idea of a responsibility to protect also implies a responsibility to prevent and responsibility to follow through".[59]

The Obama administration has yet to take a clear and unambiguous position on when to militarily intervene in distant conflicts where US security interests may not be directly at stake, but where US inaction to prevent severe human rights violations has the potential to embolden criticism of America's global leadership. However, in Obama's Nobel Lecture, the President articulated a strong belief that the use of military force "can be justified on humanitarian grounds". Obama argued that because inaction would tear at "our conscience" and may lead to a "more costly intervention later ... all responsible nations must embrace the role that militaries with a clear mandate can play to keep the peace".[60] Similarly, the Obama administration's recent Quadrennial Defense

55. Cf. Nicholas J. Wheeler, *Saving Strangers: Humanitarian Intervention in International Society* (Oxford: Oxford University Press, 2000); Edward Newman, "Human Security and Constructivism", *International Studies Perspectives*, Vol. 2, No. 3 (2001), pp. 239–251.

56. See, for example, Lawrence D. Freedman, "Writing of Wrongs: Was the Iraq War Doomed from the Start?", *Foreign Affairs*, Vol. 85, No. 1 (2006), pp. 129–134; cf. George W. Bush, "President Speaks to the United Nations General Assembly", United Nations Headquarters, New York (21 September 2004), available: <http://merln.ndu.edu/merln/pfiraq/archive/wh/20040921-3.pdf> (accessed 3 October 2010).

57. Cf. Aidan Hehir, "The Myth of the Failed State and the War on Terror: A Challenge to the Conventional Wisdom", *Journal of Intervention and Statebuilding*, Vol. 1, No. 3 (2007), pp. 307–332; Michael Innes, "Terrorist Sanctuaries and Bosnia-Herzegovina: Challenging Conventional Assumptions", *Studies in Conflict and Terrorism*, Vol. 28, No. 4 (2005), pp. 295–305; Barack Obama, "Sudan: A Critical Moment, A Comprehensive Approach" (19 October, 2009), available: <www.state.gov/r/pa/prs/ps/2009/oct/130672.htm> (accessed 5 October 2010).

58. Robert O. Keohane, "Introduction", in J.L. Holzgrefe and Robert O. Keohane, *op. cit.*, p. 9.

59. Michael Ignatieff, "State Failure and Nation-Building", in J.L. Holzgrefe and Robert O. Keohane, *op. cit.*, p. 320.

Review (QDR) emphasises that the US Department of Defense "must be prepared to provide the President with options across a wide range of contingencies", including "supporting and stabilizing fragile states facing serious internal threats, and preventing human suffering due to mass atrocities or large-scale natural disasters abroad".[61]

The US Department of Defense's Capstone Concept for Joint Operations (CCJO) outlines an important role for the US armed forces in responding to "crisis and disaster to alleviate human suffering and promote peace".[62] The idea of "failing states" and the potential need to (militarily) intervene has also been incorporated into President Obama's approach to US security policy. For example, the CCJO argues that "failure of a state often makes populations more susceptible to social movements based on ethnic or religious loyalties. These conditions invite humanitarian crises and even internal or cross-border armed conflict."[63] This illustrates how the Obama administration has begun to rhetorically and conceptually incorporate key aspects of the principle of R2P in the case of humanitarian emergencies into major policy documents. At the same time, however, a strategy and vision (multilateral or otherwise) on the questions of which states or group of states should have the right to make the decision on where, when and how to intervene, and what role existing international institutions or newly established ones should play in external interventions, has not yet been offered by Obama.

During the last presidential election campaign, however, Republican presidential candidate John McCain spurred much controversy when he presented a multilateral alternative to the UN as the key body to authorise the use of force through proposing to establish a "League of Democracies". In this new international organisation, "like-minded nations" would work together "in the cause of peace", as part of a more cooperative approach to US foreign policy and as "the core of an international order of peace based on freedom".[64] The proposed League would promote democratic values and "act where the U.N. fails to act, to relieve human suffering in places like Darfur".[65] The concept was widely criticised as a continuation of Bush's interventionist foreign policy in the name of democracy promotion and human rights, and neither President Obama nor Secretary of State Hillary Clinton have explicitly called for the creation of a new framework for international intervention. Yet rather than representing simply a "conservative" way to circumvent UN Security Council authorisation for the use of military force, the idea of establishing a new multilateral institution that is composed solely of democratic member states, and which operates under a new framework for external intervention in cases where states fail to protect

---

60. Obama, Nobel Lecture, *op. cit.*

61. Department of Defense, "Quadrennial Defense Review Report 2010", available: <www.defense. gov/qdr/images/QDR_as_of_12Feb10_1000.pdf> (accessed 5 October 2010), p. iv.

62. Department of Defense, "The Capstone Concept for Joint Operations" (Version 3.0, 2009), available: <www.dtic.mil/futurejointwarfare/concepts/approved_ccjov3.pdf> (accessed 29 November 2011).

63. *Ibid.*, p. 4.

64. Quoted in Liz Sidoti, "McCain Favors a 'League of Democracies'", *Associated Press*, 30 April 2007, available: <www.breitbart.com/article.php?id=D8OR8DTG0&show_article=1&cat=0> (accessed 20 January 2009).

65. Quoted in Kevin Whitelaw, "Better Diplomacy through a 'League of Democracies'?", *US News*, 30 June 2008, available: <www.usnews.com/articles/news/politics/2008/06/30/better-diplomacy-though-a-league-of-democracies.html> (accessed 20 January 2009).

their populations from severe human rights violations, has been widely promoted by a number of prominent US foreign policy thinkers who are not only associated with liberal internationalist traditions but are also supportive of both the Democratic Party and President Obama.

The Princeton Project on National Security, for example, has made the case for the creation of a new international organisation to "institutionalize and ratify the 'democratic peace'", a global "Concert of Democracies" on the basis that a new conception of state sovereignty alone is not sufficient to bring to a halt mass atrocities and severe violations of human rights.[66] The project emphasises that the new institution would, for the foreseeable future, not be a substitute for the United Nations, other international organisations or existing alliance systems. Rather, it would aim, first, at integrating non-Western democracies into a global democratic order that accepts "that states have a 'responsibility to protect' their citizens from avoidable catastrophe—including but not limited to genocide—and, second, that the international community has the right to act if they fail to uphold it".[67]

At the same time, the Princeton Project on National Security has also stressed that member states of the proposed Concert of Democracies should "commit themselves to accept authorization by the Concert as an equally legitimate and acceptable alternative", should the UN Security Council fail to authorise the use of force against states that violate the "responsibility to protect".[68] Prominent members of the Princeton Project on National Security include Anthony Lake, a national security advisor to Obama during the presidential election campaign, George Shultz, G. John Ikenberry and Anne-Marie Slaughter.[69] In addition, Ivo H. Daalder, a foreign policy advisor to Obama during the 2008 presidential election campaign, has also been a vocal supporter of the idea of a "Concert of Democracies" and the notion of the "responsibility to protect". In 2007, Daalder supported the argument that because "the decision of states to intervene in the affairs in another state can be legitimate only if it is rendered by the people's democratically chosen representatives rather than the personal whims of autocrats or oligarchs", it should fall to the world's democracies to both decide whether a state fails to fulfil these responsibilities and to determine the appropriate course of action, including the use of military force.[70]

Leaving aside the criticism that the idea of a concert or league of democracies as a potential substitute for the UN has received, if the Obama administration were to follow these foreign policy recommendations and push for the creation of such a new international institution, this would show strong commitment by the President to an *exclusive* ("concert") multilateral US leadership strategy rather than an "ideal" *inclusive* multilateralism.[71] For the time being, however, President Obama

---

66. G. John Ikenberry and Anne-Marie Slaughter, *Forging a World of Liberty under Law: US National Security in the 21st Century* (Princeton, NJ: Princeton University, Woodrow Wilson School of Public and International Affairs, 2006), p. 7.

67. *Ibid.*, p. 26.

68. *Ibid.*, pp. 26, 61.

69. Princeton Project on National Security, "About Us", available: <www.princeton.edu/~ppns/aboutus.html> (accessed 20 January 2009).

70. Ivo Daalder and Robert Kagan, "America and the Use of Force: Sources of Legitimacy" (The Stanley Foundation Project on Bridging the Foreign Policy Divide, 2007), available: <www.stanleyfoundation.org/publications/other/DaalderKagan07.pdf> (accessed 20 January 2009), p. 8.

71. Cf. Charles A. Kupchan and Clifford A. Kupchan, "Concerts, Collective Security, and the Future of Europe", *International Security*, Vol. 16, No. 1 (1991), p. 120.

has frequently emphasised the need for broader multilateral cooperation in responding to humanitarian crises. For example, in order to solve the crisis in Sudan and end the suffering in Darfur, Obama pointed out that the US "will seek to broaden and deepen the multilateral coalition actively working to achieve peace" in the region.[72] In 2004, Obama supported a similar position as a Senator for Illinois, stating that "Only the United States, working in concert with key nations [in particular members of the African Union], has the leverage and resources to persuade Khartoum to change its ways".[73]

Through the concept of "cooperative security", the Obama administration has acknowledged the limitations that any one country faces in responding to such humanitarian emergencies, and has accepted the need to establish arrangements that enable the US to "share the burden of maintaining security and stability" across the globe.[74] Cooperative security therefore aims at "maintaining or strengthening the global security framework of the United States and its partners", and involves a "comprehensive set" of actions among a broad spectrum of cooperative actors "that maintains or enhances stability, prevents or mitigates crises, and facilitates other operations when crises occur".[75] For the US concept of "cooperative security" to lead to the development of a new form of multilateral governance with respect to humanitarian crises, however, will require a longer-term process of embedding the "responsibility to protect" as a socially accepted norm, as well as deliberately decoupling humanitarian interventions from military actions pursued under the rubric of global norms for strategic national interests.

5. Conclusion

Regardless of whether the United States has entered a new period of hegemonic decline or "hegemonic instability",[76] how the US engages the world in the immediate future will become one of the defining features of the Obama administration's term in office. As this article has shown, after his inauguration in January 2009 Barack Obama moved swiftly to shift the character of US international engagement—at least in the case of several high profile global security issues—via a rhetorical gear change in the language of the United States executive diplomacy and the style of US interactions with other states. Whether this change in rhetorical action translates into substantive changes in practice, and especially whether the US effectively engages in a new era of multilateral decision-making, remains to be seen, although the Obama administration also faces significant domestic and international constraints that reduce the President's "room to move" on US foreign policy.

---

72. Obama, "Sudan: A Critical Moment", *op. cit.*

73. Barack Obama and Sam Brownback, "Policy Adrift on Darfur", *Washington Post*, 27 December 2005, available: <www.washingtonpost.com/wp-dyn/content/article/2005/12/26/AR2005122600547.html> (accessed 5 October 2010).

74. Department of Defense, "The Capstone Concept for Joint Operations", *op. cit.*, p. 6; for more detail see Department of Defense, "Military Contribution to Cooperative Security (CS): Joint Operating Concept" (Version 1.0, 2008), available: <www.dtic.mil/futurejointwarfare/concepts/cs_jocv1.pdf> (accessed 5 October 2010).

75. Department of Defense, "The Capstone Concept for Joint Operations", *op. cit.*, p. 10.

76. Beeson and Broome, *op. cit.*

"Multilateralism" remains an ambiguous and unwieldy concept in the study of International Relations, and one that is used far too frequently without sufficient analytical effort to pin down and disaggregate its various attributes. This article has put forward a definition of US multilateralism as a *process* of global decision-making, one which relies upon the diffusion of US power through a network of hegemonic relations with other states that are widely deemed to be legitimate (and where legitimacy is conferred by others rather than simply being claimed by the US), which gain the consent of the broader community of nations. To constitute a renewed era of US-led multilateralism, the social environment in which the United States engages other states in the future will therefore need to be characterised more by the acceptance of hegemonic leadership, self-restraint and the attraction of political support than by coercion, the use of hard sanctions to punish non-compliance and the threat of domination through military means.

On the complex issue of nuclear weapons, Obama has outlined an ambitious commitment to a nuclear weapons-free world, emphasising the importance of *inclusive multilateralism* supported by bilateral bargaining and unilateral actions. The administration's rhetoric on nuclear weapons has yet to be matched by concrete—and politically costly—actions in support of a new or strengthened architecture for global security governance to effectively fulfil these ambitious goals. Given the uncertainty surrounding the prospective returns from taking hard policy choices unilaterally in support of multilateral goals, Obama faces strong incentives to spend political capital only where there is clear political mileage to be gained from doing so.

Similarly, while Obama has moved to incorporate humanitarian intervention and the principle of the "responsibility to protect" within the US foreign and defence policymaking strategic framework, there is a substantial risk that the differences with former President George W. Bush's administration become more simply a matter of emphasis (and style) rather than the implementation of core substantive changes in US security policy. The emergence of a broad-based policy discourse in the United States oriented towards *exclusive multilateralism* when it comes to humanitarian intervention, rather than strict adherence to the principles of (relatively) more inclusive multilateralism through the United Nations, suggests the probability that Obama will struggle to clearly define and embed a new normative framework for external interventions in "failing" states that would help to mark a decisive break from the political baggage associated with the motivations of the Bush administration for the war in Iraq.

Furthermore, the global financial and economic crisis may have a lasting impact on the US ability to play a leadership role in global governance. For example, the US has experienced an image loss in the economic sphere because it was the epicentre of the crisis—as well as through its own economic malaise—without the development of "superior" plans or long-term solutions, which may have an enduring effect upon America's ability to exercise authority in global economic governance. In the security realm, the global financial and economic crisis has also increased pressure on the US budgetary environment. This comes at a time when US military expenditures have surpassed Cold War defence budgets, in particular as a result of US military engagement in Iraq and Afghanistan, thereby affecting both America's willingness and ability to project US military power abroad. Here, US international engagement in the multilateral effort to respond to the 2011 crisis in Libya is potentially a case in point. Despite strong presidential rhetoric representing a failure to exercise "America's responsibility as a leader" to protect the Libyan people from "brutal repression and a looming humanitarian crisis" as a "betrayal of who we are", from the very start of the operation Odyssey Dawn Obama assured Americans of strict limits on US military engagement in protecting Libyan civilians from harm and supporting rebel groups in their fight against Moammar Gadhafi.[77]

The paradox of the Obama administration being willing to "talk the talk" on universal moral imperatives and humanitarian intervention but indicating far less eagerness to "walk the walk" on peacekeeping and peace enforcement through open-ended military commitments and putting "boots on the ground" is not unique to the current occupant of the White House. Indeed, rather than contemporary US actions constituting a clear-cut case of "multilateralism in crisis", the empirical examples discussed in this article suggest a high degree of continuity in US multilateral engagement in global security governance in one important respect. Thus far, the United States under Obama has continued the practice common to many US presidents of expressing ambivalence about its role and responsibilities in the international system, articulating a public discourse for justifying the application of US power that embodies substantial tension between two competing sets of legitimation claims for external intervention, with one set centred on universal moral duties and the other rooted in particularistic national interests and values. How the Obama administration seeks to reconcile this tension—while addressing or avoiding the growing budgetary limits on the exercise of US military power—will be a defining marker of success for the Obama presidency, and especially whether the "Age of Obama" becomes identified as the start of a new era of multilateral security governance, or a case of a President over-promising and under-delivering on his mandate for change.

---

77. Barack Obama, "Remarks by the President in Address to the Nation on Libya at the National Defense University" (Washington, DC, 28 March 2011), available: <www.whitehouse.gov/the-press-office/2011/03/28/remarks-president-address-nation-libya> (accessed 12 April 2011).

Each Time is Different! The Shifting Boundaries of Emerging Market Debt

LENA RETHEL

Recent decades have witnessed not only a series of financial crises in both developed and developing countries, but also significant changes in the composition of overall debt. The global financial crisis of 2007–2009 highlighted the predicaments caused by rapidly rising levels of household debt, most famously in the form of so-called subprime loans, extended to riskier borrowers whose credit history and capacity to repay these loans was thought to be "less than ideal". Yet little is known about household debt levels in emerging market economies. Indeed, if we move away from (largely government) debt to foreign creditors, little is known at all about the dynamics of emerging market debt in general and the politics they imply. By focusing on so-called deleveraging episodes after crises, this article investigates the shifting boundaries of emerging market debt between the 1980s international debt crisis and the global credit crunch in the late 2000s. In so doing, it traces changes in overall debt composition. It suggests that since the 1980s, emerging market debt has been subjected to four significant trends: it has become disintermediated, domesticised, privatised and individualised. However, these changes have been largely ignored in debates on global governance reform.

Prologue: Three Decades of Financial Crises Scholarship

The global financial crisis has put debt centre stage. It has sensitised us to the struggles faced by advanced economies, be it in the form of the predicaments caused by rapidly rising levels of household debt in the United States, most famously so-called subprime loans, extended to riskier borrowers with blemished credit records and little capacity to repay, or be it in the shape of the current woes of the Eurozone. It has thus inadvertently drawn attention to the heterogeneous and evolving nature of debt itself, at least in those countries engulfed in the crisis. By contrast, emerging market debt is still largely treated as a monolithic phenomenon; not much attention has been paid to better understanding its complexities. To take one example, little is known about household debt levels in emerging market economies. Indeed, if we move away from (largely government) debt to foreign creditors, little is known at all about the dynamics of emerging market debt in general and the politics associated with it. Yet, this issue must not be ignored, for both systemic and perhaps even moral reasons. The changing dynamics of emerging market debt might affect the global financial system as a whole. Some pundits already locate emerging market debt as a source of the next financial crisis to come.[1] Moreover, there is the human toll; witness, for example, the tens of thousands of highly indebted Indian farmers who have committed suicide over the last decade.[2]

Human history is ridden with the episodic outbreak of financial crises.[3] Even in the relatively short period made up of the three decades between the collapse of the Bretton Woods regime and the outbreak of what is variously known as the global credit crunch, the subprime financial crisis, or the first world debt crisis, both developed and developing countries have repeatedly been subjected to financial crises with massive implications for economic growth and individual and collective welfare.[4] However, this article suggests that the "resolution" of each crisis has also been an expression of specific economic, political and ultimately normative commitments. In so doing, it challenges attempts to "naturalise" financial crises and the responses to them that are common to both the mainstream economics and politics literatures and emphasises their social dimension.[5]

With regard to the economics literature, Reinhart and Rogoff's recent study—to which the title of this article alludes—provides a wake-up call.[6] Their book, studying 800 years of financial crises, not only consolidates what is known about foreign government debt, but makes a strong plea for paying more attention to the issues arising from domestic debt, albeit still focused on that issued by governments. Reinhart and Rogoff's critique of how economists have dealt with emerging market debt identifies two main factors as responsible for the bias in the literature towards analyses of external government debt. Firstly, the interest of many researchers in the matter of emerging market debt was spurred by the 1980s

1. Oliver Wyman, *The Financial Crisis of 2015. An Avoidable History*, available: <http://www.oliverwyman.com/ow/pdf_files/OW_EN_FS_Publ_2011_State_of_Financial_Services_2011_US_Web.pdf> (accessed 1 May 2011).

2. Suvojit Bagcha, "Punjab Suicides Cast Shadow on Poll", BBC News, 12 April 2009, available: <http://news.bbc.co.uk/1/hi/world/south_asia/7992327.stm> (accessed 1 May 2011).

3. See, e.g., Charles P. Kindleberger, *Manias, Panics and Crashes. A History of Financial Crises*, 4th ed. (Basingstoke: Palgrave, 2000); Barry Eichengreen, *Capital Flows and Crises* (Cambridge, MA: The MIT Press, 2004).

4. See, e.g., James Brassett, Lena Rethel and Matthew Watson, "The Political Economy of the Subprime Crisis: The Economics, Politics and Ethics of Response", *New Political Economy*, Vol. 15, No. 1 (2010), pp. 1–7; James Brassett, Lena Rethel and Matthew Watson, "Introduction to the Political Economy of the Subprime Crisis in Britain: Constructing and Contesting Competence", *British Journal of Politics and International Relations*, Vol. 11, No. 3 (2009), pp. 377–381; Robert H. Wade, "The First-world Debt Crisis of 2007–2010 in Global Perspective", *Challenge*, Vol. 51, No. 4 (2008), pp. 23–54.

5. Cf. Marieke de Goede, *Virtue, Fortune and Faith. A Genealogy of Finance* (Minneapolis: University of Minnesota Press, 2005). Within this special issue, this task of repoliticising financial crises is also at the forefront of James Brassett and Nick Vaughan-Williams, "Crisis *Is* Governance: Sub-prime, the Traumatic Event, and Bare Life".

6. Carmen Reinhart and Kenneth Rogoff, *This Time Is Different. Eight Centuries of Financial Folly* (Princeton, NJ: Princeton University Press, 2009). Despite the regular occurrence of financial crises, it is a common characteristic of the period in the run up to a financial crisis that it is widely maintained that "this time is different", only to end in the typical crisis boom and bust cycle. This eponymous book serves as a harsh critique of the "this time is different" mentality by emphasising the continuity of periodic financial troubles over the centuries. This article agrees with Reinhart and Rogoff on the recurrent character of financial crises and the inherent instability of financial markets. It thus concedes that there is a high degree of continuity, at least on the abstract level, when it comes to the pathology of financial crises. Nevertheless it also suggests that an overly heavy focus on continuity bears the risk of ignoring the fact that each financial crisis has been a unique social experience and that the costs of crisis have been and can be borne in very different ways.

debt crisis, a series of defaults on high levels of external government debt.[7] Until today, the 1980s international debt crisis is perhaps the most important point of reference for many setting out to study developing country debt. The significance of this should not be ignored. It organises the academic and policy literatures and makes out-of-the-box thinking inherently difficult.[8] Undeniably, how professional groups such as economists and financial policymakers are socialised into a subject matter plays an important role in how they think about it and this also holds true for the issue of emerging market debt.[9]

Secondly, Reinhart and Rogoff point out that there is little easily available time series data on domestic debt.[10] Indeed, in addition to attempting to collate such data themselves, their research has already sparked interest in alternative conceptualisations and data sets of "debt and deleveraging" that embrace a more disaggregated understanding of debt and, by extension, the debt exposure of different economic actors such as households, corporations and banks.[11] Nevertheless, to date the availability and quality of data on external government debt and domestic emerging market debt in all its variety continues to exhibit stark variations. To put it in a nutshell, the narrow and selective treatment of the social realities of emerging market debt in the mainstream economics literature also tells an interesting story about how academic disciplines work.

However, if we look at the International Relations (IR)/International Political Economy (IPE) literature, the picture is not much better. Again, inquiries into emerging market—or developing country—debt have largely focused on its external government debt dimension.[12] In so doing, discussions have concentrated on various aspects of North–South and state–market relations.[13] More specifically,

---

7. Reinhart and Rogoff, *op. cit.*, pp. 136–137. See also Paul Krugman, *The Return of Depression Economics and the Crisis of 2008* (New York and London: W.W. Norton, 2009), p. 30.

8. Understanding this bias also helps to explain the controversial policy recommendations made by the IMF during the Asian financial crisis, especially policy prescriptions to cut government spending even though overall government deficits were low.

9. . Cf. Jeffrey M. Chwieroth, *Capital Ideas: The IMF and the Rise of Financial Liberalization* (Princeton, NJ: Princeton University Press, 2010); Mark Blyth, *Great Transformations. Economic Ideas and Institutional Change in the Twentieth Century* (Cambridge: Cambridge University Press, 2002).

10. Reinhart and Rogoff, *op. cit.*, refer to domestic government debt. The situation is even more dire when it comes to emerging market corporate and household debt. For a recent overview of the "state of the art" of developing country debt crises in the economics literature, see Barry Herman, Jose Antonio Ocampo and Shari Spiegel (eds), *Overcoming Developing Country Debt Crises* (Oxford: Oxford University Press, 2010). The issue of rising household debt in developing countries is not even mentioned.

11. See, e.g., McKinsey Global Institute, *Debt and Deleveragig: The Global Credit Bubble and Its Economic Consequences*, available at: <http://www.mckinsey.com/Insights/MGI/Research/Financial_Markets/ Debt_and_deleveraging_The_global_credit_bubble_Update> (accessed 1 May 2011).

12. For a recent contribution see, e.g., Thomas Oatley, "Political Institutions and Foreign Debt in the Developing World", *International Studies Quarterly*, Vol. 54, No. 1 (2010), pp. 175–195.

13. To get a flavour of this literature see, e.g., Stephan Haggard, *The Political Economy of the Asian Financial Crisis* (Washington, DC: Institute for International Economics, 2000); Robert H. Wade, "The Asian Debt-and-Development Crisis of 1997–?: Causes and Consequences", *World Development*, Vol. 26, No. 8 (1998), pp. 1535–1553; Stephan Haggard, Chung H. Lee and Sylvia Maxfield (eds), *The Politics of Finance in Developing Countries* (Ithaca, NY: Cornell University Press, 1994); Jeffry A. Frieden, *Debt, Development and Democracy. Modern Political Economy and Latin America, 1965–1985* (Princeton, NJ: Princeton University Press, 1991); Vinod K. Aggarwal, *Debt Games: Strategic Interaction in International Debt Rescheduling* (Cambridge: Cambridge University Press, 1996); Thomas Biersteker (ed.), *Dealing with Debt: International Financial Negotiations and Adjustment Bargaining* (San Francisco: Westview Press, 1993); Nancy Birdsall and John Williamson, *Delivering on Debt Relief: From IMF Gold to a New Aid Architecture* (Washington, DC: Center for Global Development, Institute for International Economics, 2002);

rationalist approaches tend to focus on the interests and informational uncertainties revolving around emerging market debt and restructuring episodes, while structuralist approaches take debt as yet another manifestation of the structural inequalities inherent in the contemporary world economy.[14] Reasons for this narrow approach to emerging market debt as being mainly about government debt to foreign creditors can, at least in part, be traced back to how the discipline evolved, including factors such as the looming IR legacy, especially so in the United States.[15] It is also closely linked to what were the dominant topics and paradigms at the time when IPE consolidated into a discipline in its own right in the 1970s and which have since then prevailed.[16] Nevertheless, it is one of the central propositions of this article that by subjecting to scrutiny emerging market debt and episodes of post-crisis deleveraging, it is possible to talk about very different politics dependent on what sorts of debt are involved.[17]

Thus, this article challenges those discourses about emerging market debt that are prevalent in the mainstream academic literature. It does not put forward yet another crisis theory but aims to understand how emerging market debt has changed and what the political and socio-economic implications of such change are. For this purpose, this article traces four important shifts in the nature of emerging market debt that occurred within the last three decades: the progressive disintermediation of emerging market debt; the rising importance of domestic debt *vis-à-vis* international debt; the transition from public debt to private debt; and the increasing salience of household debt.

Until the late 1980s, emerging market debt was dominated by government debt and the publicly guaranteed debt of state-owned enterprises, usually in the form of bank loans. However, this is no longer the case. Privatisation led to the (at least partial) replacement of public debt by private corporate debt. Progressive financial disintermediation and securitisation as well as changes in the provision of credit more generally have facilitated the emergence of household debt. These changes have taken place at a time when domestic debt markets have grown to previously unprecedented levels. As the power to borrow has shifted from being a largely sovereign prerogative to being a matter of the everyday, the politics of debt have changed substantially.[18] This holds true especially for the experience of emerging market economies. For both intellectual and practical reasons, these developments should not be ignored.

Miles Kahler, "Politics and International Debt: Explaining the Crisis", *International Organization*, Vol. 39, No. 3 (1985), pp. 357–382; Charles Lipson, "The International Organization of Third World Debt", *International Organization*, Vol. 35, No. 4 (1981), pp. 603–631; Barbara Stallings (ed.), *Debt and Democracy in Latin America* (Boulder, CO: Westview Press, 1989); Christian Suter, *Debt Cycles in the World-Economy: Foreign Loans, Financial Crises, and Debt Settlements, 1820–1990* (Boulder, CO: Westview Press, 1992).

14. See Donna Lee, "Global Trade Governance and the Challenges of African Activism in the Doha Development Agenda Negotiations", this issue, for a more in-depth discussion and application to the international trade regime.

15. Mark Blyth, "Torn between Two Lovers? Caught in the Middle of British and American IPE", *New Political Economy*, Vol. 14, No. 3 (2009), pp. 329–336.

16. Benjamin J. Cohen, "The Transatlantic Divide: Why Are American and British IPE so Different?", *Review of International Political Economy*, Vol. 14, No. 2 (2007), pp. 197–219.

17. It thus also constitutes yet another attempt to challenge the disciplinary boundaries and common senses of IR/IPE more generally. Cf. Michael J. Shapiro and Hayward R. Alker, *Challenging Boundaries. Global Flows, Territorial Identities* (Minneapolis and London: University of Minnesota Press, 1996).

18. Cf. John M. Hobson and Leonard Seabrooke (eds), *Everyday Politics of the World Economy* (Cambridge: Cambridge University Press, 2007).

This article puts forward the notion that by looking at the shifting boundaries of debt and indebtedness in the wake of crises, we can gain a better understanding of the economic, political and ultimately normative commitments these entail. Each crisis is a unique social experience, operating as a catalyst for rebalancing various aspects of state–market–society relations. As the politics of adjustment generate new dynamics of inclusion and exclusion, a more nuanced, historically sensitive understanding of emerging market debt is necessary. To this end, the article will draw attention to how the recent three decades of crises have fundamentally changed the politics of emerging market debt. Indeed, by looking at processes of deleveraging after crises, it becomes apparent that there have been big differences between countries and over time. Better understanding the shifting politics of debt in the wake of crises is important, because it highlights not only who bears most of the burden of adjustment, but also who might be most vulnerable to future crises (as indeed no crisis is the same).

As the dynamics of emerging market debt have changed dramatically since the public sector debt crises of the 1980s, so have its politics. These crises evolved around the debt owed by governments and state-owned enterprises, often to foreign banks. Since then, and underpinned by normative changes in relation to credit and debt, a series of important transitions towards the disintermediation, domesticisation, privatisation and individualisation of emerging market debt has taken place. Yet at the same time that individuals are increasingly exposed to the vagaries of indebtedness, the state seems to divest itself of its responsibility to protect. These changes, and their political implications, will be discussed in more detail in this article. To this end, it will proceed as follows. The next section draws attention to the changing composition of overall debt in the period between the international debt crisis of the 1980s and the global credit crunch of the late 2000s. Based on these insights, the third section will then turn to the political implications of the shifting boundaries of emerging market debt. The final section revisits the main arguments and concludes.

The Shifting Boundaries of Emerging Market Debt

Academic discussions of emerging market debt continue to focus on sovereign debt to international creditors. However, in recent years the issue of financial system development has gained growing traction with policy elites. After the financial crises of the 1990s and early 2000s and given the growing disintermediation of both the international and domestic financial systems, there was a shift in attention to the building of local financial architectures.[19] Improving access to financial services and credit has emerged as a core element of this new paradigm.[20] Nevertheless, credit and debt are two sides of the same coin and as such this transition has had significant implications for the trajectories of emerging market debt. This article synthesises recent discourses on financial system development with the literature on emerging market debt and thus provides a timely update.

The subsequent subsections look at four different aspects of changes in the composition of overall emerging market debt in the wake of the financial

---

19. See also Manuela Moschella, "IMF Surveillance in Crisis. The Past, Present, and Future of the Reform Process", this issue.

20. World Bank, *World Development Report 2002. Building Institutions for Markets* (Washington, DC: The World Bank, 2002), esp. chapter 4, pp. 75–96.

crises of the last three decades: debt disintermediation, debt domesticisation, debt privatisation and debt individualisation. In so doing, attention is drawn to the changing morphologies of emerging market debt as an important determinant of the social realities of financial crises and indebtedness. These transitions are underpinned by specific normative commitments, as will be outlined in the following.

The Disintermediation of Emerging Market Debt

In the 1980s, international credit relations became an important focus of the (newly disciplined) IPE literature, following a series of developing countries' defaults on international bank loans. The crisis was preceded by a surge in the level of public sector debt owed to foreign banks. Mexico's declaration of a moratorium on its debt servicing in August 1982 initiated a protracted period of debt renegotiation and restructuring. While it affected a wide range of developing countries, it was especially devastating for Latin America and the 1980s have often been referred to as Latin America's "lost decade".[21]

However, whereas the episode exhibited typical features of a debt boom-bust cycle, certain aspects were quite specific. In particular, it pushed the international banking system to the edge of the abyss. But therein also lies the problem in terms of the comparability of the international debt crisis and its resolution with other emerging market debt crises. By historical standards, the salience of bank loans implicated in the crisis was remarkable. In previous crises, bonds had been the dominant instruments to be defaulted on.[22] As a consequence, the extent to which the international debt crisis could, for example, be compared to the pre- and interwar international financial (dis)order was limited.[23] This also played an important part when it came to debt restructurings, especially under the auspices of creditor clubs.[24]

Processes of deleveraging played out quite differently in different countries. Nevertheless, perhaps ironically, the international debt crisis, or rather its "resolution" through the issuance of so-called Brady bonds, proved to be an important event for the resurgence of international capital markets. It set a significant precedence for the bond issuance by so-called emerging market governments.[25]

21. William Cline, *International Debt Reexamined* (Washington, DC: Institute for International Economics, 1995); Raúl L. Madrid, *Overexposed. US Banks Confront the Third World Debt Crisis* (Boulder, CO: Westview Press, 1992); Graham Bird, *Commercial Bank Lending and Third World Debt* (London: Macmillan, 1989).

22. On the series of defaults on emerging market bonds in the 1820s see, e.g., Frank G. Dawson, *The First Latin American Debt Crisis. The City of London and the 1822–25 Loan Bubble* (New Haven and London: Yale University Press, 1990).

23. Barry Eichengreen and Peter H. Lindert (eds), *The International Debt Crisis in Historical Perspective* (Cambridge, MA: The MIT Press, 1989); Susan Strange, *Casino Capitalism* (Oxford: Basil Blackwell, 1986).

24. See, e.g., Paolo Mauro and Yishay Yafeh, "The Corporation of Foreign Bondholders", IMF Working Paper No. 03/107 (1 May 2003); Barry Eichengreen and Richard Portes, *Crisis? What Crisis? Orderly Workouts for Sovereign Debtors* (London: Centre for Economic Policy Research, 1995); Christine A. Kearney, "The Creditor Clubs: Paris and London", in Thomas Biersteker (ed.), *Dealing with Debt: International Financial Negotiations and Adjustment Bargaining* (San Francisco: Westview Press, 1993), pp. 61–76.

25. World Bank, *Global Development Finance: Striving for Stability in Development Finance*, 2 volumes (Washington, DC: Worldbank, 2003); Frieden, *op. cit.*; Madrid, *op. cit.*

However, while in the process the world of international and emerging market finance was about to change dramatically, it severely limited the analytical purchase of the lessons learnt from the international debt crisis. One of these lessons was the systemic risk posed by bank loans. The progressive disintermediation of national financial systems and of the international financial system as a whole was thought to be a market-based way to mitigate this risk.

The conversion of international debt from bank loans to bonds that took place in the form of the Brady deal was only the first major move towards the disintermediation of emerging market debt, soon to be followed by even greater efforts to develop domestic bond markets, as will be discussed in the next subsection. Moreover, the disintermediation of debt issued by emerging economies was mirrored by changes in the provision of credit, notably a marked shift within private sector credit patterns from bank loans to portfolio investment. As Figure 1 shows, not only has overall middle- and low-income country debt outstanding increased dramatically, but ever since 1994, bank loans have been dwarfed by bonds. As a consequence, since the international debt crisis, or perhaps the 1980s more generally, domestic financial systems as well as the international financial system have undergone such a fundamental transformation that the insights from the debt crisis have only limited applicability.[26] As a matter of fact, this transformation was not unproblematic and arguably contributed to a new wave of financial crises in emerging markets in the 1990s.

Indeed, one of the major characteristics of the emerging market crises of the 1990s—Mexico in 1994–1995, East Asia in 1997–1998 and from there spilling over to Russia and Latin America in 1998–2002—was the volatility generated by disintermediated portfolio investment flows. It led to a renewed academic interest in "hot money", a term allegedly first used by US President Franklin D. Roosevelt in 1936 to refer to speculative short-term capital flows.[27] However, underlying the increased capital mobility that foremost gained the attention of economists and policymakers was the changing way in which debt was incurred and credit extended. The rise of international portfolio investment and the shift towards bonds as the major instruments of debt financing are two sides of the same coin rooted in and contributing to the shifting dynamics—and politics—of emerging market debt. Effectively, responses to the 1980s crisis set in motion the financial and social pathologies of the crises that were to come in the 1990s.

In terms of the transformation of emerging market debt, the "resolution" of the international debt crisis set the precedent for two further important trends: its domesticisation and privatisation. The next subsection will take a closer look at the domesticisation of emerging market debt. Its privatisation will be discussed in the subsection thereafter.

---

26. See, e.g., the contributions in Haggard *et al.*, *op. cit.*; and in Joan M. Nelson (ed.), *Economic Crisis and Policy Choice: The Politics of Adjustment in Less Developed Countries* (Princeton, NJ: Princeton University Press, 1990).

27. Rawi Abdelal, *Capital Rules. The Construction of Global Finance* (Cambridge, MA: Harvard University Press, 2007), p. 231; cf. V.V. Chari and Patrick Kehoe, "Hot Money", NBER Working Paper 6007 (1997); Hali Edison and Carmen M. Reinhart, "Stopping Hot Money", *Journal of Development Economics*, Vol. 66, No. 2 (2001), pp. 533–553; Lucio Sarno and Mark P. Taylor, "Hot Money, Accounting Labels and the Permanence of Capital Flows to Developing Countries: An Empirical Investigation", *Journal of Development Economics*, Vol. 59, No. 2 (1999), pp. 337–364.

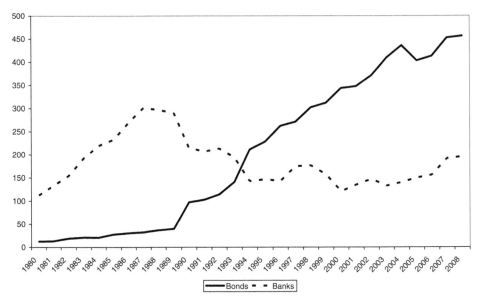

Figure 1. External Public and Publicly Guaranteed Debt Outstanding.*
Note: *Debt outstanding; low- and middle-income countries, in current US$ billion.
Source: World Development Indicators.

The Domesticisation of Emerging Market Debt

Traditionally, the IPE literature on (emerging market) debt has focused on the relationship between national governments and international financial markets.[28] Nevertheless, the last two decades have witnessed increased efforts by national policymakers and the international financial community to develop domestic debt markets as well as a series of experiments with debt contracts broadly aimed at domesticising emerging market debt. In so doing, two broader objectives can be distinguished. One of them is to reduce the role of the dollar and thus ultimately the exchange rate risk for the issuer through various attempts to de-dollarise emerging market debt.[29] The other is to establish greater jurisdictional control over the debt issued by domestic economic actors, both sovereign and corporate, and to develop national financial systems more generally.

In this regard, most important have been endeavours to develop domestic debt markets and the resulting expansion of local currency bond markets. Again, the impact of post-crisis restructuring efforts should not be ignored for both material and ideational reasons. On a material level, the restructuring of non-performing loans and the recapitalisation of banks added size to domestic bond markets. For example, in the wake of the Asian financial crisis, bonds amounting to a collective value of more than US$110 billion were issued in Malaysia, South Korea

---

28. Cf. Iain Hardie, "The Power of Markets? The International Bond Markets and the 2002 Elections in Brazil", *Review of International Political Economy*, Vol. 13, No. 1 (2006), pp. 53–77; Layna Mosley, *Global Capital, National Governments* (Cambridge: Cambridge University Press, 2003).

29. The pesofication of Argentine debt in 2002 provides an example of this trend. See Luc Laeven and Thomas Laryea, "Principles of Household Debt Restructuring", IMF Staff Position Note SPN/09/15 (26 June 2009).

and Thailand to this purpose.[30] These policies were emulated by China in the early 2000s when it cleaned up its financial system, again via the issuance of bonds.[31] This was closely linked to the discursive construction of a new financial development paradigm that was embraced by both regional financial policy-makers and the international financial community.[32]

More specifically, the growth of domestic debt markets has not been solely restricted to crisis countries and this is where ideational factors have played an important role. With the financial turmoil of the late 1990s, the perception took hold more widely that promoting domestic debt markets could serve as a protection from volatile financial flows without prohibiting them.[33] This move was facilitated by a generally more benevolent international macroeconomic climate.[34] Moreover, the growth of non-bank financial intermediaries in advanced and emerging market financial systems led to increased demand for domestic emerging market debt.[35]

As a result, the relationship between foreign debt and domestic debt has been turned on its head, at least if we take the international debt crisis of the 1980s as a benchmark. For example, Hanson demonstrates for a sample of 25 developing countries that while the share of domestic debt as percentage of total government debt amounted to only just over a third (37.7%) in 1990, by 2004 foreign government debt had been overtaken by domestic government debt (58.4%).[36] Indeed, in 23 out of 25 countries, the share of domestic debt in total government debt had increased, Argentina and Uruguay being the only exceptions. During the same period, the share of overall government debt to GDP had increased in all but four countries. This increasingly puts into question the so often assumed "foreign" market–"national" government dichotomies, thus giving rise to the emergence of new political fault lines.

Undeniably, the trend towards domestic debt in emerging market economies recasts state–market relations in a way that challenges those conventional accounts in the IPE literature that focus on the structural power of international capital.[37] More research is necessary to provide not only a more nuanced picture of efforts to "domesticate" debt, but also to better understand how these changes affect the parameters of domestic economic policymaking, the new constraints that they impose and the new spaces that they open. To this end, it is important to explore how responses to crises constitute the boundaries of future financial arrangements, their weaknesses and resilience.

---

30. Lena Rethel, "The New Financial Development Paradigm and Asian Bond Markets", *New Political Economy*, Vol. 15, No. 1 (2010), pp. 493–517.

31. Edward S. Steinfeld, "Market Visions: The Interplay of Ideas and Institutions in Chinese Financial Restructuring", *Political Studies*, Vol. 52, No. 4 (2004), pp. 643–663.

32. Rethel, "The New Financial Development Paradigm", *op. cit.*

33. Barry Eichengreen and Ricardo Hausmann (eds), *Other People's Money. Debt Denomination and Financial Instability in Emerging Market Economies* (Chicago: The University of Chicago Press, 2005).

34. James A. Hanson, "The Growth in Government Domestic Debt: Changing Burdens and Risks", World Bank Policy Research Working Paper WPS4348 (September 2007).

35. Jeffrey Carmichael and Michael Pomerleano, *The Development and Regulation of Non-Bank Financial Institutions* (Washington, DC: The World Bank, 2002).

36. Hanson, *op. cit.*, p. 4.

37. Stephen Gill and David Law, "Global Hegemony and the Structural Power of Capital", *International Studies Quarterly*, Vol. 33, No. 4 (1989), pp. 475–499.

Furthermore, the domesticisation of emerging market debt pertained not only to government debt, but also to corporate debt. Indeed, the Asian financial crisis was an important catalyst for the latter transition as policymakers identified the high foreign indebtedness of Asian corporations as one of the root causes of the crisis. This will be discussed in more detail in the next subsection.

The Privatisation of Emerging Market Debt

At the same time that emerging market debt was becoming increasingly disintermediated and domesticised, another trend was underway, namely the increasing privatisation of emerging market debt. In fact, it is one of the least discussed features of the resolution of the 1980s international debt crisis (and a number of less severe crises in Northeast and Southeast Asia) that it sped up the transition from public debt to private debt. Effectively, there are two main aspects to the privatisation of emerging market debt: increased exposure to private debt holders (over bi- and multilateral creditors) and increased indebtedness by private economic actors (often formerly state-owned corporations). On a global scale since the mid-1990s, bilateral and multilateral credit to developing countries has been dwarfed by credit provided by the private sector.[38]

With regard to the changing morphologies of emerging market debt in particular, the more important transition has been the move from public and publicly guaranteed to (at least *de jure*) privately owed debt. There have been many debates in the literature about the goods and bads of International Monetary Fund (IMF)-imposed structural adjustment programmes and the Washington consensus style policy prescriptions that became fashionable in the late 1980s. Without entering into this debate, it is sufficient to say here that their outcome proved to be incidental for the changing composition of emerging market debt. By the early 1990s, the corporatisation and privatisation of formerly state-owned enterprises was well underway in emerging markets with important implications for the shifting locus of indebtedness.[39] Figure 2 shows the rising importance of private, non-guaranteed debt in the overall external debt burden of low- and middle-income countries.

It should not be ignored that privatisation was not just ideologically motivated, but was fostered by the fiscal retrenchments of the time as states struggled with their heavy debt burdens. Moreover, these efforts were not solely restricted to countries under IMF programmes. For example, Malaysia introduced a "voluntary structural adjustment programme" in the mid-1980s that combined privatisation and fiscal retrenchment. Nevertheless, the point is that public austerity is of limited use if (newly privatised) corporations go on an international borrowing spree as happened, for example, in a range of Asian countries before the outbreak of the Asian financial crisis.

To put it differently, the effect of reductions in government debt on overall emerging market debt is not clear cut. It certainly does not automatically presage a reduction of overall debt levels. Furthermore, it opens up new questions about

---

38. World Bank, *Global Development Finance, op. cit.*; see also Liam Clegg, "Post-crisis Reform at the IMF: Learning to Be (Seen to Be) a Long-term Development Partner", this issue.

39. See, e.g., Kathryn C. Lavelle, *The Politics of Equity Finance in Emerging Markets* (Oxford: Oxford University Press, 2004).

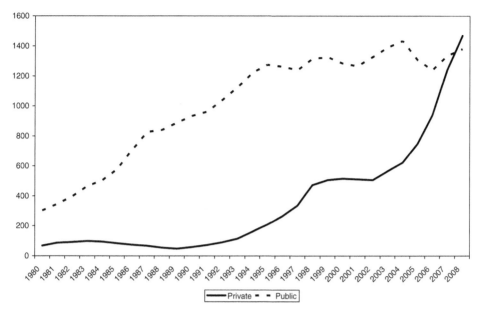

Figure 2. Private External Debt versus Public and Publicly Guaranteed External Debt.*
Note: * Debt outstanding; low- and middle-income countries, in current US$ billion.
Source: World Development Indicators.

government capacity to prevent corporate over-indebtedness, especially if governments already struggle to rein in their own indebtedness. As a matter of fact, privatisation is certainly not a panacea when it comes to tackling emerging market debt. This is even truer in cases where ultimately the state has to *de facto* bail out indebted corporations, as will be discussed below.

Thus, in the run up to the Asian financial crisis, levels of corporate leverage, the ratio of debt to equity, rose, quite dramatically in some cases, as Table 1 indicates. Facilitated by ongoing attempts to liberalise national financial systems, this private sector debt was largely short term and often owed to foreign portfolio investors, although there remained differences between countries. For example, Malaysia had a much more restrictive regulatory regime than other Asian countries. Here, three quarters of the foreign debt incurred by corporations listed on the Kuala Lumpur Stock Exchange belonged to only three (recently privatised) corporations—TNB, Telekom and Malaysia Airlines.[40] Despite government bailouts, in the aftermath of the crisis the trend towards privatisation was only temporarily reversed.

Effectively, the privatisation of emerging market debt gained new momentum with the financial crises of the 1990s and resulting efforts to promote domestic markets for both government debt and corporate debt. Table 2 shows this for the case of a range of selected Asian countries for the decade between the onset of the Asian financial crisis and that of the global credit crunch and again in 2009.

The table also reflects the two trends discussed previously, namely the disintermediation and domesticisation of emerging market debt. While the

---

40. Anita Doraisami, "The Political Economy of Capital Flows and Capital Controls in Malaysia", *Journal of Contemporary Asia*, Vol. 35, No. 2 (2005), p. 255. See also Rawi Abdelal and Laura Alfaro, "Capital and Control: Lessons from Malaysia", *Challenge*, Vol. 46, No. 4 (2003), pp. 36–53.

Table 1. Rising Leverage of Asian Corporations before the 1997–1998 Crisis.

Country	Year								
	1988	**1989**	**1990**	**1991**	**1992**	**1993**	**1994**	**1995**	**1996**
Indonesia	n.a.	n.a.	n.a.	1.943	2.097	2.054	1.661	2.115	1.878
Malaysia	0.727	0.810	1.010	0.610	0.627	0.704	0.991	1.103	1.176
S. Korea	2.820	2.644	3.105	3.221	3.373	3.636	3.530	3.776	3.545
Philippines	n.a.	n.a.	n.a.	0.830	1.186	1.175	1.148	1.150	1.285
Singapore	0.765	0.922	0.939	0.887	0.856	1.102	0.862	1.037	1.049
Thailand	1.602	1.905	2.159	2.010	1.837	1.914	2.126	2.224	2.361

Source: Stijn Claessens, Simeon Djankov and Larry H.P. Lang, "Corporate Growth, Financing, and Risks in the Decade before East Asia's Financial Crisis", World Bank Policy Research Working Paper No. 2017 (October 1998), p. 9.

Table 2. The Size of Selected Asian Local Currency Bond Markets, % of GDP.

Country	1997			2007			2009		
	Total	Gov.	Corp.	**Total**	Gov.	Corp.	**Total**	Gov.	Corp.
PRC	**12.22**	7.07	5.14	**50**	45.36	4.64	**52.3**	43.0	9.2
Indonesia	**1.94**	0.38	1.56	**20.80**	18.80	2.00	**16.6**	15.0	1.6
Malaysia	**56.36**	19.18	37.18	**84.62**	45.68	38.94	**94.2**	51.4	42.8
S. Korea	**25.07**	4.15	20.92	**136.46**	75	61.46	**113.4**	49.6	63.8
Philippines	**20.50**	20.11	0.39	**35.97**	32.76	3.21	**38.0**	33.4	4.6
Singapore	**24.79**	13.60	11.19	**69.94**	40.34	29.60	**81.9**	48.0	33.8
Thailand	**6.65**	0.19	6.46	**54.06**	37.75	16.31	**65.2**	52.1	13.2
Vietnam	**0**	0	0	**13.72**	11.60	2.12	**13.2**	12.2	1.1

Source: AsianBondsOnline.

lion's share of domestic bonds is issued by governments, with—as the 2009 data indicates—a stimulus-induced increase in the wake of the global credit crunch, the growth rates of corporate debt are striking. In all eight countries, the size of the corporate domestic bond market is bigger in 2009 than in 1997; in seven out of eight countries significantly so. In South Korea, the size of the corporate bond market even surpasses that of the government debt market. Moreover, private debt is not just corporate debt, but also, and increasingly significantly, household debt. However, the issue of rising household debt in emerging market economies will be discussed separately in the next—and final—part of this section.

The Individualisation of Emerging Market Debt

If we look at the composition of total debt to GDP levels, where available, another trend is the growth of household debt. The issue of rising household debt levels in emerging market economies has only very recently come onto the radar of policy-makers. As a consequence, there is very little data available, especially when it comes to long-term trends. Nevertheless, there are some indications that in recent years, in most emerging market economies the growth rate of household debt

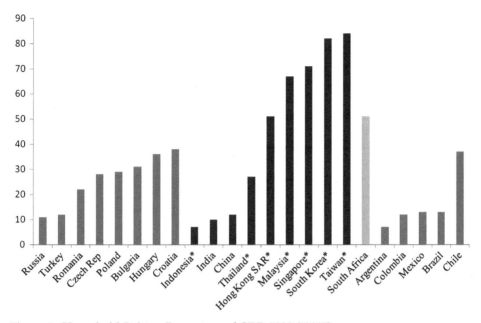

Figure 3. Household Debt as Percentage of GDP, 2008 (*2007).
Source: Financial Stability Reports of local monetary authorities; UniCredit Group;
McKinsey Global Institute.

surpassed that of corporate debt.[41] Indeed, household debt in emerging markets is on the rise both in absolute terms and in proportion to other forms of debt.

Figure 3 shows household debt levels as a percentage of GDP for a range of political economies. While this ratio has remained significantly lower in emerging market economies than in those countries at the epicentre of the global credit crunch, namely the UK and the US, for these countries it is significant. Household debt levels in Malaysia, Taiwan, South Korea and South Africa are especially striking. Moreover, it is not just the level of household debt stocks, but also their growth rates, with household debt as a percentage of GDP growing, for example, at an annualised rate of 15% in Malaysia between 1999 and 2006.[42] In South Korea, household debt as a percentage of GDP nearly doubled from 48% in 1998 to 74% in 2002.[43]

Household debt includes, but is not restricted to, mortgage debt, hire-purchase debt (e.g., for cars and other durable consumer goods) and credit card debt. Hence, the improved access to housing finance, the increased availability of credit cards and a proliferation of loans for consumer durables contributed to its recent growth. However, there are a number of more systemic factors underlying this expansion. These include longer-term trends such as the growth of the middle classes in many emerging market economies and the development of domestic financial

41. IMF, *Global Financial Stability Report. Market Developments and Issues* (Washington, DC: The International Monetary Fund, September 2006), p. 46.

42. Lena Rethel, "Financialisation and the Malaysian Political Economy", *Globalizations*, Vol. 7, No. 4 (2010), pp. 461–478.

43. James Crotty and Kang-Kook Lee, "The Effects of Neoliberal 'Reforms' on the Postcrisis Korean Economy", *Review of Radical Political Economics*, Vol. 38, No. 3 (2006), pp. 381–387.

systems—a project to which both domestic policymakers and the international financial community subscribe—which make it easier for households to access credit and go into debt. Nevertheless, as with the disintermediation, domesticisation and privatisation of emerging market debt, some of these more systemic factors very clearly originated in previous crises and policymakers' responses to them.

One such factor was an increased effort to develop local capital markets and to push ahead with progressive financial disintermediation, as discussed above. As corporations turned to capital markets to raise funds, banks increasingly targeted their lending activities at households.[44] This was encouraged by policymakers looking favourably upon, if not doing their best to make happen, domestic consumption- and credit-fuelled expansion to restore growth after crises.[45] This was especially, but not only, important in countries where extant regimes justified their actions through performance legitimacy, as rapidly expanding household credit could, at least temporarily, compensate for subdued economic growth in the wake of the crisis. Moreover, household debt is also part of the wider domesticisation of debt in that it is largely denominated in local currency, at least in most of emerging Asia and Latin America.[46]

At the moment, of course, the elephant in the room is China. By many accounts, its 2008–2009 stimulus-induced debt binge, apart from reawakening the spectre of non-performing loans to local government-linked entities, fuelled rising levels of household debt. Already, Chinese household debt had tripled from 4% of GDP in 2000 to an admittedly still low but previously unprecedented 12% of GDP in 2008.[47] Moreover, as Table 2 suggested, China is one of the few countries where the domestic corporate bond market actually grew faster between 2007 and 2009 than the government bond market. Indeed, it looks as if patterns of deleveraging and releveraging are set to continue, if not accelerate, in the wake of the global credit crunch, especially in many Asian countries. Against this context, the increased individualisation of debt is the outcome of the cascading down of debt from the collective sovereign level via privatisation and corporatisation to rising levels of household debt. However, it also means that individuals are increasingly directly exposed to the volatility of financial markets, thus giving rise to a new, individualised politics of risk.

To briefly summarise, what we have witnessed over recent decades is the disintermediation, domesticisation, privatisation and individualisation of emerging market debt. As a consequence, emerging market debt is much less monolithic and more heterogeneous than is often thought. Nevertheless, these changes should be characterised as tendentious rather than complete and irreversible, given the partial and uneven nature of trajectories of debt, like that of financialisation more generally.[48] Often they are closely interlinked, if not temporarily working in opposite directions as deleveraging in one sector can lead to

44. Ismail Ertürk and Stefano Solari, "Banks as Continuous Reinvention", *New Political Economy*, Vol. 12, No. 3 (2007), pp. 369–388.

45. Lena Rethel, "The New Financial Development Paradigm", *op. cit.*

46. As always there is an exception to the trend, with large swathes of emerging Eastern European household debt being denominated in foreign currency ("A Glow from the East", *The Economist*, 28 August 2010).

47. McKinsey Global Institute, *op. cit.*

48. Paul Langley, "In the Eye of the 'Perfect Storm': The Final Salary Pensions Crisis and Financialisation of Anglo-American Capitalism", *New Political Economy*, Vol. 9, No. 4 (2004), p. 554.

releveraging in another. The next section draws out the political implications of these shifts in the boundaries of emerging market debt.

Governing Adjustment in a Changing World

Recent contributions to this journal have shown a renewed interest in "sources of change" in the international debt regime and the evolution of responses to its crises.[49] However, as this article has demonstrated, processes of evolution and change pertain not only to how emerging market debt is dealt with, but also to the nature of this debt itself, with important consequences for its governance. To put it differently, it is important to establish not only how and by whom emerging market debt and its crises are governed, but also—and this is perhaps the more fundamental issue at stake—what exactly it is that we attempt to govern. Financial crises are important drivers of change as they act as catalysts not only for ideas about what constitutes good economic policymaking, but also for wider changes in state–market–society relations.[50] Yet they also redraw boundaries. Indeed, the financial crises of the last three decades have affected a number of these boundaries—between the domestic and the international, the public and the private, between the state and the market, between different types of markets and between the state and society.

As the previous section has shown, emerging market debt has undergone a series of transformations over the last few decades. It is perhaps less obvious, however, that these changes are also reflections of normative commitments and political choices. Thus, if we look, for example, at the progressive disintermediation of finance, we are taken back to the choices faced by policymakers in the 1980s, namely to restart the engine of global finance either by improving the liquidity of emerging market government debt by breaking it up into smaller pieces or by writing off these loans. Effectively, this was a decision between international financial stability and greater equity in global financial affairs.[51] Similarly, the domesticisation of emerging market debt, paradoxical as it might seem at first glance, can actually be taken to reflect a continuous commitment to international capital account openness, albeit interspersed with greater (notional) government control. After all, when policymakers had previously been confronted with the predicament of highly speculative international capital movements in the 1930s, they had voted to prohibit these flows, as evidenced by the closed capital accounts of the original Bretton Woods regime. This time round, at least in the long run, capital accounts were kept open.[52] But where does this leave us in terms of

49. See Candace C. Archer, "Responses to Financial Crises: An Evolutionary Perspective", *Global Society*, Vol. 23, No. 2 (2009), pp. 105–127; and André J. Broome, "When Do NGOs Matter? Activist Organisations as a Source of Change in the International Debt Regime", *Global Society*, Vol. 23, No. 1 (2009), pp. 59–78.

50. Wesley W. Widmaier, Mark Blyth and Leonard Seabrooke, "Exogenous Shocks or Endogenous Constructions? The Meanings of Wars and Crises", *International Studies Quarterly*, Vol. 51, No. 4 (2007), pp. 747–759.

51. Eleni Tsingou, "Transnational Private Governance and the Basel Process: Banking, Regulation, Private Interests and Basel II", in Andreas Nölke and Jean C. Graz (eds), *Transnational Private Governance and Its Limits* (London: Routledge, 2007), pp. 58–68.

52. Even though Malaysia introduced capital controls in 1998, these were always intended as only a temporary measure. See Government of Malaysia, *White Paper. Status of the Malaysian Economy* (Kuala Lumpur: Percetakan Nasional Malaysia Bhd., 6 April 1999).

the politics of adjustment? The remainder of this section will discuss the political implications of the changing dynamics of emerging market debt by focusing on the other two dimensions: the privatisation and individualisation of emerging market debt.

Over the last decades, access to credit has increasingly come to be perceived as a public good. While for centuries the power to borrow had largely been a sovereign prerogative and, to a lesser extent, that of a small elite, it has now turned into a mass phenomenon, although there still remain stark differences in the availability and cost of credit. Credit has been targeted at low-income classes in emerging market economies through microfinance schemes and so on, often with the active support of donor governments and the international financial institutions, especially the World Bank. Making credit broadly available has become a public policy issue of increasingly high priority. It has also served as a justification for the proliferation of exactly those forms of financial innovation that have been at the heart of the recent global financial crisis.[53]

Indeed, it could be argued that the position of individuals has been empowered as their access to credit has been made easier. However, while in many emerging market economies at first glance the increase in household debt seems to have been more than matched by a boost of asset ownership, experience suggests that asset and debt ownership are not evenly distributed across the population with regard to, *inter alia*, age, gender and income. Along these lines, more attention should be paid to the cyclical nature of house prices, given that mortgages are the biggest single component of emerging market household debt. A lesson painfully demonstrated by the recent subprime financial crisis is that house price booms and busts exhibit the same pathology as banking crises and actually often coincide with them. Indeed, house prices are more prone to sudden reversals than is often thought—an issue that holds true in both mature and emerging market economies.[54]

A more disaggregated analysis of emerging market debt could thus facilitate a better understanding of its socio-economic dimensions. Importantly, the ongoing financialisation of social life poses new demands on citizens regarding their own financial literacy and discipline as responsibility for financial well-being is increasingly shifted from the collective to the individual.[55] There is a heightened vulnerability of households that are exposed to debt in emerging market economies, especially as safeguard mechanisms and institutions tasked with the protection of financial consumers are underdeveloped. The suicide epidemic among Indian farmers bears cruel testimony to this fact. A case in point is the growing number of household debt restructurings in emerging market economies and the, albeit slow, institutionalisation of consumer debt relief regimes.

Since the late 1990s, household debt restructurings in emerging market economies have become an increasingly familiar phenomenon. Thus, what we have seen are both the creation of *ad hoc* mechanisms and the establishment of permanent agencies such as debt advice bureaus, often to complement legal mechanisms where they exist. Examples of the former were the establishment of the *Punto Final* programme in Mexico in 1998, providing government-led debt relief targeted at mortgage holders and small businesses, or the restructuring of credit

53. Leonard Seabrooke, "What Do I Get? The Everyday Politics of Expectations and the Subprime Crisis", *New Political Economy*, Vol. 15, No. 1 (2010), pp. 51–70.

54. Reinhart and Rogoff, *op. cit.*, p. 160.

55. Brassett *et al.*, "Introduction to the Political Economy of the Subprime Crisis", *op. cit.*

card debts in South Korea in 2002 and in Taiwan in 2005.[56] An example of the latter was the 2006 establishment of a Credit Counselling and Debt Management Agency in Malaysia, whose three-pronged approach to consumer debt relief consists of counselling and advice on financial management, debt management, and financial education.[57]

Unfortunately, this aspect is largely ignored in global debates surrounding the current crisis. Its conspicuous absence is reflective of a focus on the rolling out of markets, with too little attention being paid to the losers of the marketisation process. Thus, for example, as part of its World Development Indicators database, the World Bank collects information on private credit bureau coverage, i.e., the "number of individuals or firms listed by a private credit bureau with current information on repayment history, unpaid debts, or credit outstanding".[58] In contrast, however, there has been little systematic attempt so far to collect similarly comprehensive data on private debtor support. Furthermore, the emerging consumer debt regimes in emerging market economies seem to reproduce a model of financialised capitalism whose weaknesses have been so thoroughly exposed by the recent financial crisis.[59] They do not challenge, but rather condone and thus further entrench rising levels of household debt. Creditworthiness is seen as merely a function of a borrower's capacity to repay her debt; other considerations have to take second place. Importantly, the rightfulness of going into debt is never questioned. The systemic reasons of growing household debt are ignored. To put it in a nutshell, there is much more to learn about the politics of the (often state-brokered) advances of finance into the everyday life of citizens in emerging market economies.[60]

However, the disintermediation and domesticisation of emerging market debt have also induced changes for corporate borrowers. Here, the experience of advanced countries with big capital markets could serve as an important reference point. For example, Boyer suggests that financial disintermediation and the expansion of capital markets exacerbate a trajectory of uneven access to credit.[61] As a consequence, in a capital market-based financial system bigger corporations go directly to the capital market and issue bonds or equity. On the other hand, households and small and medium enterprises (SMEs) remain reliant on the banking sector. Similarly, French and Leyshon point out that there exists an intimate relationship between financial disintermediation and the emergence of new dynamics of inclusion and exclusion. More specifically, they argue that financial disintermediation leads to an "inability of intermediaries to cross-subsidize weaker borrowers and the emergence of a more direct relationship between credit risk and pricing [... that has] produced uneven financial outcomes".[62]

---

56. Laeven and Laryea, *op. cit.*

57. Rethel, "Financialisation and the Malaysian Political Economy", *op. cit.*

58. Available: <http://data.worldbank.org/indicator/IC.CRD.PRVT.ZS> (accessed 30 August 2010).

59. Paul Langley, *The Everyday Life of Global Finance. Saving and Borrowing in Anglo-America* (Oxford: Oxford University Press, 2008).

60. Rethel, "Financialisation and the Malaysian Political Economy", *op. cit.*

61. Robert Boyer, "Assessing the Impact of Fair Value upon Financial Crises", *Socio-Economic Review*, Vol. 5, No. 4 (2007), pp. 788–789.

62. Shaun French and Andrew Leyshon, "The New, New Financial System: Towards a Conceptualization of Financial Reintermediation", *Review of International Political Economy*, Vol. 11, No. 2 (2004), p. 270.

Even more importantly, it seems as if these insights, obtained from analysing processes of financial disintermediation in mature market economies such as the UK and the US, hold in the context of emerging market economies.

Indeed, there are suggestions that the so-called SME "finance gap" is bigger in emerging market economies than in advanced economies.[63] That is, recent changes in emerging market debt have, at least to some extent, been to the disadvantage of SMEs. This is exacerbated by the fact that most of the bank lending freed up by the development of capital markets—an increasingly important source of funding for big corporate borrowers—has been redirected at households. This gives rise to a two-tiered industrial finance structure: cheap(ish) and abundant financing for big corporations, expensive and restricted financing for SMEs. The differential treatment experienced by households and SMEs or by big corporations and SMEs that want to borrow illustrates the new dynamics of inclusion and exclusion that are created by the credit economy. Thus, better understanding the transformations of emerging market debt can also make us more sensitive to changing market–market relations and struggles between different factions of capital.

Moreover, there is another important aspect of corporate debt: the public–private divide is very porous. Indeed, in many cases it might be more accurate to speak of corporatisation rather than privatisation as, notably in times of crisis, the state might bail out so-called private corporations, especially where politico-business ties are close.[64] The recent financial crisis has once again demonstrated this for the case of "private" financial institutions. However, this follows a more general trend. For example, Reinhart and Rogoff suggest that public sector debt levels have increased after banking crises at an average of 86%.[65] As a matter of fact, this amount does not represent a genuine increase in public sector borrowing; it rather reflects the (often 1:1) conversion of private debt owed by financial institutions into public liabilities. It is yet another instance of "private risk becom[ing] public".[66] In so doing, it suggests an internalisation of the primacy of capital markets while reemphasising the role of the state as provider of the public good of financial stability.

From this discussion, two common themes emerge: the role of government and the question of risk. While this article has challenged the commonly held assumption that the politics of adjustment primarily afflict governments, it seems puzzling that despite the transformation of emerging market debt there remains such a pivotal, and costly, role for governments. Nevertheless, what this article has also shown is that an effective, sustainable reduction of debt is rare. Rather, what can be witnessed is a shifting of debt to other sectors or, in other words, sectoral releveraging, instead of overall deleveraging. The phenomenon of "releveraging" is especially acute after financial crises. Indeed, in some cases,

---

63. OECD, "Policy Brief: Financing SMEs and Entrepreneurs", OECD Observer (November 2006).

64. As they are in many emerging market economies. See, e.g., Ben Thirkell-White, "Indonesia and Malaysia: The Persistence of a Domestic Politico-Business Class", in Justin Robertson (ed.), *Power and Politics after Financial Crisis: Rethinking Foreign Opportunism in Emerging Markets* (Basingstoke: Palgrave Macmillan, 2008), pp. 187–211; Lavelle, *op. cit.*; Edmund T. Gomez and Jomo Kwame Sundaram, *Malaysia's Political Economy. Politics, Patronage and Profits* (Cambridge: Cambridge University Press, 1997).

65. Reinhart and Rogoff, *op. cit.*, pp. 170, 232.

66. As chapter 3 of the April 2008 Global Financial Stability Report is entitled. See IMF, *Global Financial Stability Report. Containing Systemic Risks and Restoring Financial Soundness* (Washington, DC: The International Monetary Fund, April 2008).

while the burden of debt—the locus of indebtedness—has shifted significantly, overall levels of indebtedness have hardly declined at all despite the experience of crises. Often, the state has played a key role in these processes.

Similarly, the reduction of risk has been a recurring discourse. Indeed, early advocates of the disintermediation of emerging market debt, most prominently former Wall Street banker and US Treasury Secretary Nicholas Brady, thought it to be a market-oriented way to reduce systemic risk. A similar notion also underpinned the build up to the current credit crunch. Of course, the idea that risk could be split up and sold on, and thus its systemic significance reduced, has backfired in the recent crisis.[67] It has shown the futility of the notion that, assuming a growing risk appetite among so-called sophisticated investors, risk is efficiently distributed to those with the ability to absorb it. Nevertheless, the question of who should bear the risk is one that is perhaps even less clear than that of who should bear the burden of adjustment. It seems paradoxical that risk has increasingly been cascaded down to those with the least capacity to bear it—namely households.

Effectively, the state has emerged as an important adjudicator of this issue. Despite the multifaceted character of emerging market debt, governments continue to play pivotal roles, not just traditionally as market players/borrowers, but more importantly as authorities deeply implicated in the brokering and restructuring of corporate debt and household debt.[68] In so doing, the state balances risk between different sectors, which ultimately has to be seen as an expression of its underlying normative commitments. That is, despite, or perhaps rather because of the transformation of emerging market debt, we should become more sensitive to the role of the state in monitoring, rewarding and disciplining portfolio capital and the winners and losers of this process.

Debt relations provide insights into the changing morphologies of state–market–society relations by focusing attention on issues such as who bears the burden of adjustment, what new vulnerabilities are created by the shifting loci of indebtedness and what politics of inclusion and exclusion are taking place. However, we also need to achieve a better understanding of the role of ideas and discourse, of knowledge and agency. Ultimately, global governance reform is not just the product of competing coalitions, producing winners and losers of economic adjustment. There are fundamentally normative issues at stake. The transformation of emerging market debt over the last three decades has been underpinned by a series of normative choices: the prioritisation of stability over equity, a commitment to facilitating rather than prohibiting capital mobility and a preference of the private over the public. Collectively, as the article has shown, these have served to facilitate progressive financialisation and are part of the discursive construction of economic policymaking. Ultimately, this favours a "debt repayment norm" as opposed to a "productive investment" norm.[69] By mapping recent changes in the composition of emerging market

67. Jacqueline Best, "The Limits of Financial Risk Management: Or, What We Didn't Learn from the Asian Crisis", *New Political Economy*, Vol. 15, No. 1 (2010), pp. 29–49.

68. Cf. Thomas Laryea, "Approaches to Corporate Debt Restructuring in the Wake of Financial Crises", IMF Staff Position Note SPN/10/02 (26 January 2010); Laeven and Laryea, *op. cit.*

69. Lena Rethel, "Whose Legitimacy? Islamic Finance and the Global Financial Order", *Review of International Political Economy*, Vol. 18, No. 1 (2011), pp. 75–98; cf. Timothy J. Sinclair, *The New Masters of Capital. American Bond Rating Agencies and the Politics of Creditworthiness* (Ithaca, NY: Cornell University Press, 2005).

debt, this article has rendered explicit some of the norms that underpin the contemporary global financial order. It has also challenged mainstream academic discourse for the way it continues to (mis)represent the politics of emerging market debt as a contest mainly between national governments and international financial markets. The politics of emerging market debt is a much richer tapestry than is commonly acknowledged. The boundaries are shifting, but they are easily permeable.

Conclusion: Adjusting the Boundaries

The perception is still widespread that emerging market debt consists mainly of government debt, owed to foreign creditors. However, by looking at episodes of post-crisis deleveraging, this article has traced changes in the overall composition of emerging market debt. It has argued that a range of transformations has taken place, namely the disintermediation, domesticisation, privatisation and individualisation of emerging market debt. Where exactly a country is situated *vis-à-vis* these trends depends on its own specific experience.

From this, the article has moved on to draw out the political implications of the transformation of emerging market debt. It has begun to sketch a much more nuanced picture than is usually provided by the literature's focus on North–South and state–market relations. In particular, it has elucidated four sets of normative commitments that are behind recent changes in emerging market debt regimes: the prioritisation of international financial stability over greater equity in financial affairs; a continuous commitment to open capital accounts, albeit coupled with greater government control; a preference of the notionally private over the public; and the shift towards a debt repayment norm as opposed to a productive investment norm.

By itself, improving access to credit is certainly no panacea for economic underdevelopment, especially if it ignores the new vulnerabilities that indebtedness, in its many guises, generates. Similarly, if we look at emerging market debt in its entirety, while it is important to improve international mechanisms for its governance, this on its own will not be sufficient. Indeed, certain aspects of the evolving emerging market debt regime point in a different direction. To counteract the phenomenon of rising household debt levels and the vulnerabilities it engenders, more reflection about regulation and capacity building on the national/local level is necessary.[70] The uniqueness of crisis experiences and crisis responses renders "one size fits all" solutions inherently problematic. Based on these insights, the article points towards a new research agenda that is targeted at better understanding matters of debt and financialisation in emerging market economies.

In doing this, the article has also drawn attention to the negotiation of boundaries in the social realm. This applies to the subject matter discussed—emerging market debt—but also to the disciplinary endeavour of IPE. If global governance is in crisis, then the need for well-informed reform proposals is great. For IPE to fulfil its role in this and to continue to critically interrogate commonly held wisdoms, it is important to adjust its own boundaries. This can lead to more

---

70. Grahame F. Thompson, "'Financial Globalisation' and the 'Crisis': A Critical Assessment and 'What is to be Done'?", *New Political Economy*, Vol. 15, No. 1 (2010), pp. 127–145.

sensitivity to different politics over the old "state-versus-markets" truisms: the politics of change in international political relations, the politics of the evolving nature of state–market relations, the politics of financial disintermediation, creditworthiness and financialisation, but also the politics of the discipline itself. In other words, drawing attention to the shifting politics of emerging market debt can also serve to open up new spaces for IPE, or political economy as some prefer it, as a field of inquiry.[71]

---

71. Cf. Nicola Phillips (ed.), *Globalizing International Political Economy* (Basingstoke: Palgrave, 2005); James Brassett and Christopher Holmes, "International Political Economy and the Question of Ethics", *Review of International Political Economy*, Vol. 17, No. 3 (2010), pp. 425–453.

Notes on Contributors

James Brassett is Associate Professor of International Political Economy in the Department of Politics and International Studies, University of Warwick. He is author of *Cosmopolitanism and Global Financial Reform* (Routledge, 2010), and several articles in journals such as the *European Journal of International Relations, International Studies Quarterly* and the *Review of International Political Economy.* He is currently working on a new book, entitled *Trauma and Global Ethics: The Politics of Vulnerability.*

André Broome is Associate Professor at the University of Warwick. His research focuses on the changing dynamics of international monetary relations as well as the comparative politics of economic reform, and his publications include *The Currency of Power: The IMF and Monetary Reform in Central Asia* (Palgrave, 2010).

Liam Clegg is Lecturer at the University of York. His research explores the bureaucratic dynamics shaping the operational practice of the World Bank and IMF, focusing in particular on the intersection of material and ideational power within these processes. Work exploring these themes has recently been published in *New Political Economy* and the *Journal of International Relations and Development.*

Alexandra Homolar is Assistant Professor in International Security in the Department of Politics and International Studies at the University of Warwick. Prior to joining the Department, Alexandra was Research Associate at the Peace Research Institute Frankfurt. Dr. Homolar's research explores the political economy of (inter)national security, security governance, and US foreign and security policy. She has published/forthcoming works in journals such as the *European Journal of International Relations, Review of International Political Economy,* and the *Journal of Strategic Studies,* as well as a new textbook on the concepts, origins and contemporary challenges of US security policy (Routledge, forthcoming, 2012).

Donna Lee is Professor in the Department of Political Science and International Studies at the University of Birmingham. She is Director of the research project "African Activism in the WTO" based in the Department and author of numerous articles and books on GATT/WTO trade negotiations and economic diplomacy.

Manuela Moschella is a *Nino Andreatta* Fellow at the University of Bologna, Italy. Her core research interests include the politics of change of international organisations, with a specific focus on the IMF and the reforms to the international financial architecture. She has also worked on cross-country regulatory responses to financial crises. She has published articles on these topics in a range of journals, including the *Review of International Political Economy*, *New Political Economy*, the *Journal of Public Policy*, *Comparative European Politics*, and *Comparative Economic Studies*. She is the author of *Governing Risk: The IMF and Global Financial Crises* (Palgrave, IPE Series, 2010).

Lena Rethel is Assistant Professor of International Political Economy at the University of Warwick. Her research focuses on financial system change in Asia, the emergence and challenges of Islamic finance and the relationship of finance, debt and development. Her book *The Problem with Banks*, co-authored with Timothy J. Sinclair, is forthcoming with Zed Books in 2012.

Nick Vaughan-Williams is Assistant Professor in International Security at the University of Warwick. His first research monograph, *Border Politics: The Limits of Sovereign Power* (Edinburgh, 2009, 2012), won the Gold Award of the 2011 Association of Borderlands Studies Past President's Book Competition. He is also co-author of *Critical Security Studies: An Introduction* (Routledge, 2010), co-editor of *Critical Theorists and International Relations* (Routledge, 2009), and co-editor of the Routledge *Interventions* book series.

Index

Note: Page numbers in *italics* are for tables.